DATE DUE

DEC 1 2 2001			

Critical Essays on the Theatre of Calderón

For Nancy

Critical Essays on the Theatre of

CALDERÓN

Edited by BRUCE W. WARDROPPER

NEW YORK UNIVERSITY PRESS 1965

© 1965 BY NEW YORK UNIVERSITY
LIBRARY OF CONGRESS CATALOG CARD NUMBER: 65:14336 √
MANUFACTURED IN THE UNITED STATES OF AMERICA

REPRINTED 1971

ISBN-0-8147-0425-5   cloth
ISBN-0-8147-0426-3   paper

ACKNOWLEDGMENTS

"THE DEVIL in the Drama of Calderón" by A. A. Parker, originally published under the title "The Theology of the Devil in the Drama of Calderón" as Aquinas Paper No. 32. Copyright © 1958 by Blackfriars Publications and reprinted by their permission.

"Honour and the Christian Background in Calderón" by P. N. Dunn, originally published in *Bulletin of Hispanic Studies*. Copyright © 1960 by Liverpool University Press and reprinted by their permission.

"On *La vida es sueño*" by E. M. Wilson, originally published in Spanish under the title "*La vida es sueño*" in the *Revista de la Universidad de Buenos Aires* and reprinted by their permission.

"The Structure of Calderón's *La vida es sueño*" by A. E. Sloman, originally published in *Modern Language Review* and reprinted by their permission.

"Rosaura's Role in the Structure of *La vida es sueño*" by William M. Whitby, originally published in *Hispanic Review* and reprinted by their permission.

"Calderón's Concept of the Perfect Prince in *La vida es sueño*" by Everett W. Hesse, originally published in Spanish under the title "La concepción calderoniana del príncipe perfecto en *La vida es sueño*" in *Clavileño*, and reprinted by permission of the author.

"The Figure of Fénix in Calderón's *El príncipe constante*" by Leo Spitzer, originally published in German under the title "Die Figur der Fénix in Calderóns *Standhaftem Prinzen*" in *Romanistisches Jahrbuch* and reprinted by permission of the editor and of Anna G. Hatcher.

v

ACKNOWLEDGMENTS

"Calderón's *El príncipe constante*, a Tragedy?" by Arnold G. Reichenberger, originally published in *Modern Language Notes* by the Johns Hopkins Press and reprinted by their permission.

"Calderón's Strange Mercy Play" by Edwin Honig, originally published in *Massachusetts Review* and reprinted by their permission.

"*Honor* in *El alcalde de Zalamea*" by C. A. Jones, originally published in *Modern Language Review* and reprinted by their permission.

"*El pintor de su deshonra* and the Neo-Aristotelian Theory of Tragedy" by A. Irvine Watson, originally published in the *Bulletin of Hispanic Studies*. Copyright © 1963 by Liverpool University Press and reprinted by their permission.

PREFACE

THE SPANISH GOLDEN AGE, like the Elizabethan Age in England, produced a great many dramatists, several of whom wrote masterpieces. Two, however, stand out among their fellows. Literary history has not decided whether Lope de Vega (1562–1635) or Pedro Calderón de la Barca (1600–81) is the greater. Lope is the precursor, a prolific, untidy playwright who *threw together* both works of unsurpassed beauty and shoddy pot-boilers; Calderón, the successor, *constructed* works of art which resulted from artificial, intellectual patterns. Both were deeply religious and saw their poetic worlds religiously. But while Lope tended to a penitential, affective Christianity, Calderón espoused a systematic, theological view of man and his circumstances. Two kinds of art, then, were organically united with two distinct points of view. Whether one prefers a hit-or-miss spontaneity coupled with a personal devotion or a high degree of organization embodying Christianity's answers to man's questions is largely a personal matter. It is a curious fact that Frenchmen and Americans, to judge by their scholarly and critical interests, esteem Lope, while Germans and Englishmen choose Calderón. Spanish intellectuals, though they show some preference for Lope, tend on the whole to neglect their national theatre in favor of the novel and lyric poetry.

The intellectual revival which has dominated Spain's cultural history in this century is named after the "Generation of 1898." Shocked in that year by the loss of the last vestiges of the Spanish Empire, thinkers, writers, and artists embarked on a revaluation of the Spanish past in an attempt to discover and extirpate the seeds of decay. This meant investigating the things that made Spain different from, and "inferior to," other European countries. One disturbing Spanish phenomenon which, some thought, had steered Spanish civilization into a wrong and sterile direction was the ethos of her classical theatre. A hypersensitivity to suspected conjugal infidelity frequently leads in the drama to unjustified homicide, to a blood bath, to barbarism. The Age of Enlightenment, the eighteenth century, had condemned this theatre, and the Generation of 1898 concurred. Certain peculiarly Spanish institutions—the Inquisition with its *auto da fé*, bullfighting, this exaggerated code of honor in the theatre—were held responsible for the national decline. Since honor problems do not exist, or are treated more humanely in other literary genres, the Generation's distaste for barbaric behavior suggested the easy solution of ignoring the dramatists while praising the poets and novelists. The classical theatre has practically ceased to exist in Spanish intellectual circles. Performances of plays by Lope and Calderón are rare and execrable; there is no strong tradition of producing and acting them. Calderón, whose honor plays are the most spectacularly "barbaric" of all, inevitably suffered the most neglect. The great living scholars of Spain—Ramón Menéndez Pidal, Américo Castro, José F. Montesinos, Dámaso Alonso, Rafael Lapesa—have found little to say about his work.

Non-Spanish Hispanists, on the other hand, find Spanish cultural history interesting precisely because of its peculiar institutions. The Inquisition, *cante jondo*, tauromachia exert a mysterious fascination over foreigners, who are addicted to the "Romantic Spain," the "Arabic Spain" of Andalusia. Their neglect of Calderón, with his exotic honor code, is not easy to explain. Its source, I believe, lies in a work called *Calderón y su teatro* by the revered scholar, Marcelino Menéndez y Pelayo. A young man of twenty-five when the book was published in 1881, Menéndez y Pelayo had already occupied the Chair of Literature at the University of Madrid for three years. To celebrate the bicentenary of Calderón's death he was asked by a religious organization called the Unión Católica to deliver a course of lectures on his theatre. At one fell blow the impetuous young man demolished the dramatist's reputation among Catholics and intellectuals alike. Though a considerable scholar, Menéndez y Pelayo was no critic. Whenever it was a question of analyzing a work or passing judgment on it, he charged at his target with all his prejudices flying in the wind. Like most nineteenth-century students of literature, he favored a simple, natural, spontaneous, and edifying art. And of drama he demanded well-motivated, lifelike characters set in a credible plot, free of anachronisms and incongruities. The theatre, he believed, was not the place for ideas, for symbols, for patterns, for "artificiality." Menéndez y Pelayo's published lectures remained the last word on Calderón for half a century. Even though he would, twenty-five years later, repent of his "juvenile petulance," he never repaired the injustice done by his book. Meanwhile, he acquired such a reputation as an authority that he almost singlehandedly laid down the lines of standard Spanish literary history. Calderón's insignificance—or maleficence—was the officially sanctioned view held in schools and universities at home and abroad. Hispanism had to wait for the iconoclastic decade of the 1930's before Menéndez y Pelayo's judgments would be refuted.

It was naturally enough in Cambridge that the rehabilitation of Calderón was undertaken. Before World War II Cambridge was in a critical mood. *Blast*, the Imagists, T. S. Eliot's criticism, had finally put their imprint on the academic world. I. A. Richards and F. R. Leavis were teaching that all assumptions and received ideas should be challenged and reconsidered in the light of a close textual reading. In this atmosphere E. M. Wilson and A. A. Parker began to subject Calderón's plays to what was almost technically called "scrutiny." They reached the conclusion that Calderón was the supreme dramatic artist of Spain. Wilson published his original and valuable analysis of Calderón's element metaphors, and his close readings of *El príncipe constante* and *La vida es sueño*; Parker made a painstaking edition of the former play. It was at long last possible to "read" Calderón with understanding and without prejudice. Cambridge Hispanists, finding themselves convinced of Calderón's importance, became enthusiastic advocates of his art. The cult spread to Oxford where W. J. Entwistle and his student A. E. Sloman conceived the same enthusiasm for the dramatist, though they adopted a more circumspect, traditionally scholarly approach. These are now, many articles and books later, the most renowned *calderonistas*. Their revolution has become respectable. Their views are largely accepted. The younger British students of Calderón—P. N. Dunn, C. A. Jones, A. Soons, A. I. Watson—are their disciples.

Another factor in the revaluation of Calderón was the growth of interest in the baroque. The word was not much used—not, at least, in an approving sense—before the war. Even today its limits are so ill-defined that many scholars find it prudent to evade the issues it raises. Its vogue, however, has served, if for nothing else, to focus attention on two misunderstood and unappreciated Spanish writers, Góngora and Calderón, and to confer on them a cachet of fashionable respectability. 1927, the tercentenary year of his death, saw the final acceptance of Góngora, another of Menéndez y Pelayo's victims, as a great lyric poet. Spaniards, having nothing against the lyric poetry of their Golden Age, spearheaded the crusade to rescue Góngora from three centuries of neglect and vilification. But Wilson, who performed the incredible task of translating *Las soledades* into English verse, introduced the new vogue into England. Artificiality was no longer an impediment to art. From Góngora's neopagan lyrics to Calderón's theological drama was a predictable step for the small band of English Hispanists whose religious inclination was towards a Catholic, non-Evangelical Christianity. On the other hand, German Hispanists of various religious persuasions—Ludwig Pfandl, Ernst Robert Curtius, Leo Spitzer, Helmut Hatzfeld, Wolfgang Kayser— were attracted to Góngora and Calderón by the problem of style, the *Barockstil*. Calderón illustrated beautifully all the resources of this style: *culteranismo*, *conceptismo*, a wide range of tropes, a difficult art of sound construction. He was an exemplary or textbook case who had the further advantage of moving these German scholars esthetically. More recent thinking, especially by Hatzfeld in his *Estudios sobre el barroco* (Madrid, 1964), has widened the gap between Góngora, the pre-baroque or "mannerist" poet, and Calderón, the post-baroque or *barroquista* dramatist. Nevertheless, enthusiasm for an "artificial" or "unnatural" art has never flagged in the Hispanic world which was formed in Germany.

To this intellectual ferment American Hispanism has been

largely indifferent. It has been slow to grow up, content to respect and repeat the nineteenth-century formulas of positivistic scholarship and simplistic criticism. The New Criticism, in its country of origin, has left Hispanists untouched. Still, there have been some who have found Calderón irresistible. Eunice Joiner Gates early felt the attraction of the Góngora revival; like Wilson, she moved on to an admiration for Calderón. Sturgis E. Leavitt has been for many years the dean of American *calderonistas*. Everett W. Hesse, since the war, has concentrated his scholarly endeavors on editing and discussing Calderón's works, including some of the lesser known ones. William M. Whitby, since his student days at Yale, has devoted himself to a study of the masterpieces. Edwin Honig, a writer with a Spanish background and a professor of English literature, has been led by his work as a translator to some novel interpretations of the plays. Others, like Arnold G. Reichenberger, A. D. Kossoff, Edward Glaser, and J. H. Parker, write on Calderón in the intervals of treating other, preferred, playwrights. But by and large the *comediantes* of North America continue to neglect a very great dramatist.

Spain, for the reasons already discussed, remains a peripheral contributor to Calderón studies. But an honorable exception must be mentioned. Ángel Valbuena Prat, a literary historian, wrote in 1924 a doctoral thesis which was a classification of the allegorical dramas called *autos sacramentales*. Valbuena later composed a number of more or less popular books and articles on Calderón, but they have contributed little to our deeper understanding of his difficult art.[1]

Calderón was a true son of Madrid, which had been the capital of the country since 1561. It was, by the time his plays were performed, a sophisticated urban centre far more ready for intellectual stimulation and complex entertainments than the peasant-filled overgrown village that it was when Lope de Vega was writing.

Born there in 1600, Calderón received his grammar-school

---

1 Italian studies on Calderón, though well advertised in Carmelo Samonà's book, *Calderón nella critica italiana* (Milano, 1960), have not made any noteworthy contributions in the area of *criticism*.

education at the hands of the Jesuits of the Colegio Imperial. He studied for the priesthood at the universities of Alcalá and Salamanca. After yielding to the temptation of participating in some poetic contests held in Madrid, he interrupted his ecclesiastical career to turn to writing for the stage. His first datable play is of 1623. Some travel in Italy and Flanders, some rough-housing in the streets of the capital, war service in Catalonia, the birth of a bastard daughter testify to the lively existence he led until his ordination in 1651. After this he settled down to the life of a chaplain, briefly in Toledo, and then until 1681 when he died, in Madrid. During this period of clerical respectability he wrote only religious allegories (the *autos sacramentales*) and court entertainments. The secular masterpieces belong to the first half of his life. In all, some 120 straight plays (*comedias*), some 80 *autos sacramentales*, and some 20 minor dramatic pieces have survived.

This volume aims at being representative of present-day Calderonian criticism. No more than one article by each author could be included. The interested reader must turn to the bibliography to find a basis for further study. It is hoped that the anthology will serve a useful purpose for Hispanists by presenting a cross section of current studies and by making available some essays which were not easily accessible. To the non-Hispanist, the general student of literature, it offers an introduction to a body of writing which is different, challenging, and worthwhile. The theatrelover, on the other hand, will, by sampling vicariously a drama whose ideas, techniques, and symbols are unfamiliar to him, be inevitably drawn to the plays themselves, whether in translation or in the original.

Throughout this book titles of journals are abbreviated to accord with the practice authorized by the Modern Language Association of America. While the articles have been styled in accordance with MLA principles, the authors' spelling—English, American, or idiosyncratic—has been preserved.

The authors of these essays have graciously consented to my republishing them in this collection; in some cases they have collaborated beyond the call of duty by making considerable revisions and corrections to the original text. Professor Anna G. Hatcher, the literary executrix of the late Leo Spitzer, authorized the use of his article. To all of them I give my warmest thanks.

I must also express a debt of gratitude to the Hispanic Research Council of Duke University, which generously provided funds for some typing and translating.

BRUCE W. WARDROPPER

Durham, North Carolina
August, 1964

CONTENTS

Part One

Calderón's Art and Thought

1 · The Devil in the Drama of Calderón *

by A. A. Parker

IN 1951 Sheed and Ward published a very interesting and important book entitled *Satan*, based on a French work.[1] Its thirty-
one articles, contributed by a number of writers, cover every
aspect of the subject from the existence and nature of Satan
to possession and witchcraft. This volume has prompted my
choice of subject for this paper, for the six articles comprising
Part V, "The Devil in Art and Literature," range widely from
Dante and Milton, through Balzac and Dostoievski, to several
contemporary writers like Gide and Bernanos; but nowhere is
there any mention of Calderón. Clearly the compilers and editors were unaware of the fact that this great seventeenth-century
Spanish dramatist wrote a large number of plays whose themes
require the appearance of the Devil, and that nowhere else in
world literature can we find as remarkable a presentation of
him as a dramatic character. This oversight is itself obviously
due to ignorance of the fact that Calderón must unquestionably
rank as the greatest theological dramatist that Catholicism has
yet produced. Because his religious plays are constructed on
the concepts of scholastic philosophy, which are transposed with

* *Editor's Note.* Professor Parker's essay, originally published as a
pamphlet, was delivered in the form of a lecture to the Aquinas Society
of London, whose members share theological and philosophical, rather
than literary or Hispanic, interests. For the present edition, as a glance at
the bibliography will show, the title has been modified. At the author's
request Calderón's titles and the quotations from his works are now given
in the original Spanish.

1 *Satan, Etudes Carmélitaines*, Année 27 (Paris, 1948). All references
to this work will be to the English volume.

extraordinary subtlety into the medium of poetic drama, I need offer no excuse for bringing Calderón to the attention of a Society whose primary interest lies in Thomism. The existence of this book on Satan provides me with a convenient way of doing this, by pointing to a lamentable gap in an otherwise authoritative and admirable compilation.[2]

For anyone who takes the Devil seriously he exerts that peculiar type of fascination that derives from a combination of mystery and fear. It is not surprising, therefore, that he appears as a spectacular figure—sinister, macabre, or grotesque as the case may be—in legend and in literature of every type, from the simplest folk tale to the *Divine Comedy*. Generally, however, the spectacular nature of what he is and stands for creates a gulf between the Devil of literature and the Fallen Angel of the theologian or the idea of evil evolved by the scholastic philosopher. Any one well versed in the demonology of Dante's *Inferno* and of *Paradise Lost* who turns to St. Thomas for the first time can scarcely fail to be surprised by the quite unsensational and almost matter-of-fact treatment of the demons in the *Prima Pars* of the *Summa*, and by the fact that far from holding the centre of the floor they are very much relegated to a corner. This is as it should be when Being is contemplated as a whole. But literature, apart from the *Divine Comedy*, does not take so broad a sweep, and by narrowing its focus to a point where the Devil becomes a central figure it runs the risk of over-magnifying him. This disproportion can take three main forms. First, there is the tendency to make the Devil appear as a rival of God and so as a cosmic power in his own right which can suggest, if not actually propound, a philosophy of dualism. Secondly, the necessity of personifying the Devil in anthropomorphic form makes him confront his human victim

2 The only attempt to study Calderón's Devil has been P. de la Escosura, "*El Demonio como figura dramática en el teatro de Calderón,*" *Revista de España*, xlv (1875), 337–356, 433–452. This study is inadequate: it exemplifies an outmoded approach to Calderón and belies its title by entirely ignoring his specifically theological plays. The few monographs on Calderón's philosophical ideas (of which the best is Eugenio Frutos, *La filosofía de Calderón en sus autos sacramentales* [Zaragoza, 1952]) disregard his Devil by making a division between philosophy and theology which is invalid for his drama.

as man to man, with the power to exercise a direct external influence on his will. Thirdly, the need to make the Devil a credible and forceful figure in human terms can lead to his being invested with a certain grandeur.

My purpose will be to indicate how Calderón meets these difficulties when presenting the Devil as a character on the stage, and to show that the degree of his success in avoiding theological pitfalls is the measure of his ability to utilise, within his own medium, the relevant ideas and conclusions of scholastic theology and philosophy.

His plays exemplify two quite different types of drama. One, called the *comedia*, is the type with which we are most familiar: a play which, with greater or less verisimilitude, imitates a possible action by means of characters who represent real individual men who have existed or could exist. The other type of drama, called the *auto sacramental*, derived, in unbroken continuity, from the medieval miracle and morality plays, a tradition that survived in Spain until 1765. These Spanish *autos* were performed in the open air on the feast of Corpus Christi; they employed allegory to dramatise themes from dogmatic or moral theology or from scripture; they were the representation not of an action imitating real life but of abstract ideas; and their characters were personifications of concepts, or else historical figures or supernatural beings presented in allegorical guise. This allegorical drama became, in Calderón's hands, specifically theological and philosophical,[3] and it is here that any discussion of his dramatic treatment of the Devil must begin, since it is in these plays that the Devil appears in his role as, if I may use the term, a cosmic figure.

Since the Devil appears in forty-seven of these *autos sacramentales* the material is very extensive. Thirty of these are variations on one type of theme, the dramatisation of the Fall and the Redemption. I shall confine myself to two plays of this group, selected to show the development that the treatment of the Devil undergoes. Since these *autos* are allegorical, the presentation of the Fall and the Redemption is not a dramatisation

3 For an account and analysis of this type of drama see A. A. Parker, *The Allegorical Drama of Calderón: An Introduction to the Autos Sacramentales* (Oxford, 1943).

of the first chapter of Genesis and of the Gospel narrative of
the Passion, but is an attempt to portray on the stage the ideas
behind the dogmas.

In any dramatisation of the Fall not only must the Devil
be given a leading part but his presence must also be accounted
for. The possible pitfalls can best be indicated by recalling the
kind of criticism that has been levelled against Milton. Satan
is the most impressive figure in *Paradise Lost*, so much so that
Shelley, finding Milton's God to possess no moral superiority
over his Devil, saw the poem as actually refuting the theology
it ostensibly supports. Unquestionably there is a good deal in
this criticism. In order that the rebellion against God should be
both credible and dramatic, Satan, who ought to be proud,
malicious, and foolish, is on the contrary characterised by "fortitude in adversity, enormous endurance, a certain splendid reck-
lessness, remarkable powers of rising to an occasion, [and]
extraordinary qualities of leadership." [4] Milton cannot help
sympathising with qualities such as these, and to that extent
he is on Satan's side at the beginning, and subsequently can
attempt to neutralise the effect of the first two Books only by
changing his character and degrading him.[5] But as regards the
actual Satanic rebellion the impression that remains is one of
fiery grandeur.

Calderón's first attempts to dramatise Original Sin also
exemplify this danger of making the Devil too striking and too
sympathetic a figure. One of the best examples of his earliest
autos is *El veneno y la triaca*.[6] In it Human Nature is presented
as a Princess, the daughter of a great King, who has placed her
in the Garden of the World under the care of her Understanding and served by the four Seasons. All is perfect harmony until

4 A. J. A. Waldock, *Paradise Lost and its Critics* (Cambridge, 1947),
p. 77.
5 The process of the degradation, culminating in the "unfair means"
of "cartoon-technique," has been acutely analysed by Waldock, pp. 77–92.
6 It was written in or (more probably) earlier than 1634; I cannot accept the suggestion of its modern editor that the text as we have it may
represent a revision of a later date. The only modern edition is in Calderón, *Obras completas*, III (*Autos sacramentales*, ed. A. Valbuena Prat,
Madrid, 1952), 180–197. There is an extremely poor English translation
of the opening section of the play in the Appendix to D. F. M'Carthy,
Mysteries of Corpus Christi (Dublin, 1867).

the Evening Star, as the Devil is here called, enters the Garden. He tells the Princess that he is a Prince from a foreign land who was once the favourite and Chief Minister of its King. The latter one day confided in him the secrets of his heart, showing him a portrait of the woman he had chosen to be his wife. She was so beautiful that the Evening Star became enamoured of her picture. Inflamed with the passion of love, he determined to prevent the marriage, arguing with the King that it was beneath his dignity to marry a woman of lower birth, and stating that he, the Evening Star, would be the first of his subjects to oppose this unequal marriage and to refuse to swear allegiance to her as his Queen. Nothing could move the King's resolve, whereupon the Evening Star was impelled by love of the woman in the portrait to rise in rebellion and attempt to usurp the throne. Defeated and banished from the kingdom, he has continued in exile to carry in his heart the features of the woman in the portrait, and he has come to the Garden of the World because the Princess who has listened to his story is the original of that portrait, the object of the love that caused his downfall.

This account of the Devil's revolt refers, of course, to the theological opinion that the Devil's sin was a refusal to worship the humanity of Our Lord when the plan of the Incarnation and Redemption was revealed to him; but this opposition to the Incarnation can only be attributed to envy of man—envy of the future exaltation of human nature.[7] Calderón, by here changing envy into love, links up with the older Jewish tradition found in the apochryphal Book of Enoch and, in association with Genesis 6, 1–5, accepted by the early Fathers of the Church, according to which certain of the angels in heaven became enamoured of the daughters of men and lustfully coveted their beauty.[8] In these early plays of Calderón, however, there is no suggestion of lust, but only of love. In reverting to this early legend his purpose is to endow his allegory of the Devil's temptation of woman with a poetic and dramatic force. But by presenting the Devil as the passionate and ardent lover of

7 See B. Leeming, S. J., "The Adversary," in *Satan*, pp. 22–24.
8 See *"Démon dans la Bible et la théologie juive,"* in *Dictionnaire de théologie catholique*, IV, col. 328, 336–337; *"Démon d'après les Pères,"* col. 340–358.

human nature he bestows on him a certain nobility. If we did not know what was behind the allegory, our sympathies would be entirely with the Devil. Purely on the level of poetic drama, that is to say, the Devil appears in a heroic light, as a faithful lover who has sacrificed everything for his beloved, and who humbly offers her this sacrifice as the token of his fidelity, begging her not to despise him for being poor. For though he has been banished from the Kingdom he can bring her all the riches of the world, the diamonds from the bowels of the earth, and the coral from the depths of the sea, which he offers to lay at her feet to adorn the laces of her shoe. The Devil's dramatic stature is still further enhanced by the fact that on his ardent but respectful wooing of the Princess Calderón lavishes all the grace of his poetry. This love scene is one of the most beautiful passages he ever wrote.

The Princess, like the well-bred ladies of the Spanish seventeenth-century stage, is indignant that any one should make love to her, and dismisses the Evening Star from her presence; but his wooing seems to have fired her vanity, for she lingers by the side of the streams in admiration of her own reflection and accepts with pride all the flattering service of the Seasons. Meanwhile, the Evening Star, unable to win her alive, determines to possess her dead. He places poison in an apple which he makes Death hand to her. The Princess falls sick of a strange disease, and Understanding proclaims that she will be given in marriage to any one who can cure her. A Pilgrim, who represents Our Lord, arrives by sea, cures her with the water of Baptism, the Cross and the Bread of Life, and carries her away in his ship, leaving the despairing Evening Star alone on the shore.

The simplicity of this allegory is an index of the immaturity of Calderón in this type of drama at this early stage of his career. So too is his presentation of the Devil as a faithful, self-sacrificing, and ardent lover. To represent Satan's temptation of Eve as a lover's wooing was the most obvious type of allegory in terms of poetic drama, and as such it is effective; but it is most inadequate as theology. An allegory that is near turning God and the Devil into rival suitors for the hand of Humanity, God standing on one side, Satan on the other, might seem to come perilously close to suggesting the dualism of the Manichaean heresy whereby the Devil is the antithetical counterpart to God, an *antitheos*. The only thing that saves Calderón here from falling into Manichaeism is his failure to present his Evening Star as evil at all: the only sign of malice that he shows either in his account of his revolt or in his poisoning of the apple is, in terms of the allegory, nothing more than the jealousy of a lover fighting to win his beloved. The difficulty lies in the fact that if the Devil is to appear in person to woo Humanity, he must be made attractive to her and therefore to the audience. Lastly, there is a further defect in this particular allegory: Original Sin is presented as the growth of vanity in Human Nature, but the connection between this and the Devil's wooing is tenuous only and not realised dramatically, since in fact Human Nature rejects the Evening Star's offer of his love.

Three difficulties therefore faced Calderón as a theologian if he was to continue to treat this theme in this type of drama: first, how to present the Devil as evil, secondly, how to avoid presenting him as a personified Principle of Evil, as an antithetical counterpart to the Principle of Good, and thirdly, how to connect the evil in Original Sin with the Devil's malice.

These difficulties, of course, point to a philosophical problem whose solution was offered to him by the Augustinian and scholastic doctrine of the nonsubstantiality or negative character of evil. Evil is always a privation, the lack of a good that ought to be possessed. Since, by definition, it is a deficiency, it cannot even be conceived of apart from the good of which it is a defect. Calderón had to find a way of dramatising this doctrine in his theological allegories if he was to make any progress in this type of drama. And this he succeeded in doing.

In the plays that follow his first attempts to allegorise the Fall, we find that the Devil no longer appears alone but is always paired with a companion or accomplice who is given such names as Guilt or Sin, Darkness, Night.[9] And this new

9 This applies only to the *autos* dramatising Original Sin, and not necessarily to those allegorising the Redemption only. The change can be dated approximately. In addition to *El veneno y la triaca* the Devil appears alone in the first versions of *El divino Orfeo* and *La vida es sueño*: these three plays must all have been written before 1638. The first *auto* of this

character is a dramatic counterpart to another who appears as a companion of Human Nature, and who is called Innocence, Grace, or Light. Guilt is the negation of Innocence, Sin the negation of Grace, Darkness the negation of Light. The significance of this pairing of the Devil with a negating abstraction can be brought out by a brief analysis of the allegory of any one of his mature *autos* of the Fall and the Redemption.

The one I select is *El Pastor Fido*, which is one of the last and finest.[10] I shall make no attempt to expound the full richness of the play but shall concentrate on the role of the Devil. Here he is paired with Sin (*la Culpa*), a character played by a woman. The play opens with them calling to each other from opposite ends of the stage; as the imagery of the verse suggests, they are calling to each other from across the universe. The Devil calls to Sin because he is her spirit, Sin to the Devil because she is his shadow. The two meet in the centre. What brings them together is envy—the envy of Human Nature that caused the Devil's fall from Heaven. (It should be noted that Calderón has abandoned the idea of the Devil's love for Humanity in favor of the accepted theological tradition.) This envy of man is what impels the Devil to encompass the fall of Human Nature into his arms via those of Sin.

Human Nature is in the Garden with Grace as her companion and counsellor, and with Will, Desire, Appetite,[11] and Obedience as her servants. She is not now a Princess, as she was in *El veneno y la triaca*, but a simple shepherdess aware of her lowly birth, aware that her mother was the Earth; she is not

---

kind in which the Devil appears paired is *El pintor de su deshonra* which can on technical grounds be tentatively dated c. 1645; there are eight others, all of which were written after 1651. [*Editor's Note*. Those unacquainted with Calderón's theatre may need to be told that *La vida es sueño* and *El pintor de su deshonra*, mentioned in this note, are allegorical religious rewritings, quite different from the secular plays with the same titles which are discussed in other essays in this book.]

10 It was written and performed in 1678. As the title suggests, the allegory was derived, indirectly, from the pastoral drama of Guarini. The text is in *Obras completas*, ed. cit., III, 1582–1607.

11 Calderón's thought is more Thomistic than this triple distinction would indicate. By "will" he understands the noncognitive inclination, by "desire" the will determined by the intellect (the knowledge that its object is desirable), and by "appetite" the sensitive appetite.

vain at possessing servants since she knows they are not hers
by right but by gift. In short, she is humbly grateful for the
gift of life and there is no pride in her as yet. Into this harmony,
through the Devil's envy of her happiness, there steps the figure
of Sin. She, not he, is the principal character in the drama that
follows: she it is who devises the plan for Human Nature's
downfall, and she, not he, tempts her. Yet Sin does this only
because the Devil is there: she cannot enter the garden without him. Both enter disguised, and this is important. Human
Nature, still innocent, cannot see Sin and the Devil as they
really are. The latter enters as the wolf in sheep's clothing, the
former as a gardener. In a scene of magnificently subtle poetry,
as Sin hoes around the apple tree so that the weeds may not
rob the fruit of its power to swell and ripen, she sings a song
whose burden is that a shepherdess may keep sheep but need
not keep faith [12]—the song of a cunning bawd subtly enticing a
woman to lose her purity by flattering her beauty. Human Nature listens in fascination while Sin insinuates into her mind
that there is nothing in the world as beautiful as she and therefore as worthy of being loved. The entry of Grace makes the
words of the song stick in Sin's throat, but the seed of vanity
has been sown.

How the wooing of Human Nature by the Devil in the
early play is here transformed! The Devil has now no direct
access to her. Between him and her there is the intermediary of
a crafty bawd. The bawd is sin, which is present as a possibility
in every creature with a mind and will, the possibility of the
negation or the perversion of good—here, in this allegory, as
the perversion of love. This perversion, which is potential in
Human Nature as an infidelity towards her Creator, is actualised
in the Devil in the form of envy which, St. Thomas tells us, is
the negation or opposite of charity or love of one's neighbour.
Because Sin is actualised in the Devil she is his companion;
because she is potential in Human Nature she has the direct
internal access to the human mind and will which is denied to
the Devil. That is the reason for her appearance as a dramatic

12 The couplets of the song, some of which are glossed, are taken from
one of Góngora's most splendid—and cynical—poems: "*Guarda corderos,
zagala,/ zagala, no guardes fe.*"

character. Calderón's Devil is still a lover, but now a perverted lover, and as such is evil. It is because he is a perverted lover that he takes, dramatically speaking, only a negative part in the action. The evil that matured in him as a perversion can sprout in man through sin because he, like the Devil, has a will that can be deflected from its proper object.

The proper object of the human will is God, and in the allegory of the play this is represented by the character Obedience, who symbolises Human Nature's acceptance of her status in humility, and her gratitude for the gift of life, recognised as a gift and not a right—this gratitude being her love of God. The temptation to vanity is the sign of incipient revolt, and Sin then plays her second card. Though she does the tempting, it is the Devil who gives her the snare in the form of a serpent that he plucks from his heart. To this Sin ties a ribbon and at the other end she ties an apple; making the Devil hide in a cave, she herself hides behind the tree and throws the apple at Human Nature's feet. The purpose of this is to indicate that Human Nature cannot see Sin because she has not yet committed it; for the same reason she cannot see the Devil. She can see only the apple. But the apple is attached to the Devil's serpent, which is held by Sin, because the evil inherent in the possibility of disobedience has, so far, been actualised only in the Devil. In following the apple Human Nature will move towards the Devil by following his example, but it will not be he who pulls the ribbon. Sin will do so, and the sin will be Human Nature's own. Original Sin was not the result of any compulsion on the Devil's part, for the Devil can only act on man through his imagination and his senses, not directly on his mind,[13] and Original Sin was the intellectual sin of pride. By this very careful selection of his allegorical devices Calderón is giving as exact a dramatic equivalent as possible of the precise distinctions of theology.

Sin, then, throws the apple at the feet of Human Nature and says: *"Come, y como Dios serás."* Human Nature, troubled

13 This essential aspect of the theology of the Devil will be discussed below in connection with another play where the details of the Devil's mode of temptation enter more fully into the dramatic action.

by the memory of Sin's song and by the thought of what her beauty might mean and offer, sees the apple and is at once struck by its attractiveness—if it is so lovely to look at, she asks, what will it be like when tasted? And it is now not Sin but her Will that says: *"Come della, y lo sabrás."* But Grace steps between the apple and Human Nature's Will. Desire and Appetite step forward in turn, only to find the way blocked by Grace. But Will, Desire, Appetite, and Sin all together say: *"Come, y como Dios serás."* This thought that she can cease to live in subordination and become mistress of her life in her own right takes hold of Human Nature's mind. Obedience is now the only obstacle, but its warnings and its reminder that she is but human are rejected by Human Nature, who replies: *"Por ser humana, me inclina/ mi espíritu a ser Divina."* Immediately Obedience falls to the ground and Grace withdraws. Determined to exploit the possibilities of her nature to the full, to become all that she thinks she is capable of becoming, Human Nature stoops to pick the apple. But Sin pulls it towards herself and when Human Nature, following it, picks it up and eats it, she finds herself face to face with Sin undisguised, and at the mouth of the cave where the Devil is waiting to receive her in his arms. Now, and only now, can the Devil come into contact with Human Nature. He has not pulled her: she has pushed herself into his arms, and the embrace of the two is the embrace of the perverted love that is love of self, the self-sufficiency which is the delight in oneself as if one were one's own principle, and which is the sin of pride. Pride has made Human Nature akin to the Devil, but now she discovers that she has been following a vain illusion, for the World rises against her to dispel the dream of power and greatness by showing her that she is not the mistress of life but the slave to nature in pain, suffering, and mortality. The rest of the play allegorises her rescue from sin and death by the self-sacrifice of the Faithful Shepherd, who teaches her by his example the true love of unselfish fidelity.

It will be apparent how Calderón's presentation of the Devil in this play has avoided the three pitfalls he fell into with *El veneno y la triaca.* First, he has presented the Devil as evil by making him the symbol of envy, of the perversion of love; motivated by a purely negative and destructive aim he wishes to see humanity robbed of the happiness of fulfilment because he is the spirit of disorder. Secondly, Calderón has avoided presenting the Devil as a personified Principle of Evil in antithetical rivalry with a Principle of Good, by making him subordinate to the abstract character of Sin who leads him and not he her. And Sin is presented not as a positive and constructive force but as the negation and perversion of Good. There is only one positive principle in the play and that is Love, which is the law of creation, the willing submission of the creature to the will of the Creator by submission to the law of its own nature; the abstract figure of Sin is the perversion of love by envy and pride. Thirdly, the connection between the evil of Original Sin and the Devil's malice is effected by the personification of Sin: she is the link between Satan and Man in that she is a projection of both, the turning away from order that is possible to all intelligent created beings. Through the perversion of love into the self-love of pride Man meets the Devil in Sin; both of their own accord introduce disorder into the order of the universe, but the Devil does so independently while Man follows his enticement.

My last example will be taken from Calderón's other type of drama, the *comedia*, which though not "philosophical" drama in the same way as the *auto sacramental*, exemplifies a technique that is none the less governed by a philosophical habit of mind. Here we meet the Devil in a more concrete form, with his activity more particularised—his intervention, namely, in the actual experience of an individual man. This will serve both to round off the main outline of Calderón's idea of the Devil and to clarify some of the points we have already met.

Calderón has two very fine *comedias* in which the Devil is a character, *El mágico prodigioso* and *El Josef de las mujeres*.[14] The former is one of his best-known plays. I propose to discuss it here, despite the fact that so much has been written about it,

14 The Devil or a diabolical figure also appears in *El purgatorio de San Patricio, El gran Príncipe de Fez, Las cadenas del demonio* (a play which I consider of doubtful authenticity), and *La margarita preciosa* (of which only the third act is by Calderón).

because the precise significance given to the Devil in it has passed undetected.[15]

The main action of the play dramatises, with several modifications, one of the versions of the legend of Sts. Cyprian and Justina of Antioch, according to which the magician Cyprian, falling in love with Justina, conjures his familiar spirits to bring her to him. Justina resists the temptations, and the Devil is compelled to confess himself vanquished because she is a Christian. Cyprian is converted by this evidence of a higher power than his diabolical arts, and he and Justina die as martyrs.[16] In the source, Cyprian's alliance with the Devil is presented as follows: "He invoked demons, offered sacrifices to them, swore eternal friendship and promised to recognise no other God than him who could contrive his possession of Justina." This promise of friendship and worship is changed by Calderón into a formal compact.[17]

A pact with the Devil, whereby a man signs a contract to surrender his soul to him at a specified time in return for certain benefits, was, of course, a very popular theme in medieval legend, and not only in connection with fictitious characters. Pope Silvester II, for instance, was believed a century after his death to have owed not only the great learning for which he was renowned but also his successful ecclesiastical career to a compact entered into with the Devil when he was a simple monk. In some of these stories, including one version of the Pope Silvester legend, the Devil obtains his legal payment of the man's soul; in others, however, although the Devil never on any occasion fails to fulfil his side of the bargain, the human party

15 Shelley translated a section from each act (812 lines in all), his rendering being first published in *Posthumous Works* (London, 1824). A translation of the complete play can be found in D. F. M'Carthy, *Calderón's Dramas* (London, 1873), but cannot be recommended. The adaptation by Edward Fitzgerald ("The Mighty Magician," in *Eight Dramas of Calderón* [London, 1906]) is so free that it cannot be considered Calderón at all; Fitzgerald himself had refused to publish it.

16 This is the version in the *Flos Sanctorum* of Alonso de Villegas (Madrid, 1594), fol. 321–322, which was Calderón's main source. See Max Krenkel, *Klassische Bühnendichtungen der Spanier* (Leipzig, 1885), II, 2–61.

17 This was suggested to Calderón by Antonio Mira de Amescua's play *El esclavo del demonio*, but the original features in Calderón's treatment of the compact, as described below, owe nothing to this earlier play.

to the contract defaults, breaking his vow by repentance—a fact that can provoke the cynical comment that medieval men portrayed the Devil as being more honest than themselves.[18] This impression of an honest Devil being defrauded of his legal right is one of the difficulties inherent in the theme of a diabolical pact. The other difficulty, which is the reverse corollary of the first, is exemplified by the well-known presentation of the theme in our own literature—Marlowe's *Dr. Faustus*. If the words of the play are taken literally, and the action realistically, it appears as if Faustus is prevented from repenting and so from breaking his vow by the threat of Mephistophilis to tear him to pieces if he does so, until, compelled to confirm the first pact with a second, he considers that it is too late to repent. So, in the tense and magnificent last speech, Faustus' passionate cry to God for mercy goes unheeded. This has led Santayana to assert that "This excellent Faustus is damned by accident or by predestination; he is brow-beaten by the devil and forbidden to repent when he has actually repented"; and that Marlowe was thus "on the way to reversing the Christian philosophy of life." [19] Marlowe has been convincingly defended against this accusation on the grounds that the action of the play is not to be taken realistically but allegorically.[20] None the less, the fact that the play needs to be defended against this charge is a further sign of how difficult it is to use the diabolical pact as a symbol of sin without falsifying theology. In the light of these two dangers let us note with what care and skill Calderón employs the symbol.

The opening of his play presents Cyprian as a student of philosophy who is eager to discover truth. He has walked out from Antioch into the country in order to meditate in solitude on the problem of the First Cause of the universe. The Devil appears in the guise of a traveller, tells Cyprian that he has lost his way while journeying to Antioch, and asks which is the direction. Cyprian expresses astonishment at the question, for

18 See, for instance, Arturo Graf, *Il diavolo* (Milano, 1889); Eng. trans. *The Story of the Devil* (London, 1931), pp. 141–142, 144.

19 G. Santayana, *Three Philosophical Poets* (Harvard Studies in Comparative Literature, vol. I, 1910), pp. 147, 149.

20 James Smith, "Marlowe's *Dr. Faustus*," *Scrutiny*, VIII (1939), 36–55.

the city is in full view of them and any path will take him there. The Devil replies: *"Ésa es la ignorancia, / a la vista de las ciencias / no saber aprovecharlas."* No critic has paid any attention to this remark which, together with the situation that prompted it, is not directly concerned with anything in the plot, either before or after. But it is precisely that fact that must make the reader stop and take careful note, for in Calderón's technique the apparently irrelevant remark is always a direct pointer to the understanding of the theme. The Devil here admits ignorance of a particular kind, and this is a definition both of what he is and of the form his intervention in the plot is going to take. Because it is a definition of the Devil we must stop for a moment to consider it.

One's first reaction is to be as surprised at the Devil's answer as Cyprian was at his question, for surely one cannot associate ignorance with the Devil. But Cyprian's surprise is more to the point. It is indeed a display of an odd kind of ignorance to have a city before your eyes and yet not know the way to it. Reference to St. Thomas can help us to understand what Calderón has in mind. When dealing with the sin of the fallen angels St. Thomas says that the Devil could not sin from ignorance in the sense of taking as good something that was intrinsically bad, because he had no passions to fetter his reason or understanding. But one can also sin by choosing what is good in itself, if one chooses it in such a way that one does not take into account the proper ordering of the action. He continues:

> This kind of sin does not presuppose ignorance, but only the fact that one has failed to consider what one ought to have considered. The angel sinned in this way, by using his free-will to turn towards his own good without being guided by the divine will.[21]

The whole of this passage is an answer to the objection that the angels could not sin because they were incapable of error.

21 *"Et hujusmodi peccatum non praeexigit ignorantiam, sed absentiam solum considerationis eorum quae considerari debent. Et hoc modo angelus peccavit, convertendo se per liberum arbitrium ad proprium bonum, absque ordine ad regulam divinae voluntatis."* (*Summa Theologica*, I, lxiii, 1, ad 4.)

Therefore when St. Thomas says that the Devil's sin did not
presuppose ignorance, some editors clarify the statement by adding a note to the effect that it does not presuppose the ignorance by which one does not take into consideration what one
should and could consider, this ignorance being a defect of attention.[22] Clearly the Devil was capable of this kind of wilful
ignorance.[23]

Defect of attention or lack of consideration is precisely
what Calderón's Devil means when he defines ignorance as
being in sight of knowledge but not using it. St. Thomas, when
discussing voluntary and involuntary acts, makes it clear that
defect of attention is in fact a form of ignorance. Ignorance
can be referred to the will in three ways: there is a "concomi-
tant ignorance" which produces a non-voluntary act, whereby
one does unknowingly what one would have done in any case
if the knowledge had been there (as when a man who has the
intention of killing his enemy when he next meets him, unknowingly kills him when hunting in the belief that he is shoot-
ing a stag); there is an "antecedent ignorance" which produces
an involuntary act (as when a man practising archery acciden-
tally kills a man he had not seen approaching); finally, there is
a "consequential ignorance" which produces a voluntary act.
This last is of two kinds: first, "affected ignorance," when one
refuses to acquire knowledge in order to retain an excuse for
one's wrongdoing; secondly, "the ignorance of wrong choice"
(*ignorantia malae electionis*), when one does not consider what
one ought to consider, or takes no trouble or care to acquire
the knowledge one ought to have.[24] Antecedent ignorance is,
of course, a cause of material sin only, while consequential ig-

22 So l'Abbé Drioux: "*Il ne préexige pas l'ignorance par laquelle on
prend le mal pour le bien, mais il préexige cette ignorance par laquelle on
ne considère pas en acte ce qu'on pourrait et ce qu'on devrait considérer,
et cette ignorance est un défaut d'attention.*" (*La Somme théologique de
Saint Thomas* [Paris, 1853], II, 502, n.2.)

23 [Lucifer's] sin, then, is to be found in his wilful ignoring of the
further order of his own perfection to divinity; ignorance in the sense of
lack of consideration was in the sin, surely, but *in* not preceding it, a part
and parcel of the free choice that sent the angelic hosts into hell." (W.
Farrell, O. P., "The Devil Himself," in *Satan*, p. 14.)

24 *Summa Theologica*, I, II, vi, 8.

norance is a cause of formal sin. The sin caused by the ignorance of wrong choice lies in the reason.[25]

Here, then, we have the full philosophical background to
the idea of the Devil underlying Calderón's presentation of him
in *El mágico prodigioso*. He represents that defect of reason
which is the ignorance that, through voluntary inattention to
a truth that is accessible and which it is necessary to know, leads
the will to make a wrong choice: "*Ésa es la ignorancia, / a la
vista de las ciencias / no saber aprovecharlas.*" This is a pointer
also to what will be his intervention in the play: the Devil will
act according to what he is, and his aim will be to try to make
Cyprian like himself—to induce him not to stretch out to the
knowledge he is within sight of.

This knowledge is the existence and nature of God. By the
use of his reason, aided by the pagan philosophers, Cyprian has
succeeded in postulating the necessary existence of a First Cause,
which, he further declares, must have the attributes of Unity,
Goodness, Omniscience, and Omnipotence. The difficulty with
which he is now faced is: where is this First Cause to be found.
In short, he has apprehended the existence of the God of the
philosophers. But for his intellect to be perfected he must proceed to the knowledge of the God of the Christians. That is
why the Devil appears at that precise moment and in the particular way I have described—in sight of Antioch yet asserting
that he does not know the way there. Because always when the
reason is within sight of a knowledge that is necessary for the
proper ordering of life there is the possibility that it will remain
in ignorance through deliberate inattention or distraction. The
Devil as a dramatic character thus actualises for the audience,
in visible form, a potentiality within Cyprian himself, and it is
essential for the full appreciation of Calderón's dramatisation of
the idea of the evil to realise that though as regards the stage
plot he plays an independent role, as regards the theme he is
the projection, as it were, of processes that go on within Cyp-

25 "*Utroque igitur modo contingit esse peccatum in ratione: et primo
quidem, inquantum errat in cognitione veri; quod quidem tunc imputatur
ei ad peccatum, quando habet ignorantiam vel errorem circa id quod potest
et debet scire*" (I, II, lxxiv, 5).

rian's mind, imagination, and sensibility. If the Devil is removed entirely from the action, the play as a play will of course be ruined, but the theme—the idea behind the plot—will still be complete and consistent, for all Cyprian's actions are perfectly explicable in terms of his intellect and will, and need no external supernatural influence to make them happen.

This is in accordance with the fundamental theological principle that the Devil cannot exert any direct influence on the human will: he tempts from without, but so does concupiscence from within, and the Devil's pull can have no effect unless it is combined with a push from within.[26]

The Devil cannot, as St. Thomas makes clear, act directly upon the human intellect; internally he can only act upon the imagination and the sensitive appetite.[27] Externally he can act upon the senses.[28] He acts upon the sensitive appetite by exciting the passions, though he cannot compel the will to consent to them.[29] He can act upon the imagination by causing images to appear, but he cannot produce new images which had not previously been received through sense impressions; he can only present to the imagination the objects of a man's own experience and sense knowledge.[30]

It is in accordance with these Thomistic conclusions that the Devil's temptation unfolds itself in El mágico prodigioso. He argues with Cyprian, defending pagan polytheism, but he cannot induce his reason to fall into any intellectual error. He therefore withdraws, awaiting the opportunity to entice him into the ignorance of inattention by working upon his imagination. This opportunity comes when Cyprian, who has hitherto been absorbed in his philosophical studies, makes the acquaintance of Justina and, falling in love with her, is awakened for the first time to concupiscence. Here is the distraction that can immobilise his reason in voluntary ignorance within sight of knowledge, for Justina becomes the good he now desires above all else, becomes, as he himself puts it, the God he is searching

26 See J. de Tonquédec, S. J., "Some Aspects of Satan's Activity in this World," in Satan, p. 43.

27 Summa Theologica, I, II, lxxx, 2.

28 Ibid., I, cxi, 4.

29 Ibid., I, cxi, 2.

30 Ibid., I, cxi, 3.

for. She, a Christian in a pagan city, will have nothing to do
with his advances and forbids him access to her presence. Cyprian, therefore, can satisfy his passion only by conjuring up the
form of his new god in his imagination. The Devil can therefore begin his work: this is the push from within that he needs
before his pull from without can be effective. When Cyprian
in the frenzy of passion cries out that he would barter his soul
for the possession of Justina, the Devil, in a new disguise, appears on the scene and accepts it, offering in exchange to teach
Cyprian the art of magic that will bring him what he desires;
and the contract between the two is signed. This episode shows
an original feature. In the source from which Calderón derives
the main element of his plot and, if I am not mistaken, in the
great majority of, if not all, the host of literary precedents for
a diabolical pact, the man who enters into the compact knows
that his partner is the Devil; but Calderón's Cyprian does not—
he thinks him to be a human magician. This is another example
of Calderón's fidelity to the philosophy that formed his mind,
for St. Thomas, and with him all Catholic moral theologians,
holds that sins of the flesh are less grave than sins of the mind.
The first of the three reasons St. Thomas gives [31] is that sins
of the flesh are a turning *towards* the object desired, the principal function of carnal appetite being the good of the body,
while sins of the mind are a turning *away* from God, to whom
the mind ought to be directed, and it is this turning away from
God that constitutes the nature of sin. Carnal love is not in
itself the malice of the will disordered by a deliberate, cold-
blooded judgement of the reason; the stress of physical passion
is what removes it from the intellectual sin of pride that was
the sin of Satan. That is why Cyprian does not recognise or
know the Devil, and therefore does not directly choose association with him. Only at the end, when his reason again functions
clearly, no longer blurred by passion, does he discover the Devil's
identity on realising that in subordinating the good of the mind
to the good of the body and making Justina his god, he has
abandoned himself to evil. The realisation comes when his
magic does not work. The Devil tempts Justina by evoking

31 Ibid., I, II, lxxiii, 5.

amorous suggestions in her imagination, but her will to purity, rooted in her love of God, enables her to resist. When the time comes for the Devil to fulfil his part of the bargain, all he can bring to Cyprian is a phantom Justina which, when he embraces it, turns out to be a skeleton that says: "*Así, Cipriano, son / todas las glorias del mundo*." This realisation on Cyprian's part that he has been pursuing a good that leads only to its own dissolution in death makes his intellect once more active. Why has the magic failed? Behind the radical incapacity of the carnal appetite to produce a lasting happiness there must lie a living and enduring truth, and it is the truth that once again he wants. No longer does he allow himself to be blinded by ignorance when in sight of knowledge, and the Devil's hold on him is broken.

There are three further departures here from the traditional pattern of the diabolical pact stories, two of which were suggested in Calderón's source, First, Cyprian does not recover his signed pact; it remains in the Devil's possession who finds, after Cyprian's martyrdom, that it has become blank. This indicates that as long as a man lives he is capable of mortal sin and therefore potentially in the power of the Devil until his salvation. Secondly, in nearly all the stories of diabolical pacts, the Devil fulfils his part of the bargain and it is the sinner who breaks the contract by repentance; but it is not possible to see Calderón's Devil as honest and Cyprian as dishonest, in a legal sense, for the Devil in both the play and its source is impotent to fulfil his promises because he cannot coerce the human will. Thirdly, developing a hint in his source, Calderón makes Cyprian force from the Devil's lips, one by one, the answers to his imperious questions concerning the power that kept Justina free. The Devil is compelled to tell him that the One, Good, Omniscient and Omnipotent First Cause is the God of the Christians. And this is Calderón's last word on the Devil in this play: by the very ignorance in sight of knowledge that he represents and seeks to inculcate in men, which makes him impotent to bring the happiness he promises, he is a witness to the goodness and power of God. From the knowledge of the First Cause Cyprian arrives at the knowledge of God in Faith, Hope, and Charity, and is united to Justina in the profession of his faith which they both seal by martyrdom together.

It will have been noticed that by identifying the Devil with ignorance, and specifically with the ignorance with which Cyprian of his own accord obstructs his own reason, Calderón has done in a different way the two things he did in *El Pastor Fido*: he has emphasised the fact that evil is a negation (in this case it follows from the exclusion of knowledge), and he has prevented the traditional device of externalising the Devil (as a dramatic character in his own right) from turning the human, moral struggle into a rivalry between two external, magnetic forces, each struggling to draw man's will. There are indeed two external magnets—the one is truth, which draws the reason and can alone satisfy it; the other is the carnal good that draws the sensitive appetite. But the latter is not evil *per se* and its association with the Devil does not turn him into a positive principle of evil. The moral defect lies not in the carnal appetite but in the subjection to it of the reason by clouding the latter with ignorance and so preventing its fulfilment. This defect is a disharmony in the relationship between the intellectual faculties and the sensible equipment of man and is not caused by the Devil. It is associated with him as something that, once it is there, he can encourage in order to prevent the movement of the mind from ignorance to knowledge. It is man himself who, by permitting disorder to arise within his own being, steps towards the realm of ignorance and deathly emptiness where the Devil is waiting to receive him.

Because these principles are in conformity with St. Thomas, I have thought that the subject of this paper would not be outside the interests of an Aquinas Society. Though I have dealt only with three plays, and though one superbly original dramatic subtlety has not been touched on,[32] all the essentials of Calderón's dramatisation of the Devil have, I think, been covered. I trust this has shown that Calderón is a dramatist who deserves not to be ignored by Catholic theologians and philosophers and, more particularly, that the authoritative book on Satan to which I referred at the beginning should not have omitted him from its section on the Devil in literature.

32 I have dealt with it in *The Allegorical Drama of Calderón*, pp. 82–94. See also the analysis of the Devil's dramatic function in my edition of *No hay más fortuna que Dios* (Manchester, 1949), pp. xxvi–xxxiii.

2 · Honour and the Christian Background in Calderón

by P. N. Dunn

I. THE DRAMAS OF REVENGE

Tres cosas reservó Dios para sí, y no quiso que nadie se las tomase. La primera es juzgar la intención y pensamientos de nuestros prójimos, según aquello que él mesmo dice: "No queráis juzgar, y no seréis juzgados". . . . La segunda, la honra y gloria, conforme a aquello que dice el mesmo Dios: "No daré a nadie mi gloria". La tercera cosa que reservó para sí es la venganza. Guárdate de hurtar a Dios ninguna de estas cosas.

(Fray Diego de Estella)

Hostile criticism of Calderón's "honour plays" has generally taken one of two forms. What we may call the traditional attitude regards the plays as immoral. More recently there has been a shift, a sort of moral disengagement among certain critics whose attitude is that the plays express objective sociological facts which it would be an impertinence to consider in Christian terms.[1] These writers may not be hostile to the plays themselves, but their attitude, with its implication of rigid social conformity, is ultimately damaging to Calderón's reputation. On the other hand, *El alcalde de Zalamea* has been generally esteemed for the breadth and humanity of its conception as well as for the dignity of its central character. It would be only natural for the critic to feel embarrassment in such a situation, for it is not

---

1 Américo Castro, "*Algunas observaciones acerca del concepto del honor en los siglos XVI y XVII*," RFE, III (1916); R. Menéndez Pidal, "*Del honor en el teatro español*" in De Cervantes y Lope de Vega, Colección Austral; Alfonso García Valdecasas, *El hidalgo y el honor* (Madrid, 1948); Ángel Valbuena Prat, *Historia del teatro español* (Barcelona, 1956).

easy to deal justly with a dramatist whom one believes capable of extremes of brutality and humanity in his treatment of aspects of the same theme—personal honour. Menéndez y Pelayo is the best representative of the traditional attitude, with his declaration that such plays as *A secreto agravio secreta venganza* were "*radicalmente inmorales.*" [2] He also placed *El alcalde de Zalamea* on a pinnacle above all of Calderón's other works, stating that Pedro Crespo combined justice and personal vengeance in a single act, "*confundiendo en uno (lo repito) el desagravio de su propia sangre y el desagravio de la ley moral.*" [3] If private vengeance were in fact cloaked in retributive justice, it is difficult to see how this play could escape the charge of being "fundamentally immoral." It would be ungrateful to disparage Menéndez y Pelayo for the faults which beset his great virtues, but here we have a sign of the strain produced by the apparent opposition between the "honour plays" and *El alcalde de Zalamea.*

Must we accept that human fallibility has permitted an unresolved contradiction in Calderón's work? We might prefer to allow that dramatists, like critics, are free to change their minds. We might make a third suggestion, and argue that an artist is at liberty to present different, even conflicting solutions of human problems, because these different solutions are interesting in themselves. Menéndez y Pelayo offered this possibility when he said that "*Cabe todavía otra justificación, y es que el autor, a pesar de las pretensiones dogmáticas que en algunos títulos de sus obras aparecen . . . en realidad nunca se propuso demostrar tesis ninguna, sino que eligió el asunto por sus ventajas estéticas.*" [4] As to the first suggestion, the extraordinary intellectual rigour and the commanding logic which mark Calderón's work make it difficult to believe that he held irreconcilable attitudes in different plays. Amid all the diversity of critical opinion, the supreme consistency of Calderón's work emerges with common recognition and consent. As to the second suggestion, we may change our political coat or critical theory without deeply involving our personality, but our concep-

2 *Calderón y su teatro*, 3rd ed. (Madrid, 1884), p. 279.
3 Op. cit., p. 276.
4 Op. cit., p. 281.

tion of what is right in personal relations, and especially our attitude to the demands made by conventionally acceptable codes
of behaviour are deeply rooted in our nature and highly resis-
tant to change. The more we consider these matters and weave
our feelings and intuitions into a reasoned moral scheme, the
less likely it is that we shall be either willing or able to change
the scheme. The third suggestion meets with the same objections. When Calderón gathers up conventional sentiments
about the fidelity of women, arranges them so that they reveal
a coherent and logical scheme of values, and then demonstrates
that these values can lend their support to calculated murder,
it is idle to talk of the beauty of his raw material. This is not
to say that he was indifferent to what his audience might be
expected to feel. It is only fair to notice that Menéndez y Pelayo
suggested that

> aun cabe otra justificación, y es que Calderón abominaba ex
> toto corde, y tenía por locura y aberración, estos extremos del
> principio del honor, y lo dice a cada paso en boca de sus
> personajes, que establecen así una contradicción perpetua entre
> sus palabras y sus hechos.[5]

Menéndez y Pelayo seems to have been unable to take this
possibility further.

The other critical attitude is that which takes Calderón
to be faithful mirror of the prevailing habits of thought. As
evidence, we have even been shown some moralists and writers
of manuals for priests in confessional who allowed that, in the
service of his honour, a man might commit what would otherwise be regarded as mortal sin.[6] However, these documents do
not prove that Calderón thought in the same way. Moreover,
in an interesting recent article, C. A. Jones has shown that
Castro's reading of them is entirely misleading.[7] Calderón is
generally acknowledged to be a fine analyst of motives and of
opposing loyalties, but we must not confuse Calderón's thinking with the logic of the dramatic events, or his distinctions
with the aberrant scruples of his characters. If we need authority

5 Ibid.
6 Castro, Menéndez Pidal, op. cit.
7 "*Honor* in Spanish Golden-Age Drama; Its Relation to Real Life and
to Morals," BHS, xxxv (1958), 199-210.

for Calderón's way of thinking, we can find it in the works of such writers as St. Theresa, Diego de Estella, Alejo Venegas, Juan de Ávila, to name only a few from among that great ascetic, but profoundly compassionate, tradition which is so strong a feature of the "*Siglo de Oro*." In the works of these authors we almost always find a chapter devoted to *la vana honra del mundo* or *la vanidad de los que vengan sus injurias*. In all the wealth of expression and illustration, the basic thought of these writers was clear and true to its origins: the only true honour is that which is accorded to virtuous living. This honour is imperishable because it is part of being in the community of the Mystical Body of Christ; no man may judge another man. All this was familiar ground to Calderón. If we are to overcome the apparent dichotomy, we must be prepared to show that, in spite of differences of thematic material, there is something common to the conception of such plays as *El médico de su honra* and *El alcalde de Zalamea*.

In recent years we have seen efforts being made to show that Calderón was neither an advocate of revenge nor an unquestioning accepter of accepted social attitudes.[8] Some critics, who cannot accept that Calderón is not justifying the conduct of vengeful characters, have dismissed such suggestions as "modern." Professor Parker saw in *La devoción de la Cruz* "*la condenación de un concepto extravagante del honor que pervierte lo que debiera ser el ideal de una integridad moral personal hasta convertirlo en una exaltación puramente egoísta de le categoría social.*"[9] In consequence, he has been reproached by Constandse[10] (in a Freudian analysis of Calderón and his

8 Pioneer work has been done by Professors Parker and Wilson, and I would like to acknowledge my debt to them. This new critical orientation is also evident in the recent book by Professor A. E. Sloman, *The Dramatic Craftsmanship of Calderón* (Oxford, 1958).

9 A. A. Parker, "Santos y bandoleros en el teatro español del Siglo de Oro," *Arbor*, Nos. 43–44 (1949), 409.

10 A. L. Constandse, *Le Baroque espagnol et Calderón de la Barca* (Amsterdam, 1951). "*Si Parker avait parlé ainsi de Cervantes, qui certainement identifiait honneur et vertu, qui prêchait la tolérance et la compréhension entre deux époux, il aurait pu avoir raison. . . . Le jugement de Parker est celui du vingtième siècle*" (p. 107). "*Calderón révèle son propre caractère conformiste et même 'sadique' au moyen de ces drames sanglants et cruels*" (p. 123).

work), and by Valbuena [11] for looking at Calderón from the standpoint of the twentieth century. If this is so, the sixteenth- and seventeenth-century writers mentioned above, and many others, must also be tainted with "modernity."

The sociological facts must be given their due, but only in the form in which the writer can use them—as people doing and believing, exercising or suspending judgement. A dramatist makes imaginary people in order to show them to real people who, from the point of view of moral awareness, may be scarcely more real than the imaginary ones. This is the limitation and also the opportunity which the theatre offers. It is probable that Calderón had in mind an audience which (to judge from the annals of the time and from the social observations of con- temporary novelists) contained a fair proportion of gentlemen who were susceptible of their blood, their privileges, their rank, and what the neighbours thought of them; who, at Mass, took the opportunity to spy upon the women of their household or to offer gallantries to other women; who thought it unmanly to grant another man his opinion or to fail to answer arrogance with arrogance; caught up in their catch-phrases, *"mi opinión . . . quien soy . . . lo que valgo . . . ;"* doing, in short, the conventional, bloody-minded thing, acting like dramatic clichés, mistaking humility for softness, convinced that they were good Christians and explaining, if pressed, that we cannot all be saints. When Calderón showed to these men the perfected simulacrum of themselves in his "honour plays," it was as if to say: "You are trying to have the best of both worlds and are losing both. It would be better to follow wholeheartedly and consistently a worldly canon than try to compromise with Christian values, so long as you realise what are the conse- quences to yourself and others of choosing that way. These plays do not grudge the qualities of dignity and respect, but the terrible consequences which I have shown are also latent in this exaltation of honour and conformity, even at its best."

It has become customary to say that the theocentric way of thinking remained viable in Spain for longer than in the

11 Valbuena, op. cit.; *"Calderón no podía pensar así, porque lo injusto de la ley del honor, aun sólo en apariencia de adulterio . . . llevaba im- plícita una cruenta sanción"* (p. 239).

rest of Europe. Whatever qualifications we make about this, it would surely be fanciful to interpret Calderón's plays in a way which implied a purely secular understanding of the values involved in human relations. Even Lope's cynical comedies imply a standpoint of order from which the spectacle of confusion can be vicariously enjoyed. Although Calderón has kept the action of his plays at an impersonal distance from himself, he is not practising a documentary realism. We have to overcome habits of mind produced by the nineteenth-century literary practice of controlling the spectator's or the reader's judgement, by putting a sympathetic character at the centre of the action.

The recent studies referred to above [12] mark a valuable departure from views accepted hitherto, in showing how Calderón uses character and situation so as to make demands on the moral awareness of his audience, and lead it to a critical attitude towards the code of honour. My approach is rather different, in that I wish to suggest other points at which the audience's judgement is involved. Calderón adopts, for the purposes of his "honour plays," a system of values which, in certain situations, demands killing. These values and the violence which they prescribe may be said to point, in a negative way, to the Christian values which lie outside the play, and to which Calderón subscribed.[13] But at many points in these plays we come upon examples of another relation between the values which are accepted for the play's sake, and those which shape the Christian life. This relation is that of travesty. The spiritual realities which lie beyond the fiction are present within it too, but in a perverted form, and there are a number of pointers to show how these plays are knit into their Christian context. The most notable instances, as I hope to show, are in the ambivalent symbolism of honour itself.

It is in our nature to be continually setting up false gods.

[12] Parker, op. cit.; *The Approach to the Spanish Drama of the Golden Age, Diamante* series, no. 6 (London, 1957); E. M. Wilson, "La discreción de Don Lope de Almeida," *Clavileño,* No. 9 (1951); "Gerald Brenan's Calderón," *BCom,* VI, i (1952); Sloman, op. cit.

[13] Wilson has drawn attention to the crucifix over Doña Mencía's death-bed in *El médico . . . ;* "it contrasts divine forgiveness with the cruelty of a man-made law." *BCom,* art. cit.

If we worship any of them with consistent devotion, shaping our whole life and bringing all our qualities to bear upon its service, we are creating for it a religion and a ritual. So with courtly love. Lover poets, whether or not they have been influenced by Albigensian heresies, Moslem mystics, or Andalusian poetry, have expressed their complete absorption in the object of their love in the terms of a pseudo-religion and, while speaking figuratively, they have spoken the truth. So, too, with honour. The vengeful husbands of Calderón's plays pursue honour as a supreme good, and such values as love and mercy are sacrificed to its demands. We may reasonably think of honour, then, as a religion in which the values of our own experience are inverted. In calling honour a *religion* we, in our analytical age, immediately become aware that we are speaking figuratively, and may well be afraid of speaking *merely* figuratively. But I think that Calderón stresses the resemblances to the point where we can make this equation. We can see him investing honour with the attributes of a religion, or more correctly, drawing implications from the assumptions, practice, and rhetoric of honour which will invite us to consider what kind of thing it is, and whether even its virtues can be accommodated to Christian values.

At the end of his excellent analysis of A *secreto agravio secreta venganza*, Professor Wilson makes some interesting and suggestive concluding remarks. Don Lope de Almeida is so much the master of his actions, and his feelings are so subordinated to his faith in honour, that "*es como un místico del honor.*" "*Don Juan de Silva cree en el honor; pero su discreción es menor. . . . Doña Leonor cree en el honor pero es arrebatada por sus pasiones: es una pecadora del honor.*" Don Luis de Benavides follows only his inclinations, and is "*un apóstata del honor.*" The play, then, is "*una especie de disfrazada comedia de santos.*" [14] Professor Wilson also says in this article and elsewhere that Calderón demonstrates both the cruelty and the virtues of the code of honour. I see it in a rather different way. When we follow false gods we do not leave our virtues behind. On the contrary, the dedication to them of generosity, love,

14 Art. cit., *Clavileño*, 9 (1951).

devotion, and all our care, makes the initial error that much more tragic.

It is an ancient literary *topos* that when the hero is overtaken by misfortune, he reminds his gods that he has always been their obedient servant. So in Garcilaso's *Égloga primera* the unfortunate Nemoroso complains to the goddess Lucina that

> *su reposo*
> *era seguir tu oficio, persiguiendo*
> *las fieras por los montes, y ofreciendo*
> *a tus sagradas aras los despojos.*

In *A secreto agravio secreta venganza* Don Lope makes a similar declaration, but its implications are far-reaching. In his anguish he addresses his honour and protests that he has dedicated his life and even fostered his virtues as part of his pious cult of honour: [15]

> *Yo, por no ponerte a riesgo,*
> *¿toda mi vida no he sido*
> *con el humilde, cortés,*
> *con el caballero, amigo,*
> *con el pobre, liberal,*
> *con el soldado bienquisto?* (307)

We may recall also how Don Amor, in the *Libro de buen amor*, steals the moral thunder of the "Archpriest" and subtly distorts his objections, by saying that love does not deprave, because a lover, in order to be successful, must employ the virtues. The "Archpriest" is too ingenuous and too willing to be convinced to ask whether virtues so cultivated may lose their virtue. (Don Amor is a "false god," so the parallel with honour is not surprising.) Questions such as this are the concern of the reader's rational judgement, and they occur in a great deal of the literature of the Golden Age. It seems to me to be simpler, in the end, to consider these implications in what the characters say, or do not say, first of all, before approaching the more difficult business of evaluating by reference to "character." By these means a dramatist can satisfy the moral demands of his audience

15 For the sake of convenience, all references are to the edition of L. Astrana Marín, 3rd ed. (Madrid, 1945).

without making his characters morally simple. These clues are the safeguard with which he can allow himself apparent incongruities of character, trusting that we shall see their relevance, not be disconcerted by them.[16]

The above quotation perfectly displays the piety of honour, which is a real piety, and at the same time, a travesty of true religious piety. It reveals a moral striving which, far from being God-centred or disinterested, is honour-centred and calculated. Another aspect of honour, which is widely current before Calderón [17] and which is of fundamental importance in his formulation of its ideological content, is the notion of consent. Honour is conferred as an act of grace, not as of right. *Quien soy* has its place when a course of action has to be determined, but neither virtue nor lineage is proof against dishonour. Like divine grace, which it parodies, honour may be given or withdrawn without regard to merit. So,

> Leonor es quien es, y yo
> soy quien soy, y nadie puede
> borrar fama tan segura
> ni opinión tan excelente.
> Pero sí puede (¡ay de mí!)   (298b)

If honour is a kind of religion, and religion demands an ordering of the will, then the travesty of Christianity will emerge on other levels. But in the nature of the case, we shall find further important implications for the theology of honour on these other levels. A religion has a central rite which expresses and sustains the relation between god and man. There is shedding of blood, in fact or in symbol; ritual sacrifice, either as self-giving or as propitiation. Instances of protest against the cruel acts which the code of honour demands are familiar, but the notable thing about them is the spirit in which they are uttered. The protests barely disguise the unshakeable belief that honour

16 E.g. the rectitude, generosity, etc., of men who kill for honour; the "saintliness" of Paulo in *El condenado por desconfiado*—see T. E. May, *BHS*, xxxv (1958).

17 E.g., in Lope's *Los comendadores de Córdoba:*
> Honra es aquella que consiste en otro;
> ningún hombre es honrada por sí mismo,
> que del otro recibe la honra un hombre;
> ser virtuoso hombre y tener méritos,
> no es ser honrado.   (ed. R. Acad. Esp., xi, 290b)

must have its blood sacrifice, and far from weakening that belief, they stress its power to bind. In *El pintor de su deshonra* Don Juan Roca refers, in the course of his tirade, to the *"infame rito"* which it is his duty to perform (572a). *"Infame"* expresses his human feeling, but the *"rito"* indicates that he is committed morally to an act of faith which makes his feelings of no account. The strength of these protests serves dramatically to stress the greater force of this "religion" which can override all other considerations. The bloody vengeance is an imperative to which the man of honour is bound, for *honor* imposes it as a moral duty. The protest does not weaken *honor*; it is rather a kind of sacrilege which, like swearing, testifies to the belief of the swearer. Cursing may be so wild as to be absurd, a blind swing at a target which is too big to miss, but invulnerable—like spitting at the sky. There is something of this comic wilfulness and tragic futility in the rage of Don Juan Roca with its cursing refrain: *"¡ Mal haya el primero, amén, / que hizo ley tan rigurosa !"* (572a) This style of speech is common among *graciosos*, whose job is frequently to make tragic absurdity laughable. We may recall the words of Catalinón in Act I of *El burlador de Sevilla* as he carries Don Juan ashore:

> *¡Mal haya aquél que primero*
> *pinos en la mar sembró*
> *y que sus rumbos midió*
> *con quebradizo madero!*

Phrases like *"¡Mal haya el primero que . . . !"* enable us to imagine that not only our misfortunes, but also the ways in which we can deal with them, are determined by fate. The cards have not turned up as they should: *"¡mal haya el que inventó los naipes!"* It is easy to forget that we accepted the rules of the game and knew the risks. Anger is not normally comic, so that when Calderón makes it appear so, we may presume that it is misdirected or self-deluded.

The protests emphasize honour's burden. They are also an imprecation against "the world," or against the "frail vessel" in whom honour is deposited:

> *A peligro estáis, honor,*
> *no hay hora en vos que no sea*
> *crítica, en vuestro sepulcro*
> *vivís, puesto que os alienta*

la mujer, en ella estáis
pisando siempre la huesa. (*El médico,* 200b)

¿En qué tribunal se ha visto
condenar al inocente?
¿Sentencias hay sin delito?
¿Informaciones sin cargo?
Y sin culpas, ¿hay castigo?
¡Oh locas leyes del mundo!

. . . .
. . . .

¿Quién puso el honor en vaso
que es tan frágil?
(*A secreto agravio* . . . 307–08)

If we look carefully at these speeches of protest, we find that
they are not really critical of honour and its impossible demand
for perfection, but of the human frailties which bring the sanctions of honour into operation. Vengeance can be seen as the
sacrifice of innocent blood in order to make a perverse atone-
ment for the imperfections of humanity. The law [18] of honour
assumes that human nature and the world are unredeemed and
unregenerate. It is an interesting coincidence—or is it really a
coincidence?—that this is the language of the Devil in *La creación del mundo.* Lucifer, watching the creation of Adam and
the privileges granted to Humanity, is full of resentment that
God ". . . . *derrama / en barro quebradizo honras iguales.*" [19]

Honour also has symbols which convey its spiritual content.
It appropriates to itself some of the most powerful images in
our vocabulary—gold, the sun, light—all of which have acquired
great range and depth of moral and spiritual application. These
symbols occupy a central place in the language of religious
literature, and their use in the language of *honor* is not fortuitous. St. Thomas Aquinas pointed out that the gold which was
brought by the Magi signified wisdom,[20] and Calderón's avenging husbands indeed display a stealthy prudence and tact when
their suspicions have been aroused. Since such symbols already

18 Concerning the phrase *ley de honor,* we might bear in mind the
common usage *ley* = "religion," "faith"; e.g., *ley vieja, ley nueva, ley de
Gracia, ley cristiana,* etc.
19 Lope de Vega [?], *La creación del mundo y primera culpa del
hombre* (*Obras de Lope de Vega,* Acad., III, 178b).
20 *Summa Theologica,* III, 36, viii.

have an established place in the language of Christianity, they
have an important part in the parodic movement of these plays.
Travesty, unlike more innocent kinds of analogy, seeks to wound
the thing travestied. Instead of parallel progression there is
convergence and collision. This strife between the values of
honor and the divine realities is brought to a focus in these symbols. In *A secreto agravio secreta venganza*, Don Lope de Almeida makes the well-known comparison between purging his
honour and purifying gold by fire:

> *Sacaré acendrado dél [del fuego]*
> *el honor que me ilustró,*
> *ya que la liga ensució*
> *una mancha tan cruel;*
>   *y en una experiencia tal,*
> *por los crisoles no ignoro*
> *que salga acendrado el oro*
> *sin aquel bajo metal*
>   *de la liga que tenía*
> *y su valor deslustraba.*   (313)

The refining of metals by fire has had a long life as a religious
metaphor (e.g., Zech. 13. ix; I St. Peter 1. vi-vii) and is closely
connected with other expressions of cleansing and purifying.
But if fire is a cleansing agent, we cannot forget that it is primarily the destructive element, and in fact its power to cleanse
requires a nice control of its power to destroy. There can be
righteous destruction, as when the Prophets remind the wicked
that they shall be cast into the fire, or their cities destroyed by
fire. Destruction of a different sort may hide under the euphe-
mism of cleansing.

    Men of honour reconcile themselves to their code through
bloodshed, instead of to human nature through mercy, and
usurp the vengeance which God claimed as his own. We have
already noticed that the protests against the sanctions of honour
are spoken in bitterness against human nature. Honour is a
religion of perfection, but since humanity is not perfect, men of
honour may find that they have to avenge themselves on what
they love most. They inhabit a world which is unredeemed and
epitomised by symbols of the fallen state of mankind. In *A
secreto agravio secreta venganza*, as in other plays, Calderón

takes imagery from the elements—Earth, Air, Fire, Water—so
as to indicate the effects of powerful feelings. By breaking the
usual symmetry, or by having one element usurp the function
of another, he can represent confusion or disorientation in the
mind of the speaker.[21] The elements have other claims on our
attention, too. For one thing, they have an important part in
this play, like that of the classical Furies. Moreover, we have
to bear in mind the continuance into the seventeenth century
of the traditional belief that all Creation rested on an inner
principle of orderliness, of harmony attained through authority
and obedience. If man is seen as reflecting the divine order in
his physical being and in his spiritual nature, it is reasonable
that disorder in man should be shown poetically to introduce
disruption into the macrocosm. No man is an island, and the
disruption in one man's moral being may spread by reverbera-
tion to others, and into the world, for the world is a similitude
of his moral nature, and the cohesive pattern of order is common to both. Don Lope unleashes the destructive elements
of fire and water to restore his honour, and we remember how,
after creating the world from chaos, and before the Mosaic
covenant, God punished with fire and water. Don Lope not
only usurps God's exclusive right ("Vengeance is mine, saith
the Lord"), but the manner of his revenge travesties the punishments wrought by Jehovah. More important still, while releasing
the destructive natural powers of the elements, this "cleansing"
parodies their sacramental powers. The new dispensation, in-
augurated by Christ's sacrifice, united a broken world through
love. But *honor* knows no redemption; it demands the ancient
retributive rites.

In *El pintor de su deshonra* the elements of fire and water
are symbolically belligerent. Don Juan Roca plunges into the
sea, declaring:

> que yo
> contra el fuego y contra el agua
> lidiaré igualmente. Dadme,
> ¡cielos!, o muerte o venganza.   (566b)

---

21 Wilson, *Clavileño*, loc. cit.; also "The Four Elements in the
Imagery of Calderón," *MLR*, xxxi (1936).

The language here does more than express the impossibility
of his headlong pursuit. The selfish passion of Don Álvaro has
done violence to the inherent order, and he has made the destructive elements his allies (the fire at the house, and the
abduction by sea). Don Juan's answer will be to try to suppress violence with violence: *"lidiaré igualmente."* He himself
will match the fury of the destructive elements. But if we look
at these words with other eyes than those of Don Juan, we see
that *"lidaré igulamente"* is as unrealistic as his gesture in rushing
to pursue the ship. The violence done by Don Álvaro is an
injury to Don Juan and to the moral order, which is beyond
the capacity of a man to repair. He is uttering the tragic irony
of his position: to try to do what only a god can do (and that
by self-sacrifice), is to try to fight sea and fire on equal terms.[22]

A great deal could be said about the sun, which stands for
honour, and which, at the end of *El médico de su honra*, is
blotted out in a lurid vision of honour's passion:

> *Vuelve a esta parte la cara,*
> *y verás sangriento el sol,*
> *verás la luna eclipsada,*
> *deslucidas las estrellas*
> *y las esferas borradas. . . .*   (213b)

Outwardly Don Gutierre is lamenting the death of his wife.
Doña Mencía, however, was only once called *Sol*, namely in
Act I, when Don Gutierre was countering her jealous suspicions
of Doña Leonor (Leonor was the moon; Mencía is the sun).
Apart from this one occasion, *sol* represents honour, or the
royal persons who are concerned with it. *Sol* is also implied
during Don Gutierre's interview with the King, at the beginning of Act III:

> *hasta que tirana fue*
> *la nube que turbar osa*
> *tanto esplendor en mi esposa,*
> *y tanto lustre en mi fe.*

22 Don Juan Roca's words are brief, but they range widely. The immediate reference is to the house on fire and to the abduction by sea, but
connected with these are the amorous fire of Don Álvaro and the presence
of the sea as an omen of treachery from the earliest moments of the play.

Therein, however, honour is the real subject of this discourse. Calderón withholds the common endearing use of *sol*, so that this figure shall stand unambiguously for honour which, in Don Gutierre's scale of values, is more important than the human vessel to which it is entrusted. Then, when Doña Mencía has been murdered, we are troubled by some apparent incongruities. The first is that Don Gutierre tells the other persons on the stage that the light of his world has been put out ("*Vuelve a esta parte la cara. . . .* "), giving to the word *sol* the amatory sense which has so far been excluded from the play. We might accept this as appropriate to a display of grief but for the second difficulty. The style of the passage suggests that, while he is talking about his wife, he is thinking about his honour. The apparatus of imagery—eclipse, darkness, turbulent sky—is an intensified kind of that found in the troubled monologues with which men contemplate their dishonour. We might conclude that Calderón is drawing a contrast between Don Gutierre's public expression of marital love and the private obsession with honour which has compelled him to so barbarous an act. Indeed, on Don Gutierre's own reckoning, the light of his world is not love, but honour. But it is curious that a man who, by his own standards, has removed the stain from his honour, and restored its lustre, should persist in using the language of *dishonour*, unless Calderón wishes us to understand that dishonour is in some sense beyond repair. On the level of common sense, the matter was put succinctly by Lope de Vega in his short story, *La más prudente venganza:* "*Y he sido de parecer siempre que no se lava bien la mancha de la honra del agraviado con la sangre del que le ofendió, porque lo que fue no puede dejar de ser, y es desatino creer que se quita porque se mata el ofensor, la ofensa del ofendido.*" The images of cosmic dismay used by Don Gutierre suggest that far from curing his dishonour, he has thrust a greater dishonour into the spiritual order of which he is a part, whether he respects this order or not. The terrible darkness expressed in his words can, in fact, signify the darkness of a man cut off from honour, if we understand this to mean the honour in which, as St. Paul explains, all share by virtue of God's love. This honour is the mark of a redeemed order of nature (which Don Gutierre now sees tarnished) and was bought in a manner which Don Gutierre has turned into ghastly parody. If we try to interpret, on Don Gutierre's own terms, the darkness which he has rhetorically invented, I suggest that we are left in the dark. But the spiritual darkness which he has created for himself is real enough. It is the darkness of honour's passion, an immolation without redemption. The symbol of honour's passion is already familiar to us as the symbol of another Passion, that of Love which set an ideal pattern for human life. It was accompanied by darkness and a convulsion of the heavens, but it led through darkness to the light. Don Gutierre's slaying of his sacrificial victim gives no promise of a new order; it is a consummation which puts an end to nothing except hope, and is a new beginning only in a depressing sense. He has to renew, and ask God's blessing on, his alliance with Leonor, which has already yielded honour's bitter fruits—suspicion, self-righteousness, vindictiveness, deafness to reason. The travesty is enlarged by Don Gutierre's imagining that he is a healer of honour. Again, Christ is familiar to us in the figure of a healer who shed his own blood in a manner which worldly men thought was dishonourable, in order to cure a universal wound and restore men to honour in the sight of God.

I believe that the characteristics of *honor* as they are presented in these Calderonian dramas account for the tragic inevitability, the feeling of a compulsion towards death. Professor Wilson, writing about *El médico de su honra*, has said that Doña Mencía "earned her death because she did not see how to act with such a husband in such an age." [23] While I agree that her imprudence sets the action moving towards tragedy, I do not think that the tragedy finally depends on character, although character is part of the circumstances through which tragedy is realised. Indeed, the same terrible pattern is worked out in different plays, in spite of varying degrees of responsibility. *Honor* is like a high tension cable in that, if a man dies after touching it we may say, with equal justification, that death was caused by electricity, or that it was caused by his imprudence in touching it. We might say that the violent energy of

23 *BCom*, art. cit.

honor itself is the "efficient" cause, and the imprudence or other
quality which attracts the violence is the "formal" cause. It
makes no difference to honour whether this secondary cause
is imprudence or ill-luck. In fact, Calderón makes all his victims contribute, through some weakness, to their disastrous end,
and our desire for poetic justice perhaps demands that this
should be so. We are appalled by the inexplicable suffering of
the entirely innocent. But Calderón and many other writers of
that time were astute psychologists, and they knew that our
desire for poetic justice may not always be pure. There is a
certain comfort to be had from vicarious punishment. Quevedo
lashed at his readers when he suspected that they would bring
such feelings to his work, and laid traps for them in the humiliating practical jokes of the *Buscón*. If Calderón went some
way to accommodate these feelings, he imposed conditions. If
some people in his audience felt that Doña Mencía's errors
made her death not merely *explicable* (which I understand
Professor Wilson to mean) but even *acceptable*, where could
they find a stone big enough to cast at Don Gutierre? And
while they were looking for one, would they not be giving the
self-righteous Don Gutierre his due? This takes up my earlier
remarks concerning the relation of these plays to their audience.
Calderonian men of honour embody common human characteristics carried to their logical end, because this enables the
action to acquire tragic certainty, false gods to show their true
nature, and the travesty of vital spiritual realities to be made
clear. The presence of the divine realities then has an additional
significance—the audience cannot sit in judgement, even on Don
Gutierre, without judging themselves.

The place of King Sebastian in A *secreto agravio secreta
venganza* and of King Pedro in *El médico de su honra* have
recently been revalued.[24] Accordingly, I shall make only brief
observations on how I think the kings illustrate the theme of
my argument. In each of these plays the audience is made to
perform the role of prophet, and this is important in itself. King
Sebastian will soon die at Alcazarquivir and, as Wilson has
shown, Don Lope de Almeida will presumably share his fate.

24 Wilson, arts, cit.—*Clavileño*, BCom; Parker, *The Approach*; Sloman, op. cit.

The facts concerning Sebastian which the audience might be expected to bring to their understanding of the play are equally important. He was obsessed with honour and with the glory of his throne. The shape which this obsession finally took was the desire to wage a magnificent crusade. He ignored the human factors, was destroyed, and his nation brought into servitude. He is a pathetic travesty of the Christian warrior. Herrera, in his *Canción,* crystallised the moral attitude of Spaniards, and the sense of God working behind the scenes. The presence of King Sebastian therefore contributes to the co-ordination of values in the play. In *El médico* the king is darkly forewarned of what the audience perceives with clarity: the justice-in-vengeance which is awaiting him. A destiny is shaping his end. When he hears the ominous snatches of song, there is more than the king's own sarcasm in his remark: *"¿Habla por ventura el aire?"* (211) Death by violence will be the consequence of his own acts, but the ultimate justice of it is something that we cannot reach. We know that divine providence exists, but we cannot explain it, except to say that it is not poetic justice, although it may use human retribution as an instrument. One thing, however, is clear: his end, like that of Sebastian, is foretold, and prophecy itself has a dramatic value. For unless the world has meaning, is ultimately rational, and has signs which may be read, there can be no prophecy. Prophecy implies an order behind our immediate confusion of experience. We can only guess by analogies as to *what* that order is, but we can know *that* it exists. It is possible to reason towards it by the facts and signs of faith, and not least through the patterns which are created in personal relationships.

In short, *honor* as we see it in these plays entails a structure of ideas, ritual, and symbolism which parodies the Christian pattern at each of these points. Honour's pattern and the Christian pattern cannot co-exist, because honour unbinds the destructive forces in nature and the human psyche which Christianity reconciles. I do not think, therefore, that we can properly speak of the "virtues" of the code of honour. It is interesting to notice how *honor* fares in a *comedia de santos.* In *El mágico prodigioso* the Devil tempts Justina and Cipriano through the world and the flesh, but he pays no attention to Floro and Lelio. He does not need to tempt these votaries of honour; they are his already. As we would expect, the final scene in which the Devil declares that Justina's loss of worldly reputation is pleasing to God, is lost upon them.

As Professor Sloman has said, "the society in which the innocent Mencía is brutally murdered is topsy-turvy."[25] I suggest that the various aspects of *honor*, as Calderón shows it in its "theology," its ritual, and its symbolism, also reveal a very deep and disturbing topsy-turvydom. But if we stand topsy-turvydom on its head, the result should be the world seen right-way-up. If we turn *honor* upside down we can renew our perception of the operative Christian realities which provide a "system of co-ordinates" by which to read these plays.[26]

II. EL ALCALDE DE ZALAMEA

I have drawn attention to what I believe is a fundamental quality of the "honour plays;" namely, that by purifying and drawing out the implications of honour, Calderón shows it to be a rival religion. The code of honour can, of course, encourage the practice of certain virtues, but these may be perverted by being enlisted in honour's own cause, and pressed into service in watchful spiritual warfare *against* one's neighbour. The fact that honour has its own kind of grace, its piety, its good works, implies the Christian frame of reference, which is excluded on the level of realistic action.

It is a simplification, but not too gross a one I hope, to say that *El alcalde de Zalamea* presents a possible Christian

25 Op. cit., p. 47.

26 I borrow this phrase from Professor H. D. F. Kitto's book, *Form and Meaning in Drama* (London, 1956). I find that Professor Kitto has presented the basis of my argument, with his usual clarity, though with reference to Greek tragedy:

"Our business is to see that the divine activity neither controls human activity and suffering nor renders them merely pathetic, but is rather a generalised statement about them. The divine background holds up to us, so to speak, the system of co-ordinates against which we are to read the significance of what the human actors do and suffer. The gods are a controlling element in these plays, but not in what the actors do and suffer; that is entirely their own affair. The reason for saying that the divine element controls the play is this; the dramatist does not allow the human actors to do or suffer anything which does not have significance when read against the co-ordinates." (pp. 244–45).

solution to the personal problem of the loss of worldly honour. It is a story of renunciation and, though it is less intense and less explicit in its religious motivation than *El príncipe constante*, both plays illustrate the necessary sacrifice of self. In the latter play, Don Fernando rises by means of the sacrifice of all worldly attachments, while growing in charity towards his captors, to the supernatural honour of the saints, partaking of the glory of God. The victory is extreme, and so are the temptations of "the world" which he rejects. In the life of a saint, the parallel with the life of Christ must necessarily be obvious. The death of Fernando, who is spurned and suffers insults and deep physical degradation, the victory and honour in defeat and dishonour—this pattern offers an analogy too clear to be missed. His manner of death would have been the ultimate dishonour to a Don Lope de Almeida or a Captain Don Álvaro de Ataide; but *"no sin causa eligió el Señor muerte con extrema deshonra, sino porque conoció cuán poderoso tirano es el amor de la honra en el corazón de muchos que no dudan de ponerse a la muerte, y huyen del género de la muerte si es con deshonra."* [27] Pedro Crespo is not a saint; nevertheless his experience offers a similar tragic pattern of suffering and renunciation.

We create difficulties in assessing this play if we accept the view that Calderón was a conformist in matters of conventional morality. Menéndez y Pelayo turned from the embarrassing problem of the "honour plays" and found relief in almost unreserved praise of *El alcalde de Zalamea*. Menéndez Pidal, after turning Calderón into a sort of social realist who glorified the collective sentiments of his period and milieu, merely notes this play, in passing, as *"otra comedia, refundida por Calderón,"* [28] and his few remarks refer only to the play attributed to Lope. Alfonso García Valdecasas at least faces his own difficulties frankly, though we cannot accept his solution:

El hecho es que Calderón, el último de nuestros grandes dramáticos, es el más riguroso e intransigente de todos en la ven-

27 Juan de Ávila, *Libro espiritual sobre el verso "Audi filia, et vide, etc.,"* cap. iii, included in Eugenio de Ochoa, *Tesoro de escritores místicos españoles* (Paris, 1857), II, 131.

28 In the essay "Del honor en el teatro español," in *De Cervantes y Lope de Vega* (Colección Austral), p. 157.

*ganza del honor. Más libres y desembarazados ante el tema son
los dramaturgos anteriores a él. Ha cambiado la situación
histórica de España, y ella condiciona toda la obra de Calderón.
Los principios sociales tradicionales, vigentes en el apogeo del
imperio, empezaban a vacilar. La fuerza política universal de la
monarquía estaba en franco declive. Por si fuera poco, se insinúan
sentimientos y tendencias sociales que discrepan de los principios que acompañaron a nuestra grandeza. Justamente el
honor era el más fundamental. Los elementos directivos se
aferran a las viejas formas, buscando en ellas la fortaleza de los
antecesores. No hay que hacer concesión ninguna. Todo tiende
a la rigidez, a la anquilosis. El arte de Calderón es una gran-
diosa y heroica acción defensiva.*

    *La fronda de sus parlamentos no puede inducir a error:
la obra de Calderón no tiene el brío y la lozanía de un hermoso
árbol que a todo viento extiende sus ramas, sino la pétrea
arquitectura de una fortaleza que se alza desafiando todos los
ataques. Pero en esa fortaleza alienta un gran espíritu: el que
hace triunfar la justicia en* El alcalde de Zalamea, *la libertad
moral en* La vida es sueño, *el más sublime honor en* El príncipe
constante, *la más hermosa teología en los autos sacramentales.
Y así como éstos se proponían mantener popular y vivo el cono-
cimiento de los dogmas católicos, sus dramas de honor luchaban
por mantener enhiestas las reglas de la antigua moral social.*[29]

Once again we notice in the very writers who warn us against
adopting a "modern" attitude to Calderón, a tendency to use
modern historical argument and to complete a picture of Calderón as that typically twentieth-century figure, a man divided
against himself. I have suggested already that it is hasty to
conclude that because a play is not manifestly expressing a
religious idea, it necessarily presents a world which is human-
centred and sufficient.

In *El alcalde de Zalamea* there is an explicit criticism of
accepted notions of honour. This is achieved by having as the
central character a peasant, a person not distinguished by rank,
honorific titles, or illustrious forebears. Calderón ranges against
him, for illuminating contrast, a hierarchy of men who regard
themselves as honourable by virtue of just such distinctions.
This is not to say that Pedro Crespo and his family do not re-

29 Alfonso García Valdecasas, *El hidalgo y el honor* (Madrid, 1948),
pp. 209–211.

gard themselves as honourable: he is as proud as any grandee of his good name and his clean lineage. He has good reason to feel pleased with his condition and his independence. This pride could be a real danger to him. It could become a barrier between him and knowledge of himself, as great an obstacle to the attainment of real personal identity as the attitudes assumed by the Captain or Don Mendo. The danger is averted, but even before we know this, we sympathise with Crespo in a way in which we cannot sympathise with, say, Don Gutierre de Solís in *El médico de su honra*. His pride touches our own more closely; equally real, it is also less hollow. I suspect that this is what is meant by critics who have said that here, for once, Calderón has created a character. The other persons in the play, as is usual in Calderonian drama, are associated with the central figure in that they are touched, or fail to be touched, by the issues in which he is involved. They are lesser figures in the sense that they are foils to Crespo, and they are foils, not by offering contrast between one fully rounded character and another, but by showing different degrees of awareness. They are lesser by virtue of being less clearly aware of the implications of the roles which they are acting, less perceptive of the situation in which they are placed. If Don Mendo, the Captain, the Sergeant, Juan Crespo, Rebolledo, and Don Lope de Figueroa often appear to be stock types, this is because Calderón has invented them in order to illustrate stock attitudes, commonplace ways of thinking and feeling. If a character appears to be a mere dramatic cliché, that is because Calderón wished to embody on the stage the kind of person who thinks and feels only in set attitudes, catch-phrases and all. Needless to say, Calderón does not merely put stock characters on the stage (a stage bore can be as boring as a real bore); Pedro Crespo and the clown Nuño are there to take up the catch-phrases and the bombast and make empty words do some honest work.

Grouped around Pedro Crespo are a number of persons who represent different aspects and modes of what they would all recognise as honour. The word does many duties. Although no one man's false gods have exactly the same face as any other man's, honour has the Protean quality of being all things to all men.

Oyeron que estaba uno persuadiendo a otro perdonase a su amigo y se aquietase; y respondió él ¿y la honra? Decíanle a otro, que dexase la manceba y el escándalo de tantos años; y él: no sería honra ahora. A un blasfemo, que no jurase ni perjurase; y respondía: ¿en qué estaría la honra? A un pródigo, que mirase a mañana, que no tendría hacienda para cuatro días: no es mi honra. Pues hombre de Barrabás, dijo Momo: ¿en qué está la honra? [30]

Honour can mean the outward dignity conferred by rank; pride in the superiority of birth; public respect, the good name in which a family is held, and which is most easily damaged by any scandal touching its women. All this involves degrees of self-esteem. Honour can also mean integrity, and the recognition of integrity by the world at large. This is an idea which represents honour more as an expression of the moral worth of the individual, but it still implies public consent and is vulnerable to scandal and false report. The world at large is inclined to make easy snap-judgements and can impute dishonour by misunderstanding. The only defence against this oppressive force of opinion is an unrelenting watchfulness and a correspondingly arrogant self-assertion. All this is common knowledge to readers of seventeenth-century drama. But, as Calderón made plain in such plays as A *secreto agravio secreta venganza,* if one is to tremble at *vox populi,* one could as well acknowledge it as *vox dei,* live according to its word and seek its grace. It is never easy to contract out of public opinion, least of all when self-esteem is at stake, but there may well come a time when we have to face the tyranny of opinion or become tyrants ourselves. In Crespo Calderón portrays the courage of a man who, having incurred the public stigma of dishonour, accepts it, renounces vengeance, and consequently risks the further public disgrace of being thought a coward. Crespo has an alternative course of action, that of keeping silence when the soldiers have left, and attempting to stifle any stories that go about the village. But it is clear that he can no more do this than he can take vengeance without obstructing the course of the justice which he represents as *alcalde.* The two categorical imperatives of conventional morality—revenge and secrecy—are both overruled by the de-

30 Gracián, *El Criticón* II, crisi XI.

mands of law. The phrase spoken by Crespo at the end of Act I: "*el honor / es patrimonio del alma / y el alma sólo es de Dios*" (521) [31] is of central importance in this play, but for the moment I shall mention only one aspect of its importance. In the context of Don Lope's bluster and Crespo's counter-attack of threats: "*y aunque fuera el general, / en tocando a mi opinión, / le matara*" (520) Crespo's definition of honour might appear to be merely the conventional claim of an injured man to act outside the law. He is not, of course, bound to carry out his threats if the situation really arises: as a man of conscience he clearly cannot, but he is talking to Don Lope, and Don Lope will listen only to his own kind of talk. When Crespo has the office of magistrate put upon him, he is given a dignity, an honourable rank under the Crown, and this new honour is bound up with the exercise of justice. So we realise that whatever that honour may be which is "*patrimonio del alma*," it is not the same honour to which men appeal when they take the law into their own hands. Calderón has taken away the vulgar sense of the word so that we shall have no excuse for missing the deeper sense when the play brings it out.

Crespo is a representative man, if one may be allowed the phrase. He is universally respected as a farmer, a father, and a citizen. But when his honour, his good name, is touched, he does not react as a representative man would be expected to react. Pedro Crespo's son has assumed, since the rape of his sister Isabel, that his father will avenge himself on her and on the Captain. So, at first, does Isabel when she is afraid to untie his hands. When Crespo does not kill her, but simply tells her to come home, she assumes that he will choose the way of secrecy. Juan never fully understands his father's actions in preventing him, first, from killing Isabel, then from pursuing the Captain:

> *Nadie entender solicita*
> *tu fin, pues sin honra ya*
> *prendes a quien te la da*
> *guardando a quien te la quita.*

31 In L. Astrana Marín's edition of the *Obras completas*, 3rd ed. (Madrid, 1945).

His heart is in the right place, but he has a great deal to learn.
Isabel is no less astonished when Crespo makes her bring an
action against the Captain, which will, of course, make the
matter public:

> Tú, que quisiste ocultar
> la ofensa que el alma llora,
> ¡así intentas publicarla!
> Pues no consigues vengarla,
> consigue el callarla ahora.   (538)

Pedro Crespo is a "character" in that he reacts more positively in his words and deeds than the other persons do, in
what is a common concern. In so doing, he defines the limits of
the other persons in the play. We have just observed this in relation to Juan and Isabel. The Captain, Don Mendo, Rebolledo,
Don Lope, Juan, Isabel are all cliché characters in their relation
to the common concern of honour. At the lowest level is Rebolledo, the rowdy, the time-server who respects nothing except
his own self-interest. But when it suits his interest, as when he
hopes to be given the gaming monopoly, he proclaims: "*que soy
hombre cargado / de obligaciones, y hombre, al fin, honrado /*"
(518). This is no more than any toady would say when trying
to get on the right side of his superior. Rebolledo is trying to
persuade by appealing to approved sentiments, and he shows in
a crude and naked form, uncomplicated by the ethics of social
class, how little (and how much) the word "honour" can be
made to perform. The Captain Don Álvaro de Ataide has a
powerful sense of what is due to his rank, and is blind to the
realness of persons. He is all duplicity dressed in fine words.
We may compare his conversation with the Sergeant in Act I,
which concludes: "*claro es ya / que en una villana está / ven-
dido el nombre de dama /*" (513), with the words he exchanges
with Crespo after Rebolledo has broken into the attic:

Capitán: Quien nació
> con obligaciones, debe
> acudir a ellas, y yo
> al respeto desta dama
> suspendí todo el furor.

Crespo: Isabel es hija mía,
> y es labradora, señor,
> que no dama.   (519)

The General, Don Lope de Figueroa, is interested keeping discipline and in seeing that justice is done, but he is jealous of the rights and the honour of his army. Justice means *his* justice. He embodies the kind of honour which we know as "esprit de corps," the corporate honour of an institution rather than of a social class. For this guardian of particular interests, toughness is all, and Calderón makes him talk tough. Nevertheless, he is more open to conviction than the other characters, and when Crespo talks back at him, he realises that Crespo's toughness is as real as his own. What he does not realise is that his kind of talk is being turned by Crespo into a game which anyone can play.[32] Don Mendo, the grotesque *hidalgo*, is already familiar as a stock literary figure, and at the same time he gives a good illustration of Calderón's witty procedure. His idea of honour consists in his consciousness of noble descent, which is concentrated into monomania by his poverty. Any suggestion which threatens to destroy his fantasies and make him contrast them with what he really is, is an affront to his honour. He must not be told that he is hungry, or that he would do well to marry a rich peasant's daughter. Moreover, like the *hidalgo* who is sustained by Lazarillo de Tormes, he belongs to a class which has lost social usefulness and prestige, but he retains the airs of a lord, and a nostalgia for lordly vices. If he possessed the authority which he still dreams of, he would be another Don Álvaro de Ataide. Like the Captain, he reacts to Isabel with transports of rapture on a ground of cynicism:

32 So, too, *honra* can be anybody's game, and anyone with a grudge can claim recourse to violence. Don Lope takes a military attitude towards people, and the awful possibility that what is sauce for him may also be demanded by the Crespos, and ultimately by anyone who is spoiling for a fight, has not occurred to him. To Don Lope it sounds strangely that a peasant should talk of honour and of taking satisfaction. By talking thus, Crespo can show him that in a picaresque society where men act on the right to imitate the vices of their betters (vices which may once have been chivalric virtues) Don Lope's principles set a dangerous precedent and could result in anarchy. Professor Sloman, following Sr. Dámaso Alonso, and pointing to similarities between Don Lope and Crespo, indicates that in the garden scene the two characters say the same things in different words (op. cit., p. 233). My own view is that Crespo uses words and actions similar to Don Lope's, by way of parody, in order to say something very different.

Nuño: *Y si no has*
            de casarte, ¿por qué haces
            tantos extremos de amor?
D. Mendo: *¿Pues no hay sin que yo me case*
            Huelgas en Burgos, adonde
            llevarla, cuando me enfade?   (515)

She is merely the daughter of a peasant, worth nothing more
than a day's trifling. Afterwards, she can hide her shame in a
convent. What Don Mendo boasts in his airy way to Nuño, the
Captain effectively performs. Whereas the Captain's intentions
are real beneath his false words, Don Mendo does nothing, and
his words are sound without fury. He is the shadow of his own
ideas of honour and these, in turn, are the shadow of the Captain's; he is the shadow of the shadow of a lie. He is entirely
vulnerable to Nuño's puns which draw attention to the founda-
tions on which his dream-palaces are built.

     We have been considering the secondary figures of the
play, not simply as participators in a common action, but as
people who are all "acting a part," doing and speaking lies or
half-truths. What they do is what they believe, and what people
believe is what they honour. What they say is ornament or
blanket, which nonetheless betrays what they are. For them,
honour is part of the role which they have assumed in their
world; not a patrimony, but a mortgage on their souls. Even
Juan and Isabel Crespo, who appear so conventional and respectable in their approach to their father's misfortune that the
average playgoer might accept them as exemplary, are shown,
by comparison with Pedro Crespo, to be misguided in their
zeal for duty, like Peter who cut off the ear of the High Priest's
servant. Now we must return to Pedro Crespo. The key phrase
in the play, as everyone who has read the play knows, is:

            Al rey la hacienda y la vida
            se ha de dar; pero el honor
            es patrimonio del alma,
            y el alma sólo es de Dios.   (521)

At this point Crespo is saying more than we yet realise, and
Calderón will put him to a test which will show what his words
mean in terms of living. Meanwhile, the key is also a riddle,
a type of *engañar con la verdad*. The truth which is in it has

to be brought out by events and actions. These words are thrown at Don Lope by way of repartee, in order to distinguish what is God's from what is Caesar's and, in their context (since Don Lope can only be persuaded by his own kind of words) it may appear that God is *vox populi* again. But Crespo has nothing in common with the Captain or Don Mendo. He measures people by what they are. He has rejected Juan's suggestion that he buy a title of nobility and put on the appearance of being other than what he is. But he has a practical confidence in his position as the most prosperous farmer of the district and is proud of the respect in which he is held by his neighbours. His honour is the seal upon his success and his integrity. This worldly honour is not bad, nor his pride evil. They reflect the good that is in Crespo. They could become evil if, in a situation which demanded that he relinquish them for a greater good, he were to hold blindly to them, and we would do well to remember this in the interview with the Captain in Act III. The sense of harmony which he feels in the good things which the world has given him is reflected in his invitation to Don Lope:

> *Sentaos, que el viento suave*
> *que en las blandas hojas suena*
> *destas parras y estas copas,*
> *mil cláusulas lisonjeras*
> *hace al compás desta fuente,*
> *cítara de plata y perlas,*
> *porque son, en trastes de oro,*
> *las guijas templadas cuerdas.*
> *Perdonad si de instrumentos*
> *solos la música suena*
> *sin cantores que os deleiten,*
> *sin voces que os entretengan,*
> *que como músicos son*
> *los pájaros que gorjean,*
> *no quieren cantar de noche*
> *ni yo puedo hacerles fuerza.* (523)

He is sure in and of himself, and it is no idle boast to say: "*Nunca me enajena / a mí de mí nada* (523)." The honour—the standing, the prestige—granted to him by his equals is linked to his prosperity. Valuable as it is, this is not the true "patrimony." This honour and the coming assault upon it are expressed in the following lines:

> *esta tarde*
> *salí a mirar la labranza,*
> *y están las parvas notables*
> *de manojos y montones,*
> *que parecen al mirarse*
> *desde lejos, montes de oro,*
> *y aun oro de más quilates,*
> *pues de los granos de aquéste*
> *es todo el cielo el contraste.*
> *Allí el bieldo, hiriendo a soplos*
> *el viento en ellos süave,*
> *deja en esta parte el grano*
> *y la paja en la otra parte;*
> *que aun allí el más humilde*
> *da el lugar a lo más grave.*
> *¡Oh, quiera Dios que en las trojes*
> *yo llegue a encerrarlo, antes*
> *que algún turbión me lo lleve*
> *o algún viento me lo tale!* (516)

The wheat is a golden treasure, it has drawn its substance from the beneficient powers of sun and sky working through the earth, and it will bear comparison with the sun whose golden stamp it carries. Gold, a clear sky, the sun, are all accepted images of honour, and storm-clouds crossing the fact of the sun are a frequent image of honour extinguished. But behind the favours of nature and the uncertain gifts of fortune is the providence of God, which is constant. If prosperity and esteem are the basis as well as the outward sign of honour, then honour in this worldly sense cannot be what is meant by *"patrimonio del alma."* Honour, as defined in this phrase, must be independent of a man's condition in this world, not sensitive to changes of fortune. The wind which winnows the grain from the chaff may become a storm which will wreck his honour (in the worldly sense) for there is a wind of Heaven which can test his worth, dividing him from whatever he has set his pride on, like the wheat from the chaff.[33] To be alone with the power of God, stripped of worldly honour, is not to be dishonoured. The true measure of the power of God is not its brute strength, but the withholding of that strength in giving Himself to be humiliated among men, against our worldly expectation. Alone and

33 See the words of John the Baptist in Matt. 3. xii.

stripped of his worldly credit, Crespo will have to accept his
humiliation in this true spirit of sacrifice.[34] Having robbed
Crespo of the patrimony conferred upon him by the world at
large, Calderón leaves us to judge, in the light of faith and experience what is the true *"patrimonio del alma."*

When Isabel unties Crespo's hands after her rape, she
expects him to kill her. Calderón is at some pains to impress
this on us, for she says it three times in a short space (532–33).
Moreover, after his interview with the Captain, Crespo meets
Juan who has drawn his dagger against Isabel. Calderón could
hardly have expressed more vividly the conventional view of
Crespo's duty, or juxtaposed it more tellingly against Crespo's
behaviour in the presence of the Captain. He is now *alcalde*, a
dignity in which he is responsible to the king, and he can speak
to the Captain with authority, for the Captain believes in
power. But just as he set aside thoughts of revenge, so he sets
aside his rod of office, for he comes to speak as a man to his
neighbour. He offers the Captain everything—his property, his
status, a life of slavery for himself and his son—if the Captain
will marry Isabel. He has lost credit in the eyes of the world.
Now he is willing to renounce everything to which any thread
of honour could possibly attach. When the Captain remains
adamant, Crespo throws his honour to the winds of public
gossip by referring the matter to the law. If his good name has
to be sacrificed so that justice can be done, in the name of the
king, what can it mean to say:

> Al rey la hacienda y la vida
> se ha de dar; pero el honor
> es patrimonio del alma,
> y el alma sólo es de Dios?

Calderón has shown that honour-in-the-eyes-of-the-world may
range from self-deceit to a high social good, but at its best it is
external, not patrimony of the soul. If the play has shown that
our worldly experience cannot provide a value for *honor* which
will satisfy the other term in the equation *honor = patrimonio
del alma*, then the only course is to approach the equation from
the other side. If we ask "What things are the undoubted patri-

34 Compare the ritual sacrifice demanded by the religion of honour.

mony of the soul?" we may find a value for *honor* which has been passed over.

The freedom of the understanding to judge, and of the will to choose, good and evil; divine grace freely offered, by which we can be helped to choose good and free ourselves from the trammels of instinct and from mechanical conformity with general opinion; the redemption (the first act of grace) for which God is eternally sacrificing Himself; the power, with the aid of grace, to act in our own life this healing sacrifice: all these things are *"patrimonio del alma,"* gifts with which the soul is endowed and which, like the soul itself, are given without regard to the merits of the receiver.[35] In short, these are the means by which the way is open to that corporate honour in Christ, expounded by St. Paul. Crespo has turned the other cheek to the Captain, offering him his own dishonour (in the eyes of the world), offering indeed to become the mere thing which the Captain has assumed him to be, if he will grant Isabel status and respect as a person. When Crespo ends his plea with the words:

> ¿Qué os pido?   Un honor os pido
> que me quitasteis vos mesmo;
> y con ser mío, parece,
> según os le estoy pidiendo
> con humildad, que no es mío
> lo que os pido, sino vuestro,   (536)

he is not merely asking for his credit to be restored. If the play is read as a piece of realism, this scene must present insuperable difficulties. If Crespo stands or falls by fulness and individuality of character, his character will appear inconsistent, as Professor Leavitt has declared.[36] Why does Crespo make an offer which he ought to know, and perhaps does know, will be refused? Why does a tough old man go soft and weep before the Captain? Professor Leavitt's explanation is that Calderón wanted to increase sympathy for Crespo so that the audience would accept

35 I observed earlier that honour has its theology which is a travesty of these articles of faith.

36 S. E. Leavitt, "Pedro Crespo and the Captain in Calderón's *Alcalde de Zalamea,*" *Hispania*, xxxviii (1955), 430–31.

his execution of the Captain. "In the scene between Pedro Crespo and the Captain Calderón was a practical dramatist. He sacrificed a magnificent character in order to be certain that the sympathy of the audience went to the right candidate." Why should a practical dramatist make such a disastrous muddle at a crucial point in his play, when he could have found a simpler way out of his difficulty? Professor Leavitt has convicted Calderón of using means disproportionate to his dramatic purpose; creating a climax which is superfluous to his theme, and then allowing it to slip into bathos. Suppose, however, that Crespo says what Calderón intended him to say, which is merely to affirm that Calderón is a practical dramatist. A poor man may beg money from me. His presence will also *beg* me to recognise my brother in him. If I refuse, he may reproach me. If he does not do so in words, his presence may still be a reproach to me. A deeper relation underlies that of give-and-take, as even the common usage of our language implies in this example. The dramatist who we feel has said something worth saying is he who conveys both orders of reality, who imitates what is particular and local so that we can see spiritual realities in human terms.

In the lines which I have quoted, Calderón shows what are the spiritual implications of Crespo's material offer. He is asking the Captain to recognise what unites them both, begging the Captain to look to his own Christian honour, to put himself right with his own soul and its patrimony, before God. It is not simply *"mi honor,"* but *"un honor,"* for the honour of Christians is a communion, and although no man can destroy it, he can wound it, and all share in the common hurt. But Calderón has not neglected the "verisimilitude" of this scene, because he knew that if we cannot swallow Crespo's words and actions at this point, we shall not swallow their meaning. In fact, it is simple. The Captain will either refuse to have anything more to do with the daughter of a peasant, reckoning such a marriage to be "dishonourable" in a man of his rank, or he will accept. But if he were to accept the marriage he would have to accept the "dishonour;" this would clearly require so complete a change of heart and of basic attitudes, so thorough a turning away from his old self, that it would be morally impossible for him to accept literally Crespo's offer of slavery. One advantage of having a peasant as the hero of this play (a point which, as far as I know, has been overlooked) is that we can be sure that there is no other alternative. If Crespo were a grandee, there would be the embarrassing possibility that the Captain might accept the marriage cynically, for the advantage to be had from it. If Crespo's words appear not to make sense, that is because we have made the mistake of thinking that the Captain could accept them passively; in fact the offer implies the Captain's conversion. Except he be made new, he cannot accept Crespo's sacrifice in the spirit in which it is offered, and unless he accept it in that spirit, he cannot accept it at all. The penetration of the action by sipiritual realities is clear and convincing.

By doing what needs to be done to restore Crespo's credit in the eyes of the world, the Captain would inevitably do what is necessary to restore his own honour in the sight of God. The intention of Crespo's speech, then, is not simply: "I will pay you so much to marry my daughter," but rather to persuade the Captain to appreciate that he has thrown away his *"patrimonio del alma." In effect*, Crespo's words mean: "Everything I have, my status in the world, my life and that of my son, would not be too high a price to buy back what you have lost: but you alone can make the decision, suffer this moral conversion, redeem your honour and mine." If Crespo's offer is not to be accepted, this does not mean that it is an empty pious gesture. Crespo would willingly give what he promises if it pleased God to accept it as a way of bringing the Captain to heal their common hurt. It is not a mere matter of trying to bribe the Captain to marry Isabel, for Crespo has always rejected the false honour which is mere appearances. Any credit which he purchased in this way would be worthless. The Captain cannot make any restitution to Crespo that is not conceived in charity, and which does not restore the spiritual bond of mutual honour. Crespo's action in humbling himself before the man he would like to murder, without fear or self-pity, shows the way.

The Captain, in his reply, bandies words and seeks refuge in a legal distinction. The notion of honour to which he vainly clings empties words of their meanings, as Calderón brilliantly demonstrates in these lines:

Capitán: No me puedo defender:
            fuerza es dejarme prender.
            Al Rey desta sinrazón
            me quejaré.
Crespo: Yo también
            de esotra . . .
                         . . . Dejar es bien
            esa espada.
Capitán: No es razón
            que . . .
Crespo: ¿ Cómo no, si vais preso ?
Capitán: Tratad con respeto . . .
Crespo: Eso
            está muy puesto en razón.
            Con respeto le llevad
            a las casas en efeto,
            del Concejo; y con respeto
            un par de grillos le echad
            y una cadena; y tened,
            con respeto, gran cuidado
            que no hable a ningún soldado;
            y a esos dos también poned
            en la cárcel; que es razón,
            y aparte, porque después,
            con respeto, a todos tres
            les tomen la confesión.
            Y aquí para entre los dos,
            si hallo harto paño, en efeto,
            con muchísimo respeto
            os he de ahorcar, juro a Dios.   (536–37)

The counterpointing of the Captain's empty phrases ("*esta sinrazón . . . no es razón que . . . tratad con respeto . . .*") with Crespo's use of the same words which are given full intention illustrates, on the rhetorical level, the contrast between characters that I mentioned earlier. In pricking the Captain's inflated words Crespo underlines the fact that the Captain has himself destroyed the respect offered to him. The corrupt vision, the lack of awareness in the "cliché characters" is throughout presented by means of such contrasts as these. Whereas Crespo's actions confirm his words, and the other way about, the other persons use words for the sake of evasion or self-deceit; their rhetoric is cosmetic, Crespo's is the real expression on the face.

Crespo can do nothing to regain his worldly honour. There is only one possible way for the Christian to take, and that is to renounce willingly something which God had the right to take from him, difficult as it may be. In conclusion, whereas the men of honour of seventeenth-century drama normally put their personal honour above the law, Crespo subordinates it to the observance of law, and, moreover, publicly proclaims its loss. On the other hand, the honour of the Christian (which derives from the apparently dishonourable death of his Master) is truly "patrimonio del alma" and is, as Crespo says, above human law. Human law can do nothing to right wrongs such as he has suffered. The most that he can do, as the executor of justice, is to exact the appropriate penalty, without regard to the jealousy of other institutions, and without vengeance or personal spite, *pace* Menéndez y Pelayo. Nevertheless, the world is bound to honour and esteem the man who pursues justice at the cost of his own immediate interest, risking the opprobrium of being thought judge in his own cause. The king confers this honour upon Crespo by making him *alcalde* for life, and confirms his principle that all justice is one. As to Isabel, there is no justice on earth which can take away what she has suffered. It is poor comfort for her when Crespo says: "*Hija, / ya tenéis el padre alcalde: / él os guardará justicia /* (534)." Justice, with its consequent publicity, is not what she wants. She wants redress, and her father's phrase can only speak to her in her loss if we remember its archetype in the First Epistle of St. John: "And if any man sin, we have an advocate with the Father, Jesus Christ the righteous." This is not such a great leap as may appear at first sight. Crespo is advising Isabel to trust and be patient. The popular figurative use of the phrase *tener el padre alcalde*: "to have a friend in high places" [37] allows a deepening of the sense here. Through the ordinary language of fatherly love and human justice Calderón allows us to remind ourselves of what lies behind irremediable grief and suffering: we have a Father who is also a Judge. From the point of view of the world, Isabel is ruined and there is no alternative but the conventional retirement to a nunnery. But in the religious life she may find that

---

37 *Quien tiene el padre alcalde seguro va a juicio* is given by Juan de Mal Lara in *Philosophia vulgar*, centuria novena, No. 10.

her worldly dishonour, like that of Justina in *El mágico prodi-gioso*, is pleasing to God.

To conclude these remarks, Calderón measures current conceptions of *honor* against a standard, and they are found wanting. Nevertheless, the standard is one to which a fallible man—I have not wished to imply that Crespo is perfect—can cleave in a deep personal crisis where social norms cannot serve. The fact that in this play Calderón comes nearest to a technique of realistic action should not distract our attention from the bearings by which the action is directed. Indeed, the working out of the play within an apparent realism and the careful simu-lation of a real-life situation give an immediacy which is more telling than any explicit moralising or pieties could have been. These things show the feasibility of the values which are made to stand the test. But we should not ignore the pointers which are there, beneath the currents of Crespo's practical reasoning where we become aware of sudden depths with a ground swell which resolves the movements on the surface: in the converg-ing perspectives of his figured language; in the implications of his offer to the Captain; in the special richness and valour—the "divine folly"—of his decisions. It is all so natural, so well inte-grated into the surface texture which remains unimpaired, undisturbed by special effects, or the triple underlinings of nine-teenth- and twentieth-century dramatic symbolism. And out of it comes a sane and tempered but unexpected joyousness. The events are terrible; Crespo's long harvest of respect has been swept away in the storm, but this poverty is his greatest strength. At the end, Crespo is still Crespo, and his trust is vindicated.

Pedro Crespo is not an abstraction, nor is the play a ser-mon. This play is intelligible in itself as a fiction and as a picture of what is possible, but it bears witness to the whole view of life which contains it. It points towards the divine background which gives the ultimate justification of this picture of the human condition. As Francis Fergusson has observed, "the instinct to project images of human life is basic," [38] and we may regard play-making as a kind of ritual. Ritual is an aid to understanding how the human will can be brought into

38 Francis Fergusson, *The Human Image in Dramatic Literature* (New York, 1957), p. viii.

conformity with the will of our gods. It is also a means for bringing spiritual realities forward, out of the shadows where they recede in daily life, so that the minute particulars of life may be contemplated in their true context. In short, the dramas which I have been considering in these two essays meet on the common ground of a doctrine of "imitation" which gives full value to the plausibility of words and actions, but does not circumscribe a play within these limits because the reality which they imitate will not be so bounded.[39]

39 I am grateful to Mr. T. E. May for his encouragement, and for making me clarify some points in these articles.

Part Two

La vida es sueño

3 · On *La vida es sueño.* *

by E. M. Wilson

TO ATTEMPT a new interpretation of *La vida es sueño* may well appear a rash undertaking.[1] The play is so well-known, so much has been written about it, that any novelty seems likely to be merely the result of a perverse desire for originality or at best a wrong-headed modification or distortion of what someone else has already said. Nevertheless, I undertake this task because, despite the interesting studies of Don Ángel Valbuena Prat, the criticism of seventeenth-century dramatic literature is still conducted with nineteenth-century criteria. And the appraisal of the merits of *La vida es sueño* has seemed to me to suffer particularly for this reason.

My primary objection is to the way in which modern critics employ the notion of character. They do not realise that the idea that character is the be-all and end-all of drama was not that of the eighteenth century, even, let alone, of the seventeenth. The lack of a Spanish equivalent of the *New*

* *Author's Postscript.* This article was written in 1938–39. It owes much in its arrangement to Professor James Smith, who now holds the chair of English Language and Literature at the University of Fribourg, Switzerland; Professor A. A. Parker of the University of Edinburgh suggested some sentences in the account of Segismundo's first conversion. In 1946 Don Enrique Moreno Báez translated the article into Spanish, and we added some paragraphs and deleted others in order to make it more appropriate to Hispanic readers. I have now revised slightly the original English version, added some passages from the Spanish translation and rephrased a number of sentences. I hope that the changes I have made may clarify my original interpretation without distorting it.

1 I wrote this sentence in 1946.

English Dictionary (now at last being repaired) raises difficulties for us when we try to follow the history of the word
carácter in Spanish dramatic criticism; as far as I am aware, it
was the first used as a critical term by Luzán (*Poética*, III, x),
who explained to his readers that *"lo que otras naciones llaman
Charácter, proprio de cada persona"* was *"algún género de
costumbres o inclinaciones."* Aristotle had defined character as
"that which reveals moral purpose, shewing what kind of things
a man chooses or avoids" (*Poetics*, VI, 17); Luzán's *"género
de costumbres"* may have a similar sense, like that used by other
neoclassic critics who followed him. The nineteenth-century
senses of the word were far less precise. But the age of Philip
IV seems to have ignored the word as a dramatic term, though
they might have picked it up from Aristotle. In these circumstances, though we can hardly omit the word "character" altogether from our critical vocabulary, we must be careful when
we use it of seventeenth-century plays. Calderón certainly
thought about the disposition of his plot, the problems of
verse communication, the moral questions raised by his pres-
entations and, perhaps, how certain men might be expected to
behave in certain conditions. He did not set out to make Pedro
Crespo the living incarnation of the Spanish peasantry or to
make Segismundo into "a living character."

On the first reading, *La vida es sueño* appears to most
people as an important but puzzling play. Its obvious power,
the striking scenes in the tower and in the palace, at once move
the reader deeply. No one can fail to be impressed by the
horror and atrocity of Segismundo's plight in the first scene, his
savagery when he finds himself in authority in the palace, his
expression of the vanity of life when he finds himself back in
the tower. If the verse of the first soliloquy is confused we need
not worry too much, for the refrain is a statement of the contrast between man and brute which could hardly be more
powerfully expressed: *"¿y teniendo yo más alma, / tengo menos
libertad?"* (131–132) [2] The famous second soliloquy in the
tower is immediately convincing in its simplicity;

2 References throughout this essay are to Dr. A. E. Sloman's edition,
Manchester, 1961.

> *el mayor bien es pequeño;*
> *que toda la vida es sueño,*
> *y los sueños son.*   (2185–87)

The plain statement has seldom done its work so well.

Nearly all critics of the play will admit the truth of these judgments. This play has something not to be found in ordinary versions of the folk tale of the Sleeper Awakened, such as the story of Abu Hassan in *The Arabian Nights*, or of Christopher Sly in *The Taming of the Shrew*. The play expresses a view of life, and so does the title. Some critics have too easily assumed that Calderón ought to have made us believe that all life is unreal, that no one can rely on anything, that we are all like Don Quixote, who mistook windmills for giants and a barber's basin for Mambrino's helmet. Instead of blaming Calderón for not doing what he never intended to do, I shall try to find out some of what he did. I shall look at the sub-plot as well as the main plot, at the third act as well as at the first two acts. I shall not assume that the title means what others would like it to mean. I shall try to point out how and why Segismundo is converted, how and why life is a dream, what I think the play as a dramatic whole means.

The great nineteenth-century critic, Marcelino Menéndez y Pelayo, judged *La vida es sueño* according to his criteria. He claimed that: "*La drámatica, tal como todas las escuelas la han entendido, tal como ha aparecido en todas las civilizaciones del mundo, vive de pasiones, de afectos, de caracteres humanos; no es más que la vida humana en acción y en espectáculo.*" [3] This statement is not wholly untrue, but it is too general and too sweeping. The schools of drama to which he refers have indeed represented human life, passions, characters, and feelings, but their aim has often been far more than the mere exposition of a single character or of a group of characters. From such generalizations as this he went on to assume that the more individual the character the better the play. But Aristotle, the theorist of not a minor school of drama, said that tragedy could

---

3 *Calderón y su teatro.* I quote from the edition of Madrid, 1910, p. 108.

exist without character but not without plot (*Poetics*, VI, 14).
Don Marcelino passed over the many good plays in which the
characters are stock types; he placed too much emphasis on
character in itself, not enough on plot, construction, and diction.

When he discussed the *auto* of *La vida es sueño* (which
of course is a refashioning of the *comedia*) he said—or at least
implied—that it suffered from one great weakness: "*El protagonista no es un hombre llamado Segismundo, sino el hombre
en general.*" [4] He meant this criticism of the *auto* to apply also
to the *comedia*, for later on, after mentioning Tirso's Don
Juna, he remarked: "*Calderón no alcanza nunca a crear un
tipo de esta universalidad* [i.e. *la de don Juan*]. *Segismundo
no es más que un símbolo.*" [5] It is necessary to criticise these
opinions. The assertion that a dramatic figure is a kind of Every-
man is not necessarily a fault in the play in which he is found;
how can Don Juan, a particular figure, be more universal than
Segismundo, whom the critic takes to be the symbol of all
mankind? As it stands the statement seems contradictory.
Presumably Menéndez y Pelayo meant that in some way, because he was a particular figure and not a general type, Don
Juan was superior to Segismundo. The opposite view is equally
reasonable. But our purpose is not to compare characters but
to analyse a play; even if we wanted to compare *La vida es
sueño* with *El burlador de Sevilla*, it would not suffice to set
Don Juan against Segismundo; we should also have to compare the plots, the construction, and the diction of the two
plays. I shall therefore disregard Menéndez y Pelayo's general
criticism of this play.

Don Marcelino also pointed to two defects in the play's
plan. First he said: "*En Calderón hay un salto mortal desde el
Segismundo siervo y juguete de la pasión hasta el Segismundo
tipo del príncipe perfecto, pue aparece en la tercera jornada.*" [6]
He also described the sub-plot as: "*Una intriga extraña, com-
pletamente pegadiza y exótica, que se enreda a todo el drama
como una planta parásita.*" [7] The following pages will seek to
confute these two judgments.

4 Op. cit., p. 272.
5 Op. cit., p. 394. My italics.
6 Op. cit., p. 276.
7 Op. cit., p. 278.

The Italian Hispanist Arturo Farinelli also criticised this play. He cited parallels to the story from all over the world, gave an account of Calderón's view of life, and finally criticised the play itself. His examination is to be taken seriously, and his book, diffuse and sometimes prejudiced though it is, contains much valuable information. His most important adverse criticism of the play may be summarised as follows: *La vida es sueño* is founded on a contradiction. In it there is a sceptical thesis and a religious one. The sceptical thesis is that contained in the title, "Life is a dream;" the religious one that, as good works are necessary to salvation, so they are necessary to the reform of Segismundo. The theses contradict one another, because, if life is a dream, how can a man choose the good rather than the bad? Man cannot be held morally responsible for what he does in his dreams. Calderón avoided this difficulty by inventing a particular type of dreaming, what he called "*soñar despierto*" in the *auto*. But this was a compromise; Calderón had deliberately subjugated the work of art to the improving moral lesson.[8]

At first sight this view seems plausible enough, but on further examination it does not provide a justifiable ground for criticism. Farinelli complains that Calderón's play is inconsistent because his analogy breaks down to some extent; because *all* life is not a dream in his work but only some aspect of life, he censures it. Let us however imagine a work in which the analogy held absolutely, in which man was in no way mor-

---

8 "*Sognare e operare ad un tempo, porre nel sogno la vigilanza ed accortezza dell'uomo desto, quest'è un assurdo, di cui ride la logica del poeta, al solito sì chiara e sì ferma. Ma quest'assurdo è pur necessaria conseguenza della sovrapposizione delle due tesi, che annunciano e appena si svolgono nel dramma, quella scettica, e quella religiosa. La condanna delle vanità mondane e del gioco delle apparenze e delle illusioni conduce al nirvàna buddhistico. Ma il mondo disciolto bisognava pur ricostruirlo, ricrearlo a immagine di Dio. Col vuoto e il nulla in cuore non si accede al trono dell'Altissimo. Generalizzando il sogno, come il poeta faceva, riusciva egli veramente a sollevare colle opere buone il nuovo edificio al suo Dio? Possibile non si rendesse conto della nessuna responsabilità che l'uomo ha nel sogno? . . .*" "*Dalle strette della logica il poeta poteva salvarsi, ammettendo un sognare particolarissimo, non compreso dal sognar comune, una specie di 'soñar despierto,' a cui è un'allusione fugace nell'auto. . . . Più doveva stargli a cuore la bontà della dottrina che la congruenza dell'opera sua d'arte e di fantasia.*" Arturo Farinelli, *La vita è un sogno*. Parte seconda (Torino, 1916), pp. 283–284.

ally responsible for his actions and in which he was no more
the free agent than we are in our dreams. Such a work might
contain powerful descriptions of scenes and events; it might
provide us with interesting analyses of states of mind; but it
could lead only to negation. If the statement "Life is a dream"
is pushed to its logical conclusion it means nothing is profitable;
it seems unfair to Calderón to criticise him for rejecting this
idea as pernicious or superficial.

Farinelli carried his arguments further. Calderón's thought
went one way, the dramatic action another. Finally he changed
the drama of *Life is a Dream* for that of *Honour Restored*.
Majesty and pomp are wafted away, but no breeze or dream
can remove honour. Honour, loyalty, obedience to authority,
breeding, courtesy, social usages, order, deference to the ties of
family and state, moderation: these things remain amid the
vain phantoms that constitute earthly life.[9]

Again the previous objections apply. Because Calderón considered that certain things were more valuable than others, he
is criticised for being illogical! That honour should appear as
a positive virtue in the play is, perhaps, surprising, but we may
find later on that there was some reason for it. Farinelli was
so obsessed with his own idea of the logic of the title that he
could not see how Calderón in fact applied it. I hope to shew

9 "*Il dramma, che si disse sgomentevolmente serio e di vertiginosa
profondità, offre gli strappi più vivi ad ogni seria e profonda reflessione.
Corra il pensiero da una parte, e corra dall'altra l'azione drammatica, il
poeta non se ne preoccupa. Ditegli che nel mondo del sogno a dell'illusione
deve porsi anche l'onore, ed egli si ribellerà al vostro e al suo proprio
giudizio. Nulla di chiaro riesce a veder l'uomo nell'universale fantasmagoria,
anzi non vede punto; gli si confonde ogni cosa nell'indistinto del sogno; e
Calderón obbliga tuttavia a chiaramente distinguere il raggiar dell'onore
nella vita morale degl'individui e della società. E, in conclusione, trasmuta
il dramma del sogno della vita nel dramma dell'onore restaurato. L'apre
col lamento e la sorpresa di Rosaura, venuta nella terra di Sigismondo a
vendicarsi dell'oltraggio subito; e lo chiude col trionfo della causa santa
di Rosaura e la riparazione del torto, la salvezza dell'onore. Debbon disfarsi
al soffio più tenue le maestà e le pompe; e non v'è soffio, non v'è sogno che
valga a dissolvere l'onore. Onore, lealtà, fedele sommessione al sovrano, genti-
lezza, cortesia, convenienza sociale, ordine, compattezza di vincoli nella fami-
glia e nello stato, misura, vedete quanto si salva dal complesso delle larve vane
che costituiscono il mondo e la vita terrena nell'oscillar di tutto, ammirate
tanta stabilità di principi. Se il mondo scompare, rimane la legge.*" A. Farinelli, op. cit., p. 285.

that the play is of a piece, logical, consistent, and skilfully executed, and that its importance was not merely for one particular country or century.

To understand *La vida es sueño* we need not follow Farinelli's researches through the literatures of Europe and Asia in the track of the tale of the Sleeper Awakened, or those of Father Olmedo in sixteenth-century sermons and seventeenth-century Jesuit dramas. Doña Blanca de los Ríos unearthed ten other Segismundos who occur in other *comedias* by Calderón, and Don Ángel Valbuena Prat suggested (more fruitfully) that such figures are also to be found in the *autos sacramentales*; useful though these studies may be for other purposes, they are not essential to our present one. Even to compare our *comedia* with the *auto sacramental* (as did L. P. Thomas) may mislead us, for when we return to our play we may merely reread the *auto* at greater length.[10] Instead I shall examine the play in isolation to see what it can tell us. To do this I shall trace the parts played by the different persons, beginning with Segismundo; I shall bear in mind the two detailed criticisms of Menéndez y Pelayo as well as the more general objections of Farinelli.

Segismundo describes himself or others describe him as: "*monstruo humano*" (209); "*un hombre de las fieras, y una fiera de los hombres*" (211–212); "*un monstruo en forma de hombre*" (672); "*víbora humana del siglo*" (675); "*un compuesto de hombre y fiera*" (1547); "*un hombre que de humano no tiene más que el nombre*" (1645–55). There is a terrible pathos in his first soliloquy, for his envy of the animal or of the in-

10 A. Farinelli, op. cit., Parte prima; Félix G. Olmedo, S. J., *Las fuentes de "La vida es sueño"* (Madrid, 1928); Blanca de los Ríos, "*La vida es sueño*" *y los diez Segismundos de Calderón* (Madrid, 1926); A. Valbuena Prat, *Historia de la literatura española* (Barcelona, 1937), II, 405n; L. P. Thomas, "La Genèse de la philosophie et le symbolisme dans La Vie est un songe," in *Mélanges offerts à M. Wilmotte* (Paris, 1910). Of the last work Farinelli acutely remarked: "*Ed è follia pensare raffigurino nel dramma, interamente ed esattamente, quello che raffigurano nell'auto i personaggi trascelti per la storia della rigenerazione umana; e significhi così Basilio il divino "Poder," Clotaldo l'intelligenza, Clarín la volontà o l'arbitrio, i servi i sensi, ecc.*" Op. cit., Parte seconda, p. 182.

animate almost expresses itself as a wish that he might lose his
humanity. He suffers poignantly, through no fault of his own,
and his suffering merely makes him violent. Clotaldo's teaching
has remained external to him; every impulse immediately mas-
ters him. He tries to murder Rosaura, but her gentleness sub-
dues him; he tries to resist Clotaldo and is shut up to rant in
vain at the Heavens. He is an animal, uncontrolled. Calderón
has not drawn him as a "character," a being with a private individuality, but a man in whom the animal, rather than human,
nature is dominant: a man such as any of us might have been
had we passed our early years chained up in a tower in the
desert.

In the palace Segismundo is ungovernable. In his brief
spell of power he insults the whole court from the King down,
makes love outrageously to two women, throws a servant out
of the window and tries to murder his former tutor. In this
portrayal Calderón not only describes a man who is paying off
old scores; the man is also shewn as overconfident and proud.[11]
He accepts his own power without question and takes as permanent a state of affairs that could have been permanent only
if he had acted very differently. His pride shews itself in his as-
sumption that he could do as he liked and in his manner of
speech whenever he opens his mouth. There was pride in his
defiance of the Heavens in the first act, and his pride is underlined continually in the second.

Nevertheless Segismundo is a man who has revealed certain
possibilities of redemption. When Rosaura overheard his complaints in the tower, she offended his pride by learning his
weakness; but although he threatened her, her plea moved him
to pity. In the first soliloquy, in some speeches in the palace,
in the earlier parts of his conversations with Estrella, and with
Rosaura he shews wit; wit is a human attribute that the beasts
do not possess. Even if he expresses his aspirations too proudly
some are not ignoble. If his manner is always harsh, the matter
of his speeches is sometimes correct enough: *"En lo que no es
justa ley / no ha de obedecer al Rey"* (1321–22). Most significant of all, perhaps, for his subsequent change of heart, is his

11 A. Farinelli, op. cit., Parte seconda, p. 279 and note on p. 415.

exclamation in confusion on waking up in the palace: *"Dadme, cielos, desengaño"* (1239). Although the wish to know is soon stifled (*"¿Quién me mete en discurrir?"* [1245]) and his appetites immediately resume their hold upon him, these phrases hint that Segismundo is not entirely degraded. Like King Baltasar in the *auto*, he is a personification of *tesoro escondido*, as is every man whose animal nature dominates him.

During the palace scene there are two moments in which Segismundo has to face the possibility that he may be only a figure in a dream. Basilio warns him of this; so does Clotaldo. Together they have planned to take him back to the tower if his behaviour in the palace is unpromising. So that they speak with a double meaning, but he can only understand one. The first moment occurs after Segismundo's unfilial outburst to Basilio:

Basilio: *Mira bien lo que te advierto:*
              que seas humilde y blando,
              porque quizá estás soñando,
              aunque ves que estás despierto.   *Vase.*
Segismundo: *¿Que quizá soñando estoy,*
              aunque despierto me veo?
              No sueño, pues toco y creo
              lo que he sido y lo que soy.   (1528–35)

He trusts to his senses and relies on his nature (*"un compuesto de hombre y fiera"*) to carry him through to the throne. Later, when Clotaldo interposes to preserve Rosaura, the following dialogue ensues:

[Clotaldo:] *Y no, por verte ya de todos dueño,*
             seas crüel, porque quizá es un sueño.
Segismundo: *A rabia me provocas,*
             cuando la luz del desengaño tocas.
             Veré, dándote muerte,
             si es sueño o si es verdad.   (1678–83)

In the first passage Segismundo makes clear his assurance, his belief in his own powers and in the world in which he is placed; in the second his confidence has turned to hysteria and violence. *"La luz del desengaño"* is a strange phrase to find on his lips; is he fighting against what he knows is the truth?

Overconfident after his first confusion, proud of his cruelty,

Segismundo is thwarted and taken back, drugged, to his tower. There Clotaldo easily persuades him that all his experience in the palace was a dream. There are, however, certain associations with the tower itself that underlie the process of his conversion.

Rosaura's first impressions of the tower were not very pleasant. She criticised its architecture and added:

> La puerta
> (mejor diré funesta boca) abierta
> está, y desde su centro
> nace la noche, pues la engendra dentro.   (69–72)

When she sees Segismundo chained up inside she calls it: "*una prisión oscura / que es de un vivo cadáver sepultura*" (93–4). Later she mentions its "bóvedas frías" (178). Segismundo says: "*que cuna y sepulcro fue / esta torre para mí*" (195–96). And he describes himself in the same speech as an "*esqueleto vivo*" and an "*animado muerto*" (201–2). When he wakes up again in the tower he exclaims: "*¿No sois mi sepulcro vos, / torre? Sí*" (2084–85). The tower is associated with the idea of death, and for Calderón the fear of death often represented an essential preliminary towards a new life; properly realised, the idea of man's mortality will lead men to walk along the true path of virtue. "*La memoria de la muerte*" sometimes saves the figures of Man from the devil in the *autos*; because Baltasar does not heed Daniel's reiterated warnings he is damned, and in *No hay más fortuna que Dios* the worldly figures are saved after Beauty has been changed into a skeleton. The tomblike tower is here a reminder of death; this idea may escape a careless reading of the play, but it underlies Segismundo's change of heart.

Moreover, with Calderón, death often represents the final end of disorder. And disorder has been the dominant feature of Segismundo's life up to the moment of his awakening. The portents that attended his birth, the cosmic upheavals, and the death of his mother shewed Basilio almost as clearly as did the evil horoscope what was to be expected. In the first act Segismundo wanted to murder Rosaura for an almost frivolous reason, and, though he pined for freedom, he shewed himself unfit for it by his behaviour when the guards separated him from his new source of consolation. In the palace he behaved wrongly towards every one he met: to his father he was unfilial, he rejected the servant's advice for the flattery of a buffoon, he was discourteous to Astolfo, he paid too much attention to Estrella and he shewed criminal impulses in his conduct towards Rosaura and Clotaldo. He not only stopped at nothing; he was also imprudent. When free he could use his freedom only in a misdirected and distorted way. So he wakes up in a tower that is a tomb. "*Sí, hora es ya de despertar*" (2091).

Back in the tower Segismundo dreams that he is still posturing in the palace; his real dream is a continuation of his waking life. He awakes, and Clotaldo easily persuades him that all that had happened in the palace was part of the same dream, a dream that had been inspired by the talk about the king of birds which preceded the first drugging. In dreams one does not act but is "acted upon;" in the palace Segismundo acted as his passions, not his reason, dictated: he might as well have been dreaming. For while we are awake there are objective laws outside us to which we must conform; to know these laws and how to apply them is what gives life its reality. If they are neglected man becomes the creature of his passions, he is "acted upon," and his life is no more real than a dream is. So that the palace scene became twice a dream for Segismundo: it was an unreal experience, and while it lasted he had merely acted on impulse in a dream-like way. There was, however, one moment in which his higher nature was aroused: he loved a woman, and that memory was the one thing that seemed real to him.

Segismundo awakes then to find that what had seemed real was now unreal, that what he had thought was life, was, must have been, a dream. Clotaldo's explanation of the dream convinces him; it was a dream provoked by a conversation about an eagle. Clotaldo then adds: "*que aun en sueños / no se pierde el hacer bien*" (2146–47). And Segismundo replies:

> *Es verdad; pues reprimamos*
> *esta fiera condición,*
> *esta furia, esta ambición*
> *por si alguna vez soñamos. . . .*   (2148–51)

Clotaldo's statement seems surprising, and so does Segismundo's reply to it. What Clotaldo says does not apply to ordinary dreams in which man is not responsible for his acts. But it does apply to Segismundo's life in the palace, for if he had acted more wisely he would not have found himself once more in the tower. In some way he seems to understand this, to realise that his "dream" life was a continuation of his former life in the tower, and to accept the fact that by curbing his instincts he could save himself from similar disappointments in the future. Calderón does not expressly state, but he implies, that the Prince now sees that life is not an end in itself, nor is it something that he can control. It is something with which he must come to terms. That is to say, he is not yet fully converted; he has realised that evil does not pay and should be avoided for that reason.[12] His motives are not of the highest, but they are leading him in the right direction.

Segismundo is not acting from the higest motives when he decides to turn away from impulsive and passionate action. But the turning away prepares the true conversion that will follow in the third act. Death is an awakening from the dream of life; Segismundo wakes from his life's dream in a tomblike tower which almost unconsciously puts him in mind of his latter end. Having realized that he has been in error he utters the famous soliloquy in which he equates his experience with other types of worldly experience: the king's, the rich man's, the beggar's, the merchant's, and the brawler's. He now knows that life is a dream; all life as the worldly know it. The expres-

12 I am reminded here of some ideas of Bishop Butler: "Upon the whole, if the generality of mankind were to cultivate within themselves the principle of self-love; if they were to accustom themselves often to sit down and consider what was the greatest happiness they were capable of attaining for themselves in this life, and if self-love were so strong and prevalent as that they would uniformly pursue this their chief supposed temporal good without being diverted from it by any particular passion; it would manifestly prevent numberless follies and vices. This was in a great measure the Epicurean system of philosophy. It is indeed by no means the religious or even moral institution of life. Yet, with all the mistakes men would fall into about interest, it would be less mischievous than the extravagances of mere appetite, will and pleasure: for certainly self-love, though confined to the interest of this life, is, of the two, a much better guide than passion, which has absolutely no bound, nor measure, but what is set to it by this self-love, or moral considerations." Joseph Butler, "Preface to the Sermons," in *Works* (Oxford, 1850), II, xxvi–xxvii.

sion is general: his dream is as real as his life is now that he is awake—and therefore all life is like that. He is still the dupe of Basilio and Clotaldo; he has still to understand that he was awake all the time that he thinks he was dreaming. Only then shall we be able to talk of him as truly converted.

Perhaps it is not idle to point out that the soliloquy itself establishes the nature of the dream of life. Its words are really the complete answer to the criticism of Farinelli:

> *Y la experiencia me enseña*
> *que el hombre que vive sueña*
> *lo que es hasta despertar.*
> *Sueña el rey que es rey, y vive*
> *con este engaño mandando,*
> *disponiendo y gobernando;*
> *y este aplauso, que recibe*
> *prestado, en el viento escribe. . . .* (2155–62)

The emphasis is on what one is; the king dreams in his kingship, the rich man in his riches, and so forth.[13] The word "*sueño*" applies, not to the fact that one *is*, but to *what* one is. Before, Segismundo had refused to believe that he was dreaming because he could feel what he was; now he sees that what seemed real has only the reality of a dream. The palace, his attempts to satisfy his passions, his seeming power were all untrustworthy and short-lived. Calderón here has taken the Stoics' distinction between the things that are in our power and those that are not. Our health, our property, our position are not in our power; our judgment and our power of choice are. If we live only for the things that are not in our power we are no more free than is the dreamer in his dream who cannot exercise his powers of choice, for the outside things, things not in his power, rule him. The king's life is real; but his power and honours are only "*prestados.*" The Stoic, so regarding them, would have him avoid them as far as possible; the Christian would have him use them for good ends but live by them not

13 Compare: "Thus saith the Lord, Let not the wise man glory in his wisdom, neither let the mighty man glory in his might, let not the rich man glory in his riches: but let him that glorieth glory in this, that he understandeth and knoweth me that I am the Lord. . . ." Jeremiah, IX, 23–24.

for them. External events are also outside our power, and Segismundo had wrongly assumed that he could shape them as he
would. But instead, events led to his awakening in the tower. In
his dream he had flouted the pagan precept: "Require not
things to happen as you wish, but wish them to happen as they
do happen, and you will go on well," [14] as well as the Christian
petition: "Thy will be done."

In the third act Segismundo is a man alternately swayed
by passion and by his newly acquired prudence. When the soldiers invite him to be their king he at first takes them to be
dream-figures whom he tries to drive away. He only consents
to lead them when they tell him that his "dream" foretold his
present glory; nevertheless when he accepts he is carried away
by the passion of conquest. This in turn gives way to the cau-
tious aside just before Clotado's entrance:

> Mas si antes desto despierto,
> ¿no será bien no decirlo,
> supuesto que no he de hacerlo?   (2383–85)

Until half way through the act he does not know whether he
is asleep or awake; there is a continual battle between the new
Segismundo and the old. Passionate impulses keep bursting out
and are as often repressed. One such moment occurs when
Clotaldo declares:

> Yo aconsejarte no puedo
> contra mi Rey, ni valerte.
> A tus plantas estoy puesto;
> dame la muerte.   (2407–10)

Segismundo replies:

> ¡Villano,
> traidor, ingrato! [Aparte] Mas ¡cielos!
> reportarme me conviene,
> que aún no sé si estoy despierto.   (2410–13)

Segismundo is determined to march on to victory against his
king and father and no less determined to do good lest all
should be a dream. He is engaged in a treasonable act, yet his
actions and words often belie it. His new attitude, though pref-

14 Epictetus, *The Enchiridion, or Manual*, VIII.

erable to his earlier uncurbed violence, is not only inconstant; when he corrects it, the selfish impulse peeps out again.

> *Mas, sea verdad o sueño,*
> *obrar bien es lo que importa.*
> *Si fuere verdad, por serlo;*
> *si no, por ganar amigos*
> *para cuando despertemos.* (2423–27)

A few lines before Rosaura comes onto the battlefield he appears, dressed in skins, and glories in the fact that he is a *"fiera"* in charge of an army (2660).

Rosaura's entrance brings him to his senses. In her appeal she tells him that they have seen each other three times, and the scales fall from his eyes, for, he says: *"que no es posible que quepan / en un sueño tantas cosas"* (2924–25). With this comes his last struggle, from which the new Segismundo appears trampling down the old. All his life had been a dream, and each time that he had seen Rosaura before, he had lusted for her; why not make the most of this opportunity?

> *Pues si es así, y ha de verse*
> *desvanecida entre sombras*
> *la grandeza y el poder,*
> *la majestad y la pompa,*
> *sepamos aprovechar*
> *este rato que nos toca,*
> *pues sólo se goza en ella*
> *lo que entre sueños se goza.*
> *Rosaura está en mi poder,*
> *su hermosura el alma adora.*
> *Gocemos, pues, la ocasión . . .*
> . . . .
> *Esto es sueño; y pues lo es,*
> *soñemos dichas agora,*
> *que después serán pesares.*
> *Mas con mis razones propias*
> *vuelvo a convencerme a mí.*
> *Si es sueño, si es vanagloria,*
> *¿quién por vanagloria humana*
> *pierde una divina gloria?* (2950–71)

Then comes his final triumph of disillusion, perhaps the finest statement of it in the play:

> *¿Qué pasado bien no es sueño?*
> *¿Quién tuvo dichas heroicas*
> *que entre sí no diga, cuando*
> *las revuelve en su memoria:*
> *"sin duda que fue soñado*
> *cuanto vi?"*   (2972–77)

From now on he is the reformed prince, and "*acudamos a lo eterno*" (2982) is his motto. He has triumphed over his lust, and he has found a justification for his treason: he will restore Rosaura's honour. The conflict of his action and his situation has been resolved. Rosaura is the instrument of his conversion; however we may criticise the sub-plot we must admit that it cannot be separated from the main plot without our misunderstanding the latter. Rosaura completed what Coltado began: the new Segismundo. After this his words and his conduct are harmonious and speak for themselves. He sacrifices his passion for Rosaura to the redemption of her honour and restores his conquered father to the throne of Poland.

In this analysis I hope that I have to some extent answered Menéndez y Pelayo's objections against the rapidity of Segismundo's change of heart, which after all takes place in two stages. Perhaps the scene with Clotaldo in the tower is too much compressed; but the palace scenes hinted that such a change was possible, and the developments in the last act are very well worked out. The fact that Segismundo is a symbol does not hurt the play. His experience is a representation of man's awakening from the life of the senses to that of the spirit.

Segismundo's experiences are reflected in those of other persons in the play. He trusted in his senses and in his newly found powers when he was allowed to be a prince for a few hours; he woke up, disillusioned, in the tower. Pride comes before a fall, and from the fall the proud man may become humble and prudent. Segismundo is not the only man to be humbled; Clarín, Basilio, Astolfo, a servant, and the rebel soldier have also to learn how to submit to the inevitable. They all undergo a disillusion which is less strikingly presented than Segismundo's, but which, none the less, is important to them and to the development of the plot. Each man expresses too much confidence in his own powers, deeds, or position, and each is humbled. In their different ways they too have been dreaming.

Clarín is something more than a *gracioso*, a *figura del donaire* of the common sort. He is cowardly, garrulous, humorous; he puns on his own name. But his function is not merely to give comic relief but to add to the moral lessons of the play. His vices are funny, but they are also vices. There is little hint of this at first: in the scenes with Rosaura by the tower he seems only true to type. Gradually he reveals his true nature. Despite the blows of the halbardiers he forces his way into the palace; he must see what is going on, and he relies on his impudence and lack of shame. He finds Clotaldo and obtains a situation from him by blackmail; he has guessed the relationship between Clotaldo and Rosaura:

> Y hay que, viniendo con ella [Rosaura],
> estoy yo muriendo de hambre,
> y naide de mí se acuerda,
> sin mirar que soy Clarín,
> y que si el tal Clarín suena,
> podrá decir cuanto pasa
> al Rey, a Astolfo y a Estrella.[15]   (1205–11)

But to be Clotaldo's servant is not enough for him; he immediately attempts to curry favour with Segismundo, whose temporary grandeur he looks upon as permanent.

> Señor,
> soy un grande agradador
> de todos los Segismundos.   (1337–39)

His behaviour in the palace needs no further comment. He makes Segismundo's error. The sycophant succeeds over a short term.

Disaster follows. Clarín, proud of his cleverness, falls through being too clever. He has threatened Clotaldo before; now Clotaldo can shut him up out of the way, and he does so. A Clarion that knows secrets is dangerous. Segismundo learns

---

15 See also the dialogue between Clarín and Rosaura before the battle in the last act:

Rosaura:	¡Ay, Clarín! ¿Dónde has estado?
Clarín:	En una torre encerrado. . . .
Rosaura:	¿Por qué?
Clarín:	Porque sé el secreto
	de quien eres, y en efeto, (Dentro cajas.)
	Clotaldo. . . . Pero ¿qué ruido
	es éste? (3020–3032)

a lesson from his imprisonment, but Clarín, though his dreams
have warned him, can—for his imprisonment—give only a
frivolous explanation. The moment called for more than puns
about the Council of Nicaea or the invention of burlesque saints
in a new calendar. He is interrupted by the soldiers who mistake him for Segismundo. He is puzzled, but he accepts the
first solution that his ready wit supplies, an ingenious, but
totally false, explanation of their conduct:

> ¡Vive Dios, que va de veras!
> ¿Si es costumbre en este reino
> prender uno cada día
> y hacerle príncipe, y luego
> volverle a la torre? Sí,
> pues cada día lo veo;
> fuerza es hacer mi papel.   (2242–48)

> ¿Segismundo dicen? Bueno.
> Segismundos llaman todos
> los príncipes contrahechos.   (2263–65)

He remains the clever self-seeker, and his self-seeking cannot
save him from disaster. His very cleverness continually leads
him astray. A minor example of this occurs when Clotaldo begs
for his life from Segismundo, after the latter has been acclaimed
by the rebel soldiery. Clarín, leaping to a false conclusion, mur-
murs to himself: "Yo apuesto / que le despeña del monte"
(2389–90). Segismundo, however, does not throw Clotaldo
down the mountain but pardons him.

After these earlier errors Clarín's death can be seen as a
natural consequence of his too superficial cleverness. He meets
his end by trying to escape it. The scene is among the most
powerful in the play, and we shall have to return to it when
we examine Basilio's part. Here again Clarín appears in the
double role of *gracioso* and of a man whose moral failings are
to be exposed. The speech in which he declares his intention of
hiding safely until the battle is over is a good example of humorous writing in the comic convention; but it is also an expression of cynicism and pride which deserves punishment:

Dentro unos.
> ¡Viva nuestro invicto Rey!

Dentro otros.

　　　　　　　　　　¡Viva nuestra libertad!
Clarín:　　　　　　*¡La libertad y el Rey vivan!*
　　　　　　　　　　Vivan muy enhorabuena,
　　　　　　　　　　que a mí nada me da pena,
　　　　　　　　　　como en cuenta me reciban;
　　　　　　　　　　que yo, apartado este día
　　　　　　　　　　en tan grande confusión,
　　　　　　　　　　haga el papel de Nerón
　　　　　　　　　　"que de nada se dolía."
　　　　　　　　　　Si bien me quiero doler
　　　　　　　　　　de algo, y ha de ser de mí;
　　　　　　　　　　escondido, desde aquí
　　　　　　　　　　toda la fiesta he de ver.
　　　　　　　　　　El sitio es oculto y fuerte
　　　　　　　　　　entre estas peñas. Pues ya
　　　　　　　　　　la muerte no me hallará,
　　　　　　　　　　dos higas para la muerte.　　(3041–59)

Clarín is then killed by a random shot. His dying speech makes it clear that he has at last understood where true wisdom lies: *"mirad que vais a morir, / si está de Dios que muráis"* (3094–95). All through his life he had been a clever, short-sighted opportunist; death alone could teach him the necessary lesson. Clarín dreamed he was clever and did not wake up until a few minutes before his death.

Basilio, hailed by the rival princes as the wise Thales and the learnèd Euclid, reveals his own defects as well as his good intentions in his long speech in the first act:

　　　　　　　　Ya sabéis que yo en el mundo
　　　　　　　　por mi ciencia he merecido
　　　　　　　　el sobrenombre de docto. . . .　　(604–606)

He is proud of his astrological ability and so certain of his powers of prediction that he acts upon them. Although he recognises that:

　　　　　　　　la inclinación más violenta,
　　　　　　　　el planeta más impío,
　　　　　　　　sólo el albedrío inclinan,
　　　　　　　　no fuerzan el albedrío,　　(788–791)

yet he had assumed that, as his prescience was so great, it could not be mistaken. He knew that his son's will was free, but at

the same time he assumed that it would be forced. He therefore had him reared in circumstances that made it virtually
impossible for him to make wise choices. Basilio considers that
he can mould another man's life as he pleases, and at the same
time he neglects the fact that this man's will is free. So he makes
two mistakes: one of presumption, the other of ignoring an
important human truth. The consequence is that he enables
the prediction to be fulfilled by the very means that he hoped
would avoid that conclusion. His motive was partly a good one—
to save Poland from civil war—but nevertheless his conduct
was wrong, and he involved Poland in the war he wished to
avoid. He was rash to assume that by wisdom he could control
the decrees of heaven; he was wicked to bring up a young boy
as though he were a caged beast.

At the same time Basilio's wisdom is not confined to astrology. He at least feels compelled by a rather belated Christian
charity to grant Segismundo a chance to redeem himself. Not
only that; he explains to Clotaldo how the chance is to be
given in such a way that Segismundo shall not be too much
shocked if the experiment fails; he will then see that life is a
dream, for, Basilio says:

> Podrá entender que soñó,
> y hará bien cuando lo entienda;
> porque en el mundo, Clotaldo,
> todos los que viven sueñan.   (1146–49)

These words were to prove true, as we have already seen.

Clarín meets his end by trying to escape it; Basilio finds
humiliation by trying to avoid it. Both were too confident, but
Basilio profited from Clarín's example. Basilio had never admitted that he had been unwise and unjust to Segismundo when
they met in the palace. His son's behaviour outraged and grieved
him, but he never recognised his responsibility for it. All this
was reversed after Clarín fell wounded before him to give his
dying warning:

> que no hay seguro camino
> a la fuerza del destino
> y a la inclemencia del hado.
> Y así, aunque a libraros vais
> de la muerte con huir,

> *mirad que vais a morir,*
> *si está de Dios que muráis.* (3089-95)

Not only had Basilio announced his intention of fleeing; he has also looked upon his earlier "*camino*" as "*seguro*." The voice that spoke from the dead man's wounds made him see the truths that he could not learn before:

> *que son diligencias vanas*
> *del hombre cuantas dispone*
> *contra mayor fuerza y causa.* (3105-07)

The futility of his conduct is now obvious to him; only God can decide the course of a man's life. He therefore submits, waits for his son and humbles himself before him. Basilio dreamed in his wisdom and only awakened when his schemes were defeated.[16]

Astolfo's position was rather different, but he also put too much trust in appearances. He relied on being able to escape from the working of the law of honour by trusting to his position and to his own personal merit; his false self-confidence was thus a double source of error. Notwithstanding his bravery and loyalty, Calderón made his faults exemplary too. He wronged Rosaura. When he thought he had left her forever he set about planning his political marriage to Estrella, purely to further his ambition by securing his rather doubtful right of succession to the Polish throne. When he handed Rosaura's portrait to Estrella he made clear that he was wronging Rosaura knowingly:

16 L. P. Thomas pointed out that certain attributes of the Trinity were present in the part of Basilio. Starting from the *auto* of *La vida es sueño* he detected in Basilio's long speech the working of the Trinity in it; he pointed out how certain passages exemplified Power, others Wisdom, others Love. I do not wish to deny that there is in Basilio, along with other characteristics, the germ of the notion of the Trinity found in the *auto*. This has some importance in the consideration of Segismundo's attitudes towards his father, for when Segismundo rebels he is rebelling against a divinely established order. But for the comprehension of the part of Basilio in the *comedia* we must see primarily a human being led astray by the presumption of wisdom. In interpreting any of Calderón's plays that he afterwards made into an *auto*, we must be careful not to read too much of the *auto* back into the *comedia*. The play is nearly always simplified in the process of conversion. See note 10 above.

> *Perdona, Rosaura hermosa,*
> *este agravio, porque ausentes,*
> *no se guardan más fe que ésta*
> *los hombres y las mujeres.*   (1774–77)

Although he knows the wrong he does her, he never troubles
to think of the consequences of his action; he does not see that
retribution may overtake him because of it. He is too sure of
himself to think about such things; he trusts to the distance
that he supposes lies between them (that is perhaps the world
in its most literal sense!) to carry him through, while he justifies himself because other men act in the same way. He wrongs
Rosaura. He trusts to appearances in the hope of marrying
Estrella and gaining a kingdom. Afterwards Segismundo defeats
him in battle and compels him to marry Rosaura, not Estrella.
He too is a dreamer; he dreams in his position and in the belief
that he could escape the consequences of his past actions.

Two minor characters meet disaster also through their
presumption. They are the second servant and the rebel soldier.
The servant is not afraid to speak his mind, and he reproves
Segismundo for his evil ways. He is a good man, but as soon
as he displays confidence and pride, disaster overtakes him:

Segismundo: *También oíste decir*
               que por un balcón, a quien
               me canse, sabré arrojar.
Criado 2:   *Con los hombres como yo*
               no puede hacerse eso.
Segismundo: *¿No?*
               ¡Por Dios, que lo he de probar!   (1422–27)

The soldier who headed the revolution is confident that he
will receive a good reward for his treason. When he asks for it
Segismundo sends him to be imprisoned in the tower: *"que el*
traidor no es menester, / siendo la traición pasada" (3300–01).

Segismundo, Astolfo, Basilio, Clarín, the servant, and the
soldier all trusted too much to the things of this world and all
were thwarted. Some at least, by meeting disillusion and realising what it meant, were able to rise again after their downfalls.
All were rudely awakened from their dreams.

Rosaura and Clotaldo do not appear to enter into the scheme. Moral considerations dominate both of them, and these make disillusions unnecessary. Loyalty dictates all Clotaldo's actions, honour Rosaura's. The sub-plot is the story of the conflict of these motives. Each person is swayed to some extent by the feeling of the other, but each is right in remaining true to an ideal. So Clotaldo is willing to sacrifice his daughter's honour rather than be disloyal to Basilio and to Astolfo; Rosaura to fight against her father in order to vindicate her honour.

Yet the sub-plot is still in part a reflection of the main plot. The difference is that Clotaldo and Rosaura recognise confusion when they see it, whereas the others either do not recognise it as confusion (e.g. Clarín in the tower), or trust too much to their own abilities to solve it. Clotaldo and Rosaura trust instead in principles of conduct, not in worldly importance, self-conceit, or mere cleverness. Segismundo's confusions in the palace, in the tower, on the battle-field are echoed in their doubts and conflicts. By realising the difficulties of life and by putting their trust in loyalty or honour they find their way through the labyrinth in which the others are thwarted or even destroyed. Confusion, though, is always stressed. Coltaldo, when Rosaura shews him the sword, exclaims:

> ¡Válgame el cielo! ¿qué escucho?
> Aun no sé determinarme
> si tales sucesos son
> ilusiones o verdades.   (395–398)

After Rosaura has revealed her sex he says:

> ¿Qué confuso laberinto
> es éste, donde no puede
> hallar la razón el hilo?   (975–978)

And Rosaura sees clearly her difficulties when Estrella tells her to bring the portrait:

> ¿Qué haré en tantas confusiones,
> donde imposible parece
> que halle razón que me alivie,
> ni alivio que me consuele?   (1824–27)

In his moments of trial Clotaldo is moved neither by fear of death nor by love of his daughter; Rosaura risks putting herself into Segismundo's hands in the hope of removing her dishonour. Through plot and sub-plot runs the theme of confusion; only devotion to virtue enables men and women to overcome the difficulties around them. Clotaldo and Rosaura know this from the beginning; the others have to learn it by a hard road. The sub-plot has therefore a logical justification in the plan of the play.

There is one scene in the sub-plot which particularly stresses these facts. It occurs in the last act when Clotaldo and Rosaura are brought into conflict with one another. Each is right in the course of action he or she has decided to pursue. Clotaldo has had to change his attitude towards her because Astolfo saved his life when Segismundo tried to kill him. For Rosaura the moral situation has not changed: Astolfo is still faithless, even if he rescued her father. She is therefore able to quote back at her father his earlier words: "*Vida infame no es vida*" (910), when she says:

> De ti recibí la vida,
> y tú mismo me dijiste,
> cuando la vida me diste,
> que la que estaba ofendida
> no era vida. . . .   (2592–96)

The civil war is of the greatest importance to Clotaldo; to Rosaura, in comparison with her private problem, it means nothing. The confusions of the world are such that father and daughter can both be right in taking opposite sides in pledging their loyalty to rival factions. Here is an illustration of the way in which each Christian soul has to work out his own salvation for himself.

There is another point to note in Clotaldo's part. He is loyal to his king because he is king; his loyalty asks no questions. Another author might have made him an inhuman executioner of Basilio's cruel decrees. Calderón does not attempt to palliate the enormity of Basilio's decisions, but neither does he blame Clotaldo for putting them into effect. Clotaldo is the faithful servant of an unjust master, but as the master had authority to govern, he obeyed him scrupulously. Had the servant questioned the decisions of his master he might have appeared presumptuous—like the second servant. Instead Calderón makes him loyal and humble.

The play is a carefully constructed whole. Segismundo's adventures are reflected in those of Basilio, Clarín, Astolfo, and two unnamed characters; they are contrasted with those of Rosaura and Clotaldo. (Estrella is a figure who merely serves to help the plot; I do not see how her part exemplifies a moral lesson as do the others.) There is a close correspondence between the behaviour of the characters and their fortunes and misfortunes. In this way Calderón shews how virtue and vice earn their rewards, and the plot clearly represents the workings of God's providence—except that the rewards and punishments of the future life appear in this.

We may summarise the play thus: Segismundo is a compound of pride and passion, the satisfaction of which is thwarted; so he learns to subdue his passion and to see that pride is useless in a world in which nothing is certain. He turns to follow moral precepts, at first for selfish reasons, but later for purer motives. Clarín is clever and proud of his cleverness; his early efforts meet with success, and he assumes that he can gain whatever he may want by his wits. He ignores the warning that his imprisonment might have given him and, still sure of himself, he at last meets his end by trying to avoid it. Basilio is wise and proud of his wisdom. He assumes that he can alter the decrees of the stars and that he can ignore the free will of the only man who could alter them. He is defeated in battle (which deprives him of power) and witnesses Clarín's death, which convinces him of man's impotence and his own error. Astolfo trusts to his position to evade the responsibility; but the revolution overthrows his position, and he has to right the wrong he did to Rosaura. All were proud in one way or another. All trusted to their abilities, took as permanent what was transient, thought that they could control the future in accordance with their own desires; they thought that life was too simple. In a word, all were dreaming. Clotaldo and Rosaura subordinated their lives to principles; they saw that they had difficulties to face and that the world was confusing and untrustworthy. They faced their problems with constancy, unselfishness, and prudence. For this reason they did not ride to a fall as the others did.

Plot and sub-plot depict different aspects of the same teaching. Plot and sub-plot are united also by Rosaura's part in Segismundo's conversion. When these two facts are clearly seen Menéndez y Pelayo's criticism that the sub-plot is a "parasitical growth" that has no connection with main plot is seen to be worthless.

The structure of the play is complex. We have already seen some ironies that come true or are proved false by the progress of events. Clotaldo imprisons Clarín for being a "Clarion;" Clarín had hoped to feather his nest for the same reason. Rosaura turns on Clotaldo the arguments that he had earlier used on her. Segismundo, at the end, can reprove his father, as his father had before reproved him. These are the most striking instances, but others that are hardly less so can easily be found. No detail in the play is idle. A mere compliment may serve to hint at the vanity of a king or the pride of a prince; asides shew the wit and lack of judgment of a clown.

In general, earlier criticism of this play has emphasised its fine dramatic moments. I do not wish to deny their merit or to minimise their importance. What I have tried to do is to prove that they cannot safely be isolated without serious misunderstandings. Literature teaches us both to feel and to order our feelings. In *La vida es sueño* the ordering of feelings is as important as the expression of the feelings themselves. Calderón expresses magnificently the misery of mankind [17] or the ferocity of an artificially repressed brutality, disillusion with the world or the death throes of a repentant self-seeker. Even more magnificent is the organization of the whole play.

The details are accessible to all. Can the play as a whole mean anything to those who do not share the religious outlook of the author? I think it can. We may not all be able to value all the positive qualities that Calderón holds up to us. Rosaura's honour is for us but of historical interest; Clotaldo's loyalty appears servile; Segismundo's treatment of the rebel soldier seems

[17] The misery, that is to say, of those who are dominated by their passions and are not guided by reason; this of course is not the same as the pessimistic misery of the romantic poets.

unnecessarily vindictive. Yet these are types of—they stand for —other feelings that we can respect. Clotaldo's loyalty is the type of fidelity to a just cause; Segismundo's justice represents true justice; Rosaura's honour stands for a determined self-respect. We are not yet able to feel that there is no conflict between our impulses and our reason; we have still to come to terms with the world in which we live. Calderón was conscious of these problems, he stated them, and he gave us a solution of them. His statement is of the greatest importance to us, whatever we think of the solution.

4·The Structure of Calderón's

La vida es sueño *

by A. E. Sloman

TWO ISSUES are involved in Calderón's *La vida es sueño*: a man's conversion and a woman's clearing of her honour. One centres on Segismundo, the other on Rosaura. The main issue is suggested by the title "Life is a dream;" this is Segismundo's discovery and the key to his conversion. To this central theme, with its origin in the legends of the Awakened Sleeper and of Barlaam and Josaphat, and deeply rooted in Spanish tradition, Calderón has linked the story of Rosaura, an honour episode akin to it neither in subject nor in spirit. It is this honour episode which has occasioned the most serious criticism of Calderón's famous play. Until recently, the very critics who were uananimous in placing *La vida es sueño* among the greatest of Spanish and world plays were equally unanimous in condemning its subplot, regarding it not merely as a useless adjunct, but as an action which seriously detracted from the play's unity, a parasite entwined about a noble oak.[1]

The Rosaura episode, however, is clearly neither of the nature nor dimensions of a parasite. It is no mere afterthought to fill out the required three acts. From the play's first scene

* *Editor's Note.* Quotations have been modified to make them conform to Professor Sloman's own edition of the play (Manchester, 1961).

1 Cf., for example, M. Menéndez y Pelayo: *"no existe, digo, en teatro del mundo idea más asombrosa que la que sirve de forma sustancial a esta obra; y tal, que si le quitara la parte pegadiza, y fueran más naturales, más sencillos y más nacidos de las entrañas del asunto algunos de los recursos que para desarrollar este pensamiento se emplearon, no tendríamos reparo en decir que era una obra perfecta." "Calderón y su teatro,"* in *Estudios de crítica histórica y literaria,* III, 223.

90

Rosaura is involved in the fate of Segismundo, and the characters among whom she moves and with whom she is concerned are those of the main plot: Clotaldo, Astolfo, Estrella, and Clarín. And the lines devoted to Rosaura and to the honour motive comprise very nearly one half of the play. The Rosaura episode, that is, is so inextricably bound up with Segismundo and given such prominence throughout the play that the whole dramatic structure depends upon it. Reject the subplot, and the play itself must be rejected.

Once the significance of the subplot is recognized, it is of paramount importance to see exactly how Calderón has linked it to the main episode and related it to the play's central theme. Professor Wilson's interpretation of *La vida es sueño* throws light on this aspect,[2] but the point calls for a specific analysis of the play's structure. That is the object of this brief essay. It attempts to show that, as the action of the play progresses, the two plots and the two characters on which they centre are intimately related, and that despite the two centres of interest Calderón has created a single, coherent, and integrated dramatic movement. This integration of the two plots was the essential problem of construction in *La vida es sueño*. The present essay, therefore, is primarily concerned with the parallel between Segismundo and Rosaura, and details which are not pertinent to their interrelation and which do not affect the general structural lines of the play have been omitted.

Calderón's opening scene couples Rosaura with Segismundo. Rosaura, disguised as a man, comes unawares upon the stronghold where Segismundo is imprisoned, and at once the parallel between the two characters is established. Both are dogged by misfortune: the first speech of Rosaura ends with the question "*¿Dónde halló piedad un infelice?*," and Segismundo's first words, reiterated at the beginning of his soliloquy, are "*¡Ay, mísero de mí! ¡Ay, infelice!*" Moreover, from the start, these

---

2 E. M. Wilson, "*La vida es sueño*," *Revista de la Universidad de Buenos Aires*, Tercera Época, Año IV, Nos. 3 & 4 (1946), 64: "*Precisamente el objeto de este trabajo es demonstrar que* La vida es sueño *es una obra lógica, consistente, toda de una pieza, y tan hábilmente desarrollada que sus enseñanzas trascienden con mucho la época y el país donde se escribió.*"

two victims of misfortune respect and pity each other: knowing
the fate of Segismundo, Rosaura observes: *"Temor y piedad en
mí / sus razones han causado"* (I, 173–174), and to Segismundo's
"Who's there?" she replies: *"No es sino un triste ¡ay de mí! /
que en estas bóvedas frías / oyó tus melancolías"* (I, 177–179).
Segismundo, for his part, mysteriously moved by the presence
of Rosaura, checks his natural impulse to attack her:

> *tú solo, tú, has suspendido*
> *la pasión a mis enojos,*
> *la suspensión a mis ojos,*
> *la admiración aloído.*
>   *Con cada vez que te veo*
> *nueva admiración me das,*
> *y cuando te miro más*
> *aun más mirarte deseo.*   (I, 219–226)

And when Rosaura is discovered by Clotaldo he pledges his life
for her safety:

> *Primero, tirano dueño,*
> *que los ofendas y agravies,*
> *será mi vida despojo*
> *destos lazos miserables;*
> *pues en ellos, vive Dios,*
> *tengo de despedazarme*
> *con las manos, con los dientes,*
> *entre aquestas peñas, antes*
> *que su desdicha consienta*
> *y que llore sus ultrajes.*   (I, 309–318)

From the first, therefore, there is a bond of sympathy between
Segismundo and Rosaura: they are companions in misfortune.
The words of Rosaura underline the parallel:

> *Sólo diré que a esta parte*
> *hoy el cielo me ha guïado*
> *para haberme consolado,*
> *si consuelo puede ser,*
> *del que es desdichado, ver*
> *a otro que es más desdichado.*   (I, 247–252)

Clotaldo provides a further link, for, as we are soon to
learn, he is at once Segismundo's gaoler and Rosaura's own
father, and is concerned with the fortunes of both. He discovers
the reason for Rosaura's visit to Poland and guesses at her

identity; but, by the King's order, she must be placed under arrest. When the scene ends, Segismundo has been returned to his prison cell and Rosaura is under sentence of death.

Scene 2 brings hope for both Segismundo and Rosaura. King Basilio discloses the long-guarded secret that he has a son Segismundo who, because of his horoscope, has been secretly imprisoned; and he announces his decision to bring him to the palace for one day, to afford him an opportunity of giving the lie to the stars' prediction. Basilio's decision means trial freedom for Segismundo; and it means life to Rosaura, for, since it no longer matters that she knows the whereabouts of Segismundo's prison, she is reprieved.

And at this point the fortunes of Segismundo and Rosaura are shown to be not only closely related but interdependent. Rosaura tells Clotaldo that her grievance is against Astolfo, and one clearly that can only be removed by his marrying her:

> *Juzga advertido*
> *si no soy lo que parezco,*
> *y Astolfo a casarse vino*
> *con Estrella, si podrá*
> *agraviarme. Harto te he dicho.* (I, 969–973)

But Basilio has announced that, should Segismundo fail to redeem himself during his stay at the palace, he will consent to the marriage of Astolfo and Estrella, that they may be joint heirs to the Polish throne. The failure of Segismundo, therefore, since it will confirm the marriage of Astolfo to Estrella, implies the failure of Rosaura.

This parallel between the fortunes of Segismundo and Rosaura is maintained in Act II. In the first scene Clotaldo's description of the drugging of Segismundo and his transfer to the palace is followed by Clarín's announcement that his mistress Rosaura has shed her disguise and, under the name of Astrea, is maid of honour to Estrella. The way is thereby prepared for a second meeting of Segismundo and Rosaura. Of all Segismundo's palace experiences his meeting with Rosaura is the most significant. Whilst Clotaldo, Basilio, Astolfo, and the second servant are the victims of his anger and passion for revenge, the feminine beauty of Estrella and Rosaura attracts and intrigues him. But with Rosaura there is something more than physical attraction, though in this respect she is evidently superior to Estrella.[3] She is strangely familiar to Segismundo: "*Pero ¿qué es lo que veo?*" (II, 1578); "*Yo he visto esta belleza / otra vez*" (II, 1580–81); "*Ya hallé mi vida*" (1583). He pleads with her to stay, and only when she refuses is he provoked to attack her. That this meeting with Rosaura is something totally different from Segismundo's other palace experiences is clear from his own confession to Clotaldo in the following scene.

Segismundo has at least aired his grievance against his father Basilio, "tyrant of his free will;" but his behaviour has served only to confirm the verdict of the stars, and he is to return of his prison tower. In the portrait incident with which the palace scene ends, Rosaura too confronts the person responsible for her misfortune, Astolfo, and she succeeds in embarrassing him and alienating him in the eyes of Estrella. But the failure of Segismundo augurs ill for the cause of Rosaura.

In scene 2, Segismundo is again in prison under the eye of his gaoler Clotaldo; and he is readily persuaded that his palace sojourn was but a dream. But of all his experiences, one was unique:

> *De todos era señor,*
> *y de todos me vengaba.*
> *Sólo a una mujer amaba;*
> *que fue verdad, creo yo,*
> *en que todo se acabó*
> *y esto solo no se acaba.*   (II, 2132–37)

Rosaura has been responsible for the one occasion when he curbed his will for revenge, the experience which remains as the only truth and only reality of his palace stay. Segismundo's resolve at this point to control his cruel nature, which has been shown to be a first stage towards his later conversion,[4] follows directly upon this recollection of his meeting with Rosaura.

Act III opens with the rescue of Segismundo. Though

---

3 "*Pues ¿cómo, si entre flores, entre estrellas, / piedras, signos, planetas, las más bellas / prefieren, tú has servido / la de menos beldad, habiendo sido / por más bella y hermosa, / sol, lucero, diamante, estrella y rosa?*"
4 Cf. Wilson, art. cit., p. 68.

suspecting that this liberation is a second dream, he resolves to
do good, and even spares Clotaldo, allowing him to join forces
with King Basilio to oppose him. In a new scene at the palace,
Clotaldo brings news of Segismundo's rescue; then, alone with
Rosaura, he refuses to take the life of Astolfo to clear her
honour. Segismundo himself is unwittingly responsible for Clotaldo's refusal: Astolfo has won the gratitude of Clotaldo by
coming to his rescue when he was attacked by Segismundo
and, after Segismundo's behaviour at the palace, he is for Clotaldo the only acceptable heir to the Polish throne. Clotaldo
at all events is not prepared to meet the demands of Rosaura.

So it is that the play comes full circle with the reuniting of
Segismundo and Rosaura. The very speech in which Clarín
announces the approach of Rosaura seems to parody the opening lines of the play which preceded their first meeting; and,
as before, Rosaura is dressed as a man and Segismundo is in
skins. Rosaura delivers a long speech to Segismundo in which
she recalls their two previous meetings and, for the first time in
the play, gives a full account of her birth and misfortune; and
she ends by laying emphasis on their common interests. As a
woman she comes to plead for her honour; as a man she pledges
to support him against his father:

> *Ea, pues, fuerte caudillo,*
> *a los dos juntos importa*
> *impedir y deshacer*
> *estas concertadas bodas;*
> *a mí porque no se case*
> *el que mi esposo se nombra,*
> *y a ti porque, estando juntos*
> *sus dos estados, no pongan*
> *con más poder y más fuerza*
> *en duda nuestra victoria.*
> *Mujer vengo a persuadirte*
> *al remedio de mi honra,*
> *y varón vengo a alentarte*
> *a que cobres tu corona.*
> *Mujer vengo a enternecerte*
> *cuando a tus plantas me ponga,*
> *y varón vengo a servirte*
> *cuando a tus gentes socorra. . . .*
> *Y así piensa que si hoy*

> *como a mujer me enamoras,*
> *como varón te daré*
> *la muerte en defensa honrosa*
> *de mi honor; porque he de ser,*
> *en su conquista amorosa,*
> *mujer para darte quejas,*
> *varón para ganar honras.*   (III, 2892–2921)

This reunion scene is, as Professor Wilson has pointed out,[5] all-important in the process of Segismundo's conversion. Rosaura, and Rosaura only, can convince Segismundo that his visit to the palace was real. And only in the knowledge of this can his conversion be complete—the knowledge, that is, that life itself is as fleeting and unreal as a dream. Rosaura is the means of Segismundo's conversion.[6]

More than that, however, Rosaura is the proof of Segismundo's conversion. Segismundo is clearly in love with Rosaura; he was strangely attracted by her at their first meeting in Act I; at the palace in Act II his arrogance leads him to attack her when she dares to stand against him. Now, too, his first reaction is force:

> *Rosaura está en mi poder,*
> *su hermosura el alma adora.*
> *Gocemos, pues, la ocasión;*
> *el amor las leyes rompa*
> *del valor y confianza*
> *con que a mis plantas se postra—*   (III, 2958–63)

words which recall those of Act II: "*y así, por ver si puedo, cosa es llana / que arrojaré tu honor por la ventana*" (1644–45). But he overcomes his natural impulse and, far from dishonouring her, resolves to be the very champion of her honour: "*¡Vive Dios! que de su honra / he der ser conquistador / antes que de mi corona*" (III, 2989–91). He calls his men to arms and abruptly takes leave of her:

---

5 Art. cit., pp. 70–71.
6 For a careful analysis of the meaning of *La vida es sueño*, cf. Leopoldo Eulogio Palacios, "*La vida es sueño*," *Finisterre*, II, No. 1 (1948), 5–52. But there is only a passing reference to Rosaura, and the conversion of Segismundo is taken to be complete at the end of Act II (p. 51). It is hoped that the present essay will direct attention to the essential and indispensable role of Rosaura.

> Rosaura, al honor le importa,
> por ser piadoso contigo;
> ser crüel contigo agora.
> No te responde mi voz,
> porque mi honor te responda;
> no te hablo, porque quiero
> que te hablen por mí mis obras;
> ni te miro, porque es fuerza,
> en pena tan rigurosa,
> que no mire tu hermosura
> quien ha de mirar tu honra. (III, 3005–15)

In the battle which follows Rosaura's servant Clarín is killed. Clarín, attempting to evade the battle, is the one person who dies. His dying words are an insistence on the inevitability of death and on the futility of trying to avoid one's fate: *"que no hay seguro camino / a la fuerza del destino / y a la inclemencia del hado"* (III, 3089–91). These words recall those of Basilio in an earlier scene of Act III:

> Poco reparo tiene lo infalible,
> y mucho riesgo lo previsto tiene;
> si ha de ser, la defensa es imposible,
> que quien la excusa más, más la previene.
> ¡Dura ley! ¡Fuerte caso! ¡Horror terrible!
> Quien piensa que huye el riesgo, al riesgo viene. (2452–57)

Basilio has tried to change the course of events by imprisoning Segismundo, just as Clarín has tried to avoid his own fate; and like Clarín, he has failed. The words of the dying Clarín convinced Basilio of the error of his ways, but his inference—"¡ . . . *son diligencias vanas / del hombre cuantas dispone / contra mayor fuerza y causa!*" (3105–07)— is wrong, and he is corrected by Clotaldo:

> Aunque el hado, señor, sabe
> todos los caminos, y halla
> a quien busca entre lo espeso
> de dos peñas, no es cristiana
> determinación decir
> que no hay reparo a su saña.
> Sí hay, que el prudente varón
> victoria del hado alcanza. (III, 3112–19)

Segismundo is soon to give ample proof of such *prudencia*. Clarín, as servant of Rosaura, belongs, strictly speaking, to the

secondary action; but his role of *gracioso* has here given way to
a tragic role of particular relevance to the main theme. Clarín
himself provides an example of the interlinking and interrelation of the characters of the two plots in the mind of Calderón.

Basilio's error is underlined when Segismundo enters in the
final scene. Basilio has failed lamentably to change the course
of fate, and, as the stars decreed, finds himself kneeling before
his son. One person only has the power to overcome what fate
has decreed for Segismundo: Segismundo himself, by his own
free will.

> *Sentencia del cielo fue;*
> *por más que quiso estorbarla*
> *él, no pudo. ¿Y podré yo*
> *que soy menor en las canas,*
> *en el valor y en la ciencia,*
> *vencerla?—Señor, levanta,*
> *dame tu mano; que ya*
> *que el cielo te desengaña*
> *de que has errado en el modo*
> *de vencerte, humilde aguarda*
> *mi cuello a que tú te vengues;*
> *rendido estoy a tus plantas.*   (III, 3236–47)

Segismundo has again triumphed over his arrogant self.

Clotaldo, Rosaura, and now Basilio owe their honour and
their lives to Segismundo, sure proof of his conversion. Arrogance has given way to humility, cruelty to mercy. But the
greatest and final proof of his conversion is still to come. The
sparing of Clotaldo, Rosaura, and Basilio bears witness only to
the self-restraint of the new Segismundo. Self-denial provides
the crowning proof. And it is Rosaura who makes this possible.
Segismundo sacrifices the woman he loves for the sake of her
honour. We have his own words for it:

> *Pues que ya vencer aguarda*
> *mi valor grandes victorias,*
> *hoy ha de ser la más alta*
> *vencerme a mí.—Astolfo dé*
> *la mano luego a Rosaura,*
> *pues sabe que de su honor*
> *es deuda y yo he de cobrarla.*   (III, 3255–61)

Since Calderón's *La vida es sueño* is composed of two quite
dissimilar plots, the strength of its structure depends on their

combination and interlinking. Plot and subplot are perfectly blended. Rosaura not only makes possible the conversion of Segismundo, but she provides the supreme proof of his conversion. Segismundo, in turn, is responsible for the clearing of Rosaura's honour.

The problem presented by a double plot and Calderón's achievement are thrown into relief if *La vida es sueño* is set against Lope de Vega's *Fuente Ovejuna*. The two plots of Lope's play derive from chapter thirty-eight of the Second Part of Rades y Andrada, *Crónica de las tres Órdenes y Cavallerías de Santiago, Calatrava y Alcántara* (Toledo, 1572): first, the capture of Ciudad Real by the Order of Calatrava and its later recapture by the armies of Fernando and Isabel, and second, the rising of Fuente Ovejuna against its Commander Fernán Gómez de Guzmán. These plots have much in common: both are historical, both show the common people supporting and protected by the Monarchy in opposition to the Order of Calatrava, and in both, right is on the side of the monarchy and the people. As well as these historical links, Lope makes Fernán Gómez, the tyrant Comendador, persuade the young Maestre of Calatrava to attack Ciudad Real, and take a leading part in the actual capture of the town. Both actions of *Fuente Ovejuna* are in the same spirit. But the technique of Lope is to isolate rather than unite them. The Fuente Ovejuna episode is expanded and elaborated. The outrages of the Comendador are particularized and shown against a traditional rustic background, and every significant incident is represented on the stage in action: the reception for the Comendador, the gifts of the village, the detaining of Laurencia, Fernando's clash with the Comendador, the Comendador's protest, the molesting of Jacinta, the defence of Mengo, permission for the marriage of Frondoso and Laurencia, the wedding celebration, its interruption by the Comendador, the decision to attack the Comendador, the attack itself, the death of the Comendador, the decision for concerted action, the arrival of the investigator, the questioning, and finally the King's pardon. All this action occupies some four-fifths of the play. The Ciudad Real episode, on the other hand, is used merely as a backcloth against which the incident at Fuente Ovejuna is set. The incident is not elaborated nor do its characters assume any particular importance. And it is presented as a narrative proceeding in short scenes of its own, used by Lope to break into the all-important events at Fuente Ovejuna. The narrative is eked out to provide bridge scenes for the main action. Though linked to the main action in spirit and though providing emphasis for Lope's theme, it is by no means essential to the play. Indeed, with but minor alterations, the play could stand with the secondary action removed.

Calderón's *La vida es sueño* could hardly provide a greater contrast. Here the subject matter of the secondary action is totally unrelated to that of the main action; the tone of the two actions, as Sr. Valbuena has remarked,[7] is often quite different. For all this, however, Calderón has achieved a unity wholly lacking in *Fuente Ovejuna*. Two plots are woven together to form a single pattern, so much so that it may be misleading to speak of two plots. From the first scene to the last, Rosaura is intimately linked with the fortunes of Segismundo, and Clarín, Clotaldo, and Astolfo contribute to both main plot and subplot. The two episodes, so unlike in character, have been carefully fitted together to form one dramatic movement; its culmination in Astolfo's acceptance of the hand of Rosaura signifies at once the clearing of Rosaura's honour and the final proof of Segismundo's conversion.

7 ". . . En la intriga subordinada al tema esencial, de Rosaura y sus amores con Astolfo y rivalidad ante Estrella, la galantería se enreda en el discreteo frívolo, muy lejos de la intensidad de los problemas de la existencia y del propio carácter del protagonista." *Calderón* (Barcelona, 1941), p. 137.

5. Rosaura's Role in the Structure of

La vida es sueño

by William M. Whitby

MARCELINO MENÉNDEZ Y PELAYO[1] and Arturo Farinelli[2] complained of the excessive role which Rosaura plays in Calderón's *La vida es sueño*. They also held that Segismundo's conversion is too rapid to be convincing.[3] It has become increasingly evident, however, thanks to three recent analyses of the play,[4] that it is precisely Rosaura's role which explains the apparent rapidity of Segismundo's transformation.

Edward M. Wilson[5] has argued that the key to Segismundo's conversion lies to a great extent in Rosaura's role. Federico Michele Sciacca[6] has explained that the prince, through seeing the beauty of Rosaura and Estrella, glimpses the eternal form of feminine beauty. This in turn gives him a vantage point outside of the life dream from which, seeing it for what it is, he may know that it is in fact a dream. Albert E. Sloman has focussed the light of analysis more sharply on Rosaura herself[7] and on the honor episode in which she is the

---

1 See his *Calderón y su teatro*, 4th ed. (Madrid, 1910), pp. 264–279; esp. p. 278.

2 See his *La Vita è un sogmo* (Torino, 1916), II, 260, 285–286.

3 Menéndez y Pelayo, pp. 265, 275–277; Farinelli, II, 276–278.

4 Edward M. Wilson, "La vida es sueño," *Revista de la Universidad de Buenos Aires*, 3a Epoca, Año IV, núms. 3 y 4 (1946), 61–78; Michele Federico Sciacca, "Verdad y sueño de La vida es sueño, de Calderón de la Barca," *Clavileño*, Año I, núm. 2 (marzo-abril, 1950), 1–9; Albert E. Sloman, "The Structure of Calderón's *La vida es sueño*," *MLR*, XLVIII (1953), 293–300.

5 Wilson, pp. 70–71, 77.

6 Sciacca, pp. 4-5.

7 Sloman, op. cit. He says in a note (p. 297), "It is hoped that the

principal figure. He demonstrates how this episode and the main action "have been carefully fitted together to form one dramatic movement." [8]

My purpose is to examine in greater detail the manner in which Rosaura's presence awakens in Segismundo a consciousness of his true nature and brings about his conversion. I shall assume, for the purposes of this discussion, that the prince's conversion is the result of his attaining knowledge about himself and about the world.[9] What he must learn about the world is that it offers fleeting, unreal pleasures, and eternal values, among which his senses alone cannot distinguish. Before his conversion can be fully realized, he must also learn what it means to be *"un compuesto de hombre y fiera"* (II.vi.561).[10] In order that he may come to know himself and the world, there must be an awakening of his spiritual faculties. Just as he must discover that his brute instinct cannot tell him whether he is awake or dreaming, he must learn that, on the other hand, his memory and understanding can find intelligible order amidst the world's confusion of sensory phenomena. So that he may prudently apply his will

present essay will direct attention to the essential and indispensable role of Rosaura."

8 Sloman, p. 300. Further support of this position is found in Wolfgang Kayser, "Zur *Struktur des* Standhaften Prinzen *von Calderón*," in *Gestaltprobleme der Dichtung*, hrsg. von Richard Alewyn, Hans-Egon Hass, Clemens Heselhaus (Bonn: H. Bouvier, 1957). Kayser says that Rosaura *"gehört vielmehr unlöslich und dramaturgisch viel überzeugender als die Fénix im Príncipe constante zur Struktur des Dramas"* (p. 78). To appreciate the degree of support which Kayser's assertion lends to the defense of Rosaura's role, one must take into account the recent studies (including Kayser's own) which have put to rout the complaints that Fénix's role in *El príncipe constante* is of an episodic nature. Cf. Bruce W. Wardropper, "Christian and Moor in Calderón's *El príncipe constante*," MLR, LIII (1958), 512–520, and my article, "Calderón's *El príncipe constante:* Fénix's Role in the Ransom of Fernando's Body," BCom, VIII (1956), No. 1, 1–4.

9 The traditional position, represented by Menéndez y Pelayo (pp. 275–276) and Farinelli (II, 276–278), makes Segismundo's conversion dependent upon the deception practised on him by Basilio and Clotaldo, which results in the prince's blind acceptance of the dogma as taught to him by his tutor.

10 Here and throughout the present discussion of this play, unless I otherwise indicate, I cite from Augusto Cortina's recent edition (Calderón de la Barca, *La vida es sueño; El alcalde de Zalamea*, Clásicos Castellanos [Madrid, 1955]).

to the restraint of his animal impulses and to the assertion of his noble human nature, he must be able to consider in retrospect the actions engendered now by his lower nature, now by his higher one. These are necessarily the indispensable steps to his conversion. The part which Calderón has assigned to Rosaura in bringing them about will be explored in the following paragraphs.

Sloman has pointed out how the fortunes of Rosaura and Segismundo run parallel courses. At the beginning of the play, they are both without honor. Their fathers separately make attempts to restore honor to them, but in each case the attempt fails. Basilio, anxious to keep order in the kingdom, has his son shut up again in his cell; Clotaldo, inspired by the same fears, proposes to send Rosaura to a convent. Both Segismundo and Rosaura must seek justice later in their own way, joining forces for this purpose. In the end, both are acknowledged publicly by their fathers and gain their rightful status. It might almost be said that the similarity in their situations is so close that it approaches identity. This is important, because, as we shall see, the question of Rosaura's identity is crucial to Segismundo's discovery of his own—to his knowledge of self.

When Segismundo awakens to find himself back in his cell, Clotaldo treats as a dream what the prince is certain was real (his experiences in the palace). The prince is deceived by Clotaldo with regard to what has actually happened and so believes that he has dreamed his palace experiences. But since he feels the reality of his being in the palace as distinctly as the reality of his being in prison, he equates the two states of being. Since he only dreamed that he was in the palace, he also only dreams that he is in prison. Hence, all of life is a dream. But we cannot hold Segismundo responsible at this point for a complete understanding of what this means. The premises on which he has based this view of life are false ones, the result of a deception contrived by Clotaldo and Basilio. Conflicting with this view of life is another, more practical one. In this view, he considers his prison existence reality—waking—and his palace stay illusion—dreaming. Because he also holds this other view, he refuses at first to go with the soldiers when they come to free him. They are not real, he thinks, but shadows which his deceitful senses conjure up. What he has learned up to this point is that his senses are not to be trusted.

But why, then, does he finally go with the soldiers? It is because in the midst of the other "dream" he had glimpsed a reality: the image of feminine beauty.[11] This image, incarnated in Rosaura and impelled by his love for her, had become so indelibly stamped on his memory that it remained when the rest of the dream ended:

> sólo a una mujer amaba—
> que fué verdad, creo yo
> en que todo se acabó
> y esto solo no se acaba.   (II.xviii.1147–50)

Because of this reality, he must have a strong suspicion, in spite of what Clotaldo has told him, that his palace experiences were real.

While in a larger sense, perhaps, Segismundo is seeking reality, what he is certainly seeking is himself in that reality. He does not formulate the question, Who am I?—not in so many words. But first in the palace, and then once more in the prison, he doubts the identity of which he had formerly been certain. At any rate, the answer to the question, Who am I? is not expressed adequately in a name: Segismundo. The answer is a statement of what the inquirer is in relation to the world, his *"circunstancias"* in the Ortegan sense of the word. This is what Segismundo seeks—his identity. And running parallel to his quest of his own identity is his quest of the identity of Rosaura. *"¿Quién eres?"* he asks Rosaura when they first meet in his prison (I.ii.193). He sees her again in the palace and again asks her, *"¿Quién eres, mujer bella?"* (II.vii.604). The matter of who Rosaura really is—that is, who she is in relation to her own circumstances—is not at all important, except as these circum-

---

11 Sciacca, pp. 4–5. It is difficult not to agree completely with this critic throughout his penetrating analysis. Nevertheless, when he warns that the image of beauty which Segismundo glimpses is not *"la de una mujer (Estrella o Rosaura), sino de la mujer; esto es, la belleza femenina como tal, independientemente de esta o aquella encarnación"* (p. 4), one must add a counter-warning that it is only by the force of his love for Rosaura that this image is impressed on the prince's consciousness.

stances include Segismundo. But she does intercalate in the long
narration of her history (III.x.503–730) enough about her
identity, as this concerns Segismundo, to answer his question,
"*¿Quién eres?*" At the same time, and by the same token, she
gives him the answer, albeit incidentally, to the underlying
question, "*¿Quién soy yo?*"

Closely related to the confused distinctions which, in the
second act and part of the third, Segismundo makes between
sleeping and waking, is the hint of a division of the play into
night and day. This division corresponds to the dreaming and
the awakened prince. In the opening scenes of the play, Rosaura
and Clarín arrive at the door of Segismundo's prison as the sun
is setting in the outside world. Rosaura describes the prison as
the womb of night.[12] As she enters, the temporal impression of
night is left behind, and in its place there is a spatial impression,
figurative of the night of Segismundo's consciousness. In the
third act, when Rosaura arrives to aid and seek the aid of Segismundo, her first words to him are these:

> *Generoso Segismundo,*
> *cuya majestad heroica*
> *sale al día de sus hechos*
> *de la noche de sus sombras. . . .* (III.x.503–506)

Now regardless of what the real time of day is as Rosaura
speaks these lines, it is clear that symbolically it is dawn in Segismundo's consciousness. The outside world is day, while the
prison was night. Certainly, in the most positive and practical

12 "*Desde su centro / nace la noche, pues la engendra dentro*" (I.i. 71–
72). Rosaura also speaks of the fact that the building is deprived of the
light of the sun:

> *Rústico nace entre desnudas peñas*
> *un palacio tan breve,*
> *que al sol apenas a mirar se atreve:*
> *con tan rudo artificio*
> *la arquitectura está de su edificio,*
> *que parece, a las plantas*
> *de tantas rocas y de peñas tantas*
> *que al sol tocan la lumbre,*
> *peñasco que ha rodado de la cumbre.* (I.i.56–64)

Then, as they enter the tower in which Segismundo is imprisoned, she no-
tices a light so weak and flickering that it makes "*más tenebrosa / la oscura
habitación con luz dudosa*" (I.i.89–90).

view which Segismundo has of his situation, this is the first time
he has left his prison. In this scene, in which Rosaura, through
the exegesis she gives, will enable Segismundo to form a coherent picture of his reality, she welcomes him into the waking
world. In the first scenes of the play she had entered into the
night of his prison, bringing light to his sleeping consciousness.
In the first act, at the time of their first encounter, what he says
to her at one point unmistakably draws attention to the effects
she has on his eyes:

> Con cada vez que te veo
> nueva admiración me das
> y cuando te miro más.
> aun más mirarte deseo.
> Ojos hidrópicos creo
> que mis ojos deben ser:
> pues, cuando es muerte el beber,
> beben más, y desta suerte,
> viendo que el ver me da muerte,
> estoy muriendo por ver.   (I.ii.223–232)

Then, in his palace meeting with Rosaura, the prince implies
in his speech that for him her presence is equivalent to light:

> Oye, mujer, detente:
> no juntes el ocaso y el oriente,
> huyendo al primer paso;
> que juntos el oriente y el ocaso,
> la luz y sombra fría,
> serás sin duda síncopa del día. (II.vii.586–591)

When she attempts to leave, he says,

> No has de ausentarte, espera.
> ¿ Cómo quieres dejar de esa manera
> a oscuras mi sentido ?   (II.viii.638–640)

The action of the play portrays his groping, at first unconsciously, then more and more consciously, for his reality. The
only light to his senses as he seeks his way out into the daylight
of this reality is the fugitive figure of Rosaura. But finally, as
he emerges from the night of his prison into a world for him
still peopled with shadows, Rosaura appears to him for a third
time. Here, perhaps prophetically, as though in anticipation of

the light she is about to bring to his reason, he says, "*Su luz me ciega*" (III.ix.500).[13]

In the first act, then, when Segismundo is immersed in the shadows of his spiritual night, Rosaura arouses his desire to see. In the second act, he tries to keep the light which her presence brings to him. But he is unable to do this, relying as he does not on reason but on physical force. In the third act, when he "comes forth to the day of his deeds from the night of his shadows," the light which he receives from Rosaura is there in blinding strength.

Now that the scene has been laid for the dénouement, we can proceed to the analysis of Rosaura's precise effect on Segismundo in the two earlier encounters. The purpose of this analysis is to discover how her appearance and the identification which she makes of herself in this third encounter complete the prince's grasp of his own identity in reality. Rosaura says:

> *Tres veces son las que ya*
> *me admiras, tres las que ignoras*
> *quién soy, pues las tres me viste*
> *en diverso traje y forma.*   (III.x.525–528)

What sort of impressions did Rosaura make on Segismundo on these three occasions? The first time, Segismundo thought she was a man:

> *La primera me creíste*
> *varón en la rigurosa*
> *prisión. . . .*   (III.x.529–531)

But not only was Segismundo deceived with regard to her sex. Rosaura reminds him that on that occasion, "*tú de mirarme te asombras*" (III.x.668). There were three things about Rosaura's person which at that time fanned the spark of Segismundo's noble nature, which had lain smothered through all the years of his imprisonment. He said to her on the occasion of that first meeting,

13 I am indebted to Robert G. Mead, Jr., who read this article in MS, for the suggestion that the letters of Rosaura's name may be rearranged to spell the word "Auroras." While it cannot be affirmed with certainty that Calderón had this in mind, in view of the foregoing analysis it seems probable that he did.

> *Tu voz pudo enternecerme,*
> *tu presencia suspenderme*
> *y tu respeto turbarme.*   (I.ii.190–192)

In her voice very possibly he sensed that she like himself was an unfortunate being; secondly, he could not fail to marvel at her beauty, even though she was dressed as a man; and most important of all, she inspired in him a feeling of respect or reverence for her which disturbed him profoundly.

Certainly, when she entreats him to spare her life, her speech cannot fail to appeal to his human qualities:

> *Si has nacido*
> *humano, baste el postrarme*
> *a tus pies para librarme.*   (I.ii.187–189)

Rosaura makes an appeal to the human half of his nature, and the appeal is answered.

How much was Segismundo affected by Rosaura's beauty in this scene? It is difficult to say with assurance, since no mention is made of beauty, and then, of course, Rosaura is dressed as a man. Yet it is hardly possible to attribute to mere curiosity the prince's eagerness to feast his eyes on the traveler. It is evident from the passage which begins, "*Con cada vez que te veo*" (cited more fully above), that he was struck by Rosaura's beauty. Now, since the prince was not aware that he was looking at a woman, he must have been impressed with beauty *per se*—or possibly even womanly beauty *per se*—unprovocative of the desire for possession. If the beauty he saw could have been possessed—that is, if he had known it could be possessed—perhaps his admiration would then have been transformed into desire, as it was later, in the palace, when he saw Rosaura as a woman.[14]

---

14 In his *Symposium*, Plato speaks of man's yearning for immortality, which when he first happens upon a particular embodiment of beauty, urges him to "beget." Some men, "teeming in body . . . acquire an immortality . . . by getting children." Others, pregnant in soul, "in their souls still more than in their bodies conceive those things which are proper for soul to conceive and bring forth" (*Plato, with an English Translation*, V: *Lysis, Symposium, Gorgias*, trans. W. R. M. Lamb, Loeb Classical Library [London and New York, 1925], p. 199). Segismundo, being "*un compuesto de hombre y fiera*," may be affected either in "body" or in "soul" by Rosaura's beauty. In Act I, when she is dressed as a man, her

In this first meeting, however, his admiration was transformed into, or mingled with, the respect which he felt for this particular being. The beauty he saw in Rosaura, then, must always remain in his mind as a vivid image fused with the idea of respect for the rights of others. Although he was not yet conscious of its true meaning, it was an image of what he was seeking: his own nobler self.[15]

On the occasion of the second encounter between Rosaura and Segismundo, he saw her as a woman: "*La segunda me admiraste / mujer, . . .*" (III.x.533–534). With his eyes, that is, he saw her as a particular woman, tempting possession. She therefore became the object of his unrestrained appetite. But when he first saw her, on this second occasion, he admired her, as he had in the first encounter, and once again asked who she was. Although he was certain he had seen her before, he could not remember where or in what circumstances. He groped awhile for the connecting thread:

> *¿Pero qué es lo que veo?*
> . . . .
> *(Yo he visto esta belleza*
> *otra vez.)*
> . . . .

---

beauty strikes his soul, and he conceives a virtuous act: namely, his attempted defense of her and Clarín against his jailers. In the palace (Act II), Rosaura being dressed as a woman, her beauty affects predominantly his body, with the result which we know. In Act III, the beauty of Rosaura, who this time is dressed as a woman but armed as a man, stirs both his body and his soul. His soul having begun to win out, he denies his body the sight of her and explains:

> *ni te miro, porque es fuerza*
> . . . .
> *que no mire tu hermosura*
> *quien ha de mirar tu honra.* (III.x.821–824)

15 Plato, in his *Symposium*, has Socrates say that "in general all who feel desire, feel it for what is not provided or present; for something they have not or are not or lack; and that sort of thing is the object of desire or love" (p. 171). The same dialogue (with Agathon) ends with Socrates' conclusion that "if Love lacks beautiful things, and good things are beautiful, he must lack good things too" (p. 173). Rosaura is not, when all is said and done, the real object of Segismundo's desire. She merely serves to embody the beauty which, in Platonic terms, is a kind of visible symbol of the good (and therefore beautiful) things which Segismundo lacks at first and finally acquires through learning to assert his noble nature.

> ¿Quién eres? Que sin verte
> adoración me debes, y de suerte
> por la fe te conquisto,
> que me persuado a que otra vez te he visto.
> ¿Quién eres, mujer bella?　(II.vii.592–604)

The image—the form—which his eyes transmitted to his mind became fused and confused with the image formed in their first meeting; Rosaura, recalling the palace episode, says,

> . . . aquí me viste
> otra vez confuso, y otra
> con el traje de mujer
> confundiste entrambas formas;　(III.x.679–682)

In this second encounter, then, the two forms became fused in Segismundo's mind in one image of beauty. But when he asked Rosaura who she was, she replied,

> . . . Soy de Estrella
> una infelice dama.　(II.vii.605–606)

When she deceived him by assuming a different identity, that of Astrea, he was deprived of the possibility of associating the present image with the one formed earlier. He could not identify consciously the image of pure beauty, with which had been mingled respect and noble impulses, with the sight of "Astrea's" particular beauty. There was therefore no counterbalance to his bestial nature. When "Astrea" attempted to leave, he was furious at the thought of losing something to which he had a right. The *"respeto"* which in the earlier meeting he had felt for Rosaura's person continued to act in a subconscious way as a check on his base actions, but he was bent on overcoming all obstacles to his *"gusto:"*

Segismundo: *Harás que de cortés pase a grosero,*
　　　　　　　porque la resistencia
　　　　　　　es veneno cruel de mi paciencia.
Rosaura:　　*Pues cuando ese veneno,*
　　　　　　　de furia, de rigor y saña lleno,
　　　　　　　la paciencia venciera,
　　　　　　　mi respeto no osara ni pudiera.
Segismundo: *Sólo por ver si puedo*
　　　　　　　harás que pierda a tu hermosura el miedo,
　　　　　　　que soy muy inclinado
　　　　　　　a vencer lo imposible: . . .　(II.viii.645–655)

He did, of course, proceed with his attempt to conquer this fear and respect which her beauty caused him to feel. He prevented her leaving and tried to possess her by force.

As a result of these two meetings, Rosaura became two separate persons in Segismundo's consciousness: an unidentified traveler and Astrea. This must have been the state of his consciousness when he saw her for the third time, approaching on a swift horse:

> La tercera es hoy, que siendo
> monstruo de una especie y otra,
> entre galas de mujer
> armas de varón me adornan. (III.x.537–540)

When Clarín saw Rosaura, he said, "*¡Vive Dios, que es Rosaura!*" But Segismundo did not name her. He said merely, "*El cielo a mi presencia la restaura*" (III.ix.502). It is apparent by his later speech that he first thinks of her as three different persons, each of which corresponds to one of the three times he has seen her. He begins by calling her "*esta mujer*":

> Si soñé aquella grandeza
> en que me vi, ¿cómo ahora
> esta mujer me refiere
> unas señas tan notorias? (III.x.739–742)

"*Esta mujer*" is still not identified, for Segismundo has not yet succeeded in putting the pieces together. As he tries to fit them into place, he decides at one point that it would be best to enjoy the fleeting moment. Where the Cortina edition ("Clásicos Castellanos"),[16] from which I am citing, gives the reading, "*Rosaura está en mi poder*" (III.x.767), the Zaragoza edition (1636) reads, "*Astrea está en mi poder.*"[17] As Astrea, Rosaura

16 The Cortina edition is basically the text of the play as we have known it since Juan de Vera Tassis y Villaroel published it in 1685 in the *Primera parte de comedias del célebre poeta español, Don Pedro Calderón . . .* (see Cortina's remarks immediately following his *prólogo*; see also Milton A. Buchanan, ed., *La vida es sueño. Comedia famosa de D. Pedro Calderón de la Barca.* 1636, I [Toronto: University of Toronto Library, 1909], 102–104).

17 Buchanan's edition, p. 131, line 2958. Buchanan calls this "surreptitious" Zaragoza edition "B." It appeared in 1636 in the *Parte Treynta de Comedias famosas de Varios Avtores.* I do not propose to argue here that B is more authentic than the version with which we are familiar. Nor shall

had tempted Segismundo before, and it is certainly logical to suppose that when the temptation assails him again it is because he is thinking of *"esta mujer"* as Astrea. Then, he comes to the point in his reasoning at which he decides to seek eternal values:

> *acudamos a lo eterno,*
> *que es la fama vividora*
> *donde ni duermen las dichas*
> *ni las grandezas reposan.*   (III.x.791–794)

At this moment, *"esta mujer,"* Astrea, and the unfortunate traveler become identified as one person, Rosaura. Here, the Zaragoza edition shows no variation from the Cortina edition:

> *Rosaura está sin honor;*
> *más a un príncipe le toca*
> *el dar honor que quitarle.* (III.x.795–797)

Now that the three persons which Segismundo has seen in the three different scenes have been identified as one, the prince is no longer confused. It is the linkage between the first two of these scenes which brings about the crystallization of his personality. Until now he has thought of the palace episode as a dream (within the life dream) and of the prison experience as waking (within the life dream). In terms of his conduct with respect to Rosaura, he had acted nobly in his prison and basely in the palace. Now the object of these manifestations of both of his natures is identified as one person, and he realizes in this moment that both natures exist in him together, on one plane of existence. They are not, as he had thought, separated by the division line between dreaming and waking. The combination of Segismundo's two natures is symbolized, and made clear to him in the final act, in the person of Rosaura, who fittingly refers to herself as *"monstruo de una especie y otra."*

That which was reality in all of his encounters with Rosaura corresponded to his higher self—nobility of feeling expressed in his reverence for Rosaura's beauty, and nobility of action through the exercise of virtue. The truth of ultimate reality,

---

I make the mistake of choosing the best readings from different versions. It is helpful, nevertheless, to cite this variant reading to show how the play may have been understood by some of Calderón's contemporaries.

therefore, becomes reconciled to Segismundo's own existence. Through recognizing that his own being is a manifestation of the dualism of reality, he is enabled to live the truth through virtuous action. And Rosaura, of course, is the means by which he arrives at this solution.

Finally, there is no longer any basis for Menéndez y Pelayo's and Farinelli's objections to the considerable extent of Rosaura's role. Not only does the honor episode involving her parallel and then blend into the main action, as Sloman has pointed out, but it now appears undeniable, in the light of the further evidence presented in this article, that she is, as Wilson has said, the key to Segismundo's conversion. The conversion itself is not, Menéndez y Pelayo and Farinelli to the contrary, overly rapid. For, as we have seen, the prince's spiritual growth, which is to bring about his conversion, begins in Act I and is not complete until Act III, Scene x, when he clearly comprehends his own nature in its relation to reality and thenceforth acts in accordance with that knowledge.

6 · Calderón's Concept of the Perfect Prince in *La vida es sueño* *

by Everett W. Hesse

SEVERAL STUDIES in recent years have deepened our appreciation and understanding of Calderón's masterpiece *La vida es sueño*. In 1946 Edward M. Wilson made a cogent analysis of the play, showing among other things, that the secondary action is closely integrated with the main action, and all the characters with the exception of Rosaura and Clotaldo are victims of an exaggerated pride and an overconfidence in themselves which precipitates their ultimate downfall.[1] Several years later Leopoldo Eulogio Palacios presented what he called a "new" interpretation of the play based on two opposing viewpoints on life, the one conceived as pride, and the other as a dream.[2] Michele Federico Sciacca a few years ago detailed the suggestion already made by previous critics and by Calderón himself that Rosaura is the only woman Segismundo truly loves, and that she is the dominant factor in the prince's conversion.[3] Later I shall attempt to demonstrate that Segismundo's love for Rosaura is only one of the elements which impels the prince to change his conduct. In this essay I propose to examine Calderón's concept of the perfect Christian prince, and to show that it consists principally of an exaltation of the virtue of prudence, and to a lesser degree of temperance. Both virtues

---

* *Editor's Note.* For this English version of the essay, some of the footnotes have been abbreviated, and some excised.

1 "La vida es sueño," *Revista de la Universidad de Buenos Aires*, Tercera Época, Año IV, Nos. 3 & 4 (1946), 61–78.

2 "La vida es sueño," *Finisterre*, II (1948), 5–52.

3 "Verdad y sueño de La vida es sueño, de Calderón de la Barca," *Clavileño*, I, No. 2 (1950), 1–9.

are acquired after a process of re-education with marked emphasis on reason which is derived, in general terms, from the moral philosophy of Seneca, and the ethical system and philosophical teachings of Saint Thomas Aquinas as expounded in the *De Regimine Principum*, a detailed program of the duties of the prince, and the *Summa Theologica* which contains an account of the social justice that it is the prince's duty to promote. I shall also attempt to point out in some detail the Thomistic psychology, scholastic rationalism, and the anti-Machiavellian implications. It is difficult to determine conclusively whether Calderón acquired his concepts directly from the fountainhead or indirectly from the most of Thomistic apologists, neo-Stoics, and anti-Machiavels of the sixteenth and early seventeenth centuries.

Through the centuries philosophers have wrestled with the perplexing problem of man's behavior in society. Christianity teaches the doctrine of original sin which represents man as having fallen from a state of grace. Man has been corrupted by the fall, but he can be redeemed by the sacrifice of Christ if he allows the freely given grace of God to work in him. According to St. Thomas sin stems from ignorance, malice, and passion. Sin is a willful breaking of a divine law, a transgression which deprives the soul of eternal salvation. Man, however, has been offered the hope of everlasting life by the Son of God. Man must accept Christian teachings and merit a heavenly reward by faith and works.

It was only reasonable that philosophers in their desire to perfect man should give special attention to the education of the ruler of the state, the head of the body politic. Beginning with Marcus Aurelius there is a long list of treatises on the education of princes and on the perfect government. María Angeles Galino Carrillo, in her book *Los tratados sobre educación de príncipes* (Madrid, 1948), lists about one-hundred works on the subject written in Spain in the sixteenth and seventeenth centuries, excluding treatises in Latin.

It was commonly believed that there were three moving forces which played an important part in the drama of man's life: God, Fortune, and man himself. St. Thomas has remarked that it is "Divine Providence which disposes everything for the best" (De Reg., Chap. III), and so if man is prudent he will cooperate with God. Fortune, which was largely a poetic "fiction" or pure superstition, but which had been incorporated into the Christian scheme of things since the Middle Ages, was necessary and useful to explain the otherwise inexplicable.[4] The blows of Fortune had to be borne stoically, for she was blind and unpredictable, and while her blows could not be avoided their effect could be mitigated through a virtuous Christian life.

As for man, he was supposed to have a spark of the divine in him. Man had the power to reason. Covarrubias defined reason as the faculty which distinguishes man from the beasts. According to St. Thomas (De Reg., Chap. I) ". . . in the individual man the soul rules the body; and among the parts of the soul, the irascible and the concupiscible parts are ruled by reason." In the prevailing concept of the hierarchy of the faculties, reason occupied the lowest rung. Superior to it were understanding and will. In the seventeenth century, however, many writers often confused the reason and the understanding and some included memory among the higher faculties.

The reason and the understanding had no capacity for action. They merely supplied the will with the basis for action. The will, the executive part of the soul, directed man's conduct toward good or evil, depending on whether the guide was reason or passion. The great problem of seventeenth-century writers, then, was the education of the will. The distinction between the voluntad and the libre albedrío was often lost in the confusion. The Jesuits followed St. Thomas in the belief that the will could be educated through habit (Thomistic habitus). Padre Andrés Mendo in his El príncipe perfecto (1622, pp. 39–60), expressed it well when he wrote: "No nacen en nosotros las inclinaciones; imprímense, como en cera blanda, en la niñez, y van creciendo. Lo que uno obra en años mayores es eco de lo que aprendió en los juveniles."

While the will was able to act for good if guided by reason, and was all important to sixteenth- and seventeenth-century moralists, in the Calderonian concept of the perfect Christian

4 Cf. Calderón, No hay más Fortuna que Dios, ed. A. A. Parker (Manchester, 1949), p. 6, verses 104–125.

prince it is the reason and prudence which are exalted over the will; for as St. Thomas remarked "intellect is nobler than will." The Angelic Doctor also believed that the intellect was superior to the will because it sought *verum* and not *bonum*.[5] The intellect deliberates the issues. The will terminates the deliberation and makes the choice when one of the particular issues appears to it to give it satisfaction. Both powers are needed for the operation of the *libre albedrío* which is at the basis of human liberty.

Of the four cardinal virtues discussed by St. Thomas prudence occupies the preeminent position.[6] It is the only intellectual virtue and is at the basis of all moral habits. The other subsidiary virtues of the intellect, (i.e., understanding, science, wisdom, and art) can exist without the moral, but not prudence, for it is the right knowledge about things to be done. It is in itself a complete virtue, for it makes the whole man good. As a Christian virtue it is said to govern man's relation with God. Of prudence Fray Luis de Granada wrote in his *Guía de pecadores*, 1556,

> . . . *a la prudencia pertenece conocer el fin de todas nuestras obras, que es Dios, y enderezar a él todo lo que hiciéremos, examinando sutilmente la intención que tenemos en las obras que hacemos, para ver si buscamos puramente a Dios o si buscamos a nosotros. . . .*[7]

In the Calderonian concept of the ideal Christian prince, prudence is composed of two main elements: moderation and knowledge of self. Prudent moderation—the old Aristotelian idea of the "golden mean"—would teach the prince to control his passions so that he might act in accordance with reason. The reasonable act is the prudent act. The rule of reason according to St. Thomas is like the rule of a king—sweet, gentle, and enlightening. The rule of passion he compares with the rule

---

5 R. E. Brennan, *Thomistic Psychology: A Philosophic Analysis of the Nature of Man* (New York, 1941), p. 237.

6 *Summa*, I^a-II^{ae}, QQ, 55–67.

7 *Clásicos castellanos* (Madrid, 1929), p. 196. See also the discussions of "discretion" and its differentiation from "prudence" by A. A. Parker (*No hay más Fortuna que Dios*, pp. 77–92) and by Margaret J. Bates (*"Discreción" in the Works of Cervantes: A Semantic Study* [Washington, 1945]). See also L. E. Palacios, *La prudencia política* (Madrid, 1947).

of a despot—blind, cruel, and harsh. When man follows the dictates of reason he acts like a man, but when he obeys his passions he acts like an animal.

In the early part of the play Calderón depicts Segismundo as a beast ruled by his primitive passions. Rosaura sees Segismundo in the dimly lit cell of the prison, dressed in skins like a beast and remarks: *"en el traje de fiera yace un hombre"* (96).[8] Although Segismundo has the outward appearance of a beast he is, nevertheless, a human being endowed with reason.

In the opening stanza of Segismundo's famous soliloquy on liberty, Calderón broaches the problem of original sin: *"el delito mayor / del hombre es haber nacido"* (111–112). As the prince's horoscope portended a rule of tyranny, the Heavens were perfectly justified in fulminating their wrath against Segismundo on the occasion of his birth. The ruler, like other mortals, must take his chances in life, hoping to merit salvation when overtaken by death, the great leveler of society. Since the prince places himself on an equality with his fellow men, he wonders what he has done to deserve his protracted captivity. He compares his status as a prisoner with that of a bird, beast, fish, and stream which are free. Segismundo is cognizant that he is endowed with a soul, a better instinct, and life, but yet is denied the God-given privilege of liberty (167–171), and the sphere of activity of his free will has been greatly curtailed.[9] Although man is born in original sin he is not bound to follow the path of sin. He may, if he so desires, choose the path of righteousness.

8 References are to *La vida es sueño*, ed. Martín de Riquer (Barcelona, 1945).

9 The idea of the superiority of animals to man, at least in some aspects, was not new. It harks back to antiquity, where in Pliny's *Historia naturalis* one finds a passage dealing with the frailty of human strength compared with that of animals. The notion became popular in the Renaissance. See Battista Gelli, *La Circe* (1549), in *Opere* (Firenze, 1855), pp. 9–147: Ulysses asks a number of animals whether they wish to return to manhood or stay as they are. The majority prefer not to exchange the wretchedness of a man for the happiness of a beast. The elephant, however, argues the point, stating that man like the beast must depend on his senses for intellection. But when Ulysses counters that man is endowed with reason and a free will to act upon the dictates of his judgment, thus placing him at the apex of creation, the elephant is convinced and asks to be returned to his former human status.

The majestic *décimas* represent Segismundo's reaching and striving for something higher—the divine gift of freedom. They show that he has the ability to reason, and Thomistic doctrine teaches that "the roots of human liberty are lodged in man's rational nature since his intellect knows the universal meaning of value." [10]

When Segismundo realizes that it was not his old mentor Clotaldo but Rosaura who has overheard his lamentation, his self-respect is destroyed, and his pride wounded by the fact that a stranger should know his weaknesses. Seizing Rosaura, he is about to yield to his irascible appetite:

> *Pues la muerte te daré,*
> *porque no sepas que sé*
> *que sabes flaquezas mías.* (180-3)

Rosaura, prostrating herself at his feet, appeals to his humanity:

> *Si has nacido*
> *humano, baste el postrarme*
> *a tus pies para librarme.* (187-9)

When Clotaldo discovers Rosaura and Clarín talking to Segismundo he orders them to surrender or be shot, as they have violated the king's edict that no one see the captive prince. Segismundo calling Clotaldo a *"tirano dueño"* (309), boastfully threatens suicide if a hand is laid on Rosaura. He realizes that he has done wrong in losing his temper and concedes: *"que bien hacéis en quitarme / la libertad"* (330-1).

King Basilio has imprisoned his son to spare his beloved Poland the rule of a tyrant as predicted by the stars:

> *que yo, Polonia, os estimo*
> *tanto, que os quiero librar*
> *de la opresión y servicio*
> *de un rey tirano, porque*
> *no fuera señor benigno*
> *el que a su patria y su imperio*
> *pusiera en tanto peligro.* (761-7)

In the Thomistic political system tyranny is one of the greatest catastrophes which can happen to a government:

10 Brennan, p. 222.

. . . it is clear [states St. Thomas] from what has been said that diligent zeal must be exercised in order that the interests of the multitude be so safeguarded with regard to their king that they may not fall under a tyrant. First it is necessary that the man who is raised up to be king by those to whom this office belongs, should be of such character that it is improbable he should fall into tyranny. (*De Reg.*, Chap. VI).

Basilio's imprisonment of his son, then, is understandable. In addition he has taken appropriate measures to overcome his son's predicted tyrannical nature. Under the tutelage of the venerable Clotaldo, Segismundo informs us that:

> la política he estudiado,
> de los brutos enseñado,
> advertido de las aves,
> y de los astros süaves
> los círculos he medido. (214–18)

Later Basilio informs Astolfo and Estrella of Segismundo's education:

> solo Clotaldo
> le ha hablado, tratado y visto.
> Éste le ha enseñado ciencias;
> éste en la ley le ha instruido
> católica, siendo solo
> de sus miserias testigo (754–59)

Aware that he has given too much credence to astrology which Calderón has elsewhere dubbed a "*dudosa ciencia*," [11] Basilio suffers pangs of remorse. He realizes that it is not Christian charity to take away from his own flesh and blood the human and divine right to rule, and that by attempting to thwart the rule of a tyrant he himself has become a tyrant (773–79). With the knowledge that the stars do not force the will but merely incline it, he decides to put his son to the test. Segismundo is to be drugged and brought to the palace where all are to obey him. Basilio then sets the criteria by which his son is to be judged. If the prince is "*prudente, cuerdo y benigno*" (809), he will be acceptable as a ruler. Basilio's concept of the perfect ruler is one who through prudence conquers himself by supressing his primitive passions:

11 *El mayor monstruo los celos*, Act I.

> *o se mitiga, o se templa*
> *por lo menos, y, vencido*
> *con valor y con prudencia*
> *se desdice; porque el hombre*
> *predomina en las estrellas.*   (1107–11)

If, however, Segismundo shows himself to be "*soberbio, osado, atrevido / y cruel*" (817–18), he will be returned to prison, and Basilio will consider his obligation fulfilled. Against the affirmative standards of prudence and its complementary virtues of temperance and to a lesser degree justice and fortitude on the one hand, Calderón places on the other the negative standards of pride, rashness, insolence, and cruelty, which are vices against prudence—the highest cardinal virtue, and the one which guides the moral virtues.

When Segismundo awakens in the palace he is astounded by the luxury of the surroundings, and once accustomed to the splendor and the service, he enjoys them: "*Dejarme quiero servir / y venga lo que viniere*" (1246–47). Segismundo has no thought of duties and responsibilities to be assumed because of his rise to power; he thinks only of momentary pleasures.

First to render obeisance to Segismundo is Clotaldo, his aged mentor, who maltreated him in prison (1265). Clotaldo explains the situation to the new ruler and adds that the king, Basilio, will fill in the details. Segismundo becomes angry and vaunts his pride and power, blaming Clotaldo for not having revealed the secret of his royal identity to him long before. Segismundo's anger is human and understandable. He accuses Clotaldo of being a traitor, a flatterer of the king, and a cruel tyrant to him. In his rage he threatens the old man's life. A servant tries to intervene, and Segismundo threatens to hurl him out of the window. Segismundo argues that it is not necessary to obey the king who sets up an unjust law:

> *En lo que no es justa ley*
> *no ha de obedecer al rey;*
> *y su príncipe era yo.*   (1321–23)

When Segismundo addresses Astolfo with the greeting "*Dios os guarde*" (1351), the latter identifies himself as a grandee and his cousin, and therefore his equal and worthy of more honor than he has hitherto received. Whereupon Segismundo insults him, stating that in any future meeting "*le diré a Dios que no os guarde*" (1363). Segismundo is angry that Astolfo does not remove his hat, and the servant, trying to justify the latter's conduct, states that Astolfo is a grandee and thus enjoys the privilege of wearing his hat in the presence of royalty. Segismundo lacks respect and consideration. The servant points this out to him.

The third visitor is Estrella. When Segismundo, overcome by her great beauty, tries to kiss her hand, a servant, perceiving Astolfo's anxiety, points out that such conduct would not be prudent. Segismundo, motivated by his pleasure and vexed by the servant's remarks and suggestions, throws him off the balcony, yielding completely to his irascible appetite. The selfish side of Segismundo's nature, together with overtones of Machiavellianism, can be observed in the explanation of his conduct: "*nada me parece justo / en siendo contra mi gusto*" (1417–18). Then Astolfo advises him to be more gentle and mild: "*que lo que hay de hombres a fieras, / hay desde un monte a palacio*" (1434–5). Segismundo then threatens Astolfo. His impetuosity finds justification in Machiavellian philosophy:

> . . . I am well persuaded that it is better to be impetuous than cautious. For Fortune is a woman who to be kept under must be beaten and roughly handled; and we see that she suffers herself to be more readily mastered by those who so treat her than by those who are more timid in their approaches. And, always, like a woman, she favours the young, because they are less scrupulous and fiercer, and command her with greater audacity.[12]

Basilio is disappointed by the ungainly conduct of his son who he hoped would overcome the predictions of fate. Segismundo reproaches his father for his unjust severity in treating him like a monster instead of like a human being. An argument ensues and Segismundo states he has lost his "*libertad, vida y honor*" (1516). The father urges his son to be "*humilde y blando*" (1529). With vain boasting, Segismundo argues that his right to the crown cannot be taken away from him:

> *ya informado estoy*
> *de quien soy y sé que soy*
> *un compuesto de hombre y fiera.*   (1545–7)

12 Machiavelli, *The Prince*, Chap. XVII.

Both Machiavelli and St. Thomas recognized the dual nature of man, the animal, and the human elements. But while the former would use the animal instincts whenever it was expedient, the latter would suppress them and subordinate them to the rule of reason. Segismundo from his studies knows that man is a microcosm and a reflection of the macrocosm:

> *Leía*
> *una vez en los libros que tenía*
> *que lo que a Dios mayor estudio debe,*
> *era el hombre, por ser un mundo breve.* (1562–5)

This concept of man as a little world in himself, the product of God's benevolence, was not new. It had been common enough in the literature of previous centuries. But the notion served Calderón's purpose in underlining man's supremacy in the hierarchy of created things, his dual nature with a perishable body but an immortal soul, and his endowment with reason. Man might wallow in the mud, but he could also reach for the stars.

Segismundo sees Rosaura again and tries to woo her. She becomes annoyed by his attentions. Although the prince recites a very flowery, affected speech on his love for her, she disdains him scornfully:

> *Tu favor reverencio.*
> *Respóndate retórico el silencio:*
> *cuando tan torpe la razón se halla,*
> *mejor habla, señor, quien mejor calla.* (1620–22)

Rosaura asks his permission to leave; he refuses to allow her to go away in such a violent frame of mind. When she threatens to leave without his permission, Segismundo's irascibility increases, and in another Machiavellian tone he intimates that he gets what he wants by fair means or foul:

> *Harás que de cortés pase a grosero,*
> *porque la resistencia*
> *es veneno cruel de mi paciencia.* (1631–33)
> ....
> *que soy muy inclinado*
> *a vencer lo imposible.* (1640–41)

He boasts that he threw a servant out of the window and threatens: "*y así, por ver si puedo, cosa es llana / que arrojaré tu honor por la ventana"* (1644-45). Rosaura reproaches him for his repugnant brutishness and asks what else can one expect of a man who has the name of human (1655), but acts like a rash, inhuman, cruel, proud, and barbarous tyrant. Segismundo admits he is a tyrant (1666), and yielding to his concupiscible appetite, he menaces Rosaura. Clotaldo intervenes, and a second time he provokes Segismundo's ire (1671). The prince's pride is again wounded and he calls Clotaldo a *"viejo caduco y loco"* (1672). Clotaldo discreetly urges Segismundo to be *"más apacible, si reinar deseas"* (1677), warning that it may all be a dream. Segismundo's rage increases as he realizes that Clotaldo is attempting to disillusion him (1680-01).

Before the prince can inflict any bodily harm on Clotaldo, Astolfo intrudes, reasoning that the old tutor has found sanctuary at the duke's feet. At that comment Segismundo draws his sword and threatens Astolfo: *"también sabré vengarme, con tu muerte"* (1703). The king emerges in time to halt the duel and asks his son if he doesn't respect old age? Segismundo in desperation fulminates against his own father, predicting that he will also humble him and take vengeance on him:

> *Acciones vanas,*
> *querer que tenga yo respeto a canas;*
> *pues aun ésas podría*
> *ser que viese a mis plantas algún día;*
> *porque aun no estoy vengado*
> *del modo injusto con que me has criado* (1714-19).[13]

This is the last straw. Basilio is convinced that his son is the monster the horoscope foretold, and orders that he be drugged, returned to the tower and informed that all which occurred in the palace was a dream.

Later, impelled by an insatiable curiosity, Basilio visits the prison as Segismundo begins to talk *"entre sueños."* Here a mental conflict holds sway and precipitates the process of the conversion. For the first time Segismundo admits: *"Piadoso*

13 Another instance of the abuse of parental authority is found in *La devoción de la Cruz*, where Curcio wants his daughter Julia to marry the man he has selected for her; otherwise she must enter a convent. See A. A. Parker, *"Santos y bandoleros en el teatro español del siglo de oro," Arbor,* Nos. 43-44 (1949), 395-416.

príncipe es / el que castiga tiranos" (2064–5). But reason has not yet triumphed over instinct as the prince blusters: *"muera Clotaldo a mis manos, / bese mi padre mis pies"* (2066–7). Once Segismundo regains consciousness, the memory, which gains definite advantages from its proximity to reason, plays an important role in recalling the past experiences. Reason, then, begins to function more and more in Segismundo, and we see the emergence of the intelligence over instinct. However, doubts and confusion still assault the prince in his dilemma in which he cannot discriminate dreams from reality:

> Ni aun agora he despertado;
> que según, Clotaldo, entiendo,
> todavía estoy durmiendo,
> y no estoy muy engañado;
> porque si ha sido soñado
> lo que vi palpable y cierto,
> lo que veo será incierto,
> y no es mucho que, rendido,
> pues veo estando dormido
> que sueñe estando despierto.   (2098–2107)

Clotaldo prudently advises Segismundo: *"que aun en sueños / no se pierde el hacer bien"* (2146–7). Segismundo has decided to accept the suggestion of Clotaldo, and the advice given previously by his father. In the closing soliloquy of Act II he agrees to subject his inordinate appetites and rash impulses to the rule of reason:

> Es verdad; pues reprimamos
> esta fiera condición,
> esta furia, esta ambición.   (2148–50)

The conversion of Segismundo is not due primarily to the influence of Rosaura as Sciacca and others have contended. The transmutation is much more complex than that, and is effected by a number of factors operating simultaneously. One of these is the education of the prince. We are led to conclude that his mentor Clotaldo has been prudent and discreet by the advice he offers in the play (1677, 2146–7). We know that among other things Segismundo has been instructed in the Catholic faith (754–59), and in the art of governing (*"la política"* of

214). We may assume that he was familiar with some of the many treatises on the governance of princes.

The principal factor is the *desengaño* Segismundo experiences when he awakens in the prison tower after being king for a brief period. He thinks his life as king was a dream and concludes that all life like a dream is ephemeral. In the last act this *desengaño* is a deterrent which restrains him from evil. Segismundo dreads awakening back in the tower from another *desengaño*: "*que cuna y sepulcro fue / esta torre para mí*" (195–6).[14] Segismundo has been shaken by the events before his last speech in Act II. He has been lifted from the depths of despair to the heights of power, then hurled down into the abyss without being able to explain satisfactorily what has happened to him. It is as though he had been given a modern psychiatric shock treatment. His mind is in an extreme state of suggestibility. What more natural, therefore, than that the hint that he has been dreaming should, with Clotaldo's speech (2140–47), be seized upon by him as offering the only reasonable conclusion to be drawn from the recent hectic events?

Still another factor in the conversion is the use made by Segismundo of a kind of Thomistic rationalization and scholastic dialectics before and after the *desengaño*. In the five trials of Act III Segismundo uses his reason to help him deliberate the issues carefully before arriving at a decision. This is a manifestation of the prudent man which now gains the ascendancy.

When people come to acclaim him their new king, Segismundo, remembering his previous experience, wonders whether he again is to dream of a grandeur which time will eventually dissipate. After three rhetorical questions(2307–17), he wants none of it, for, disillusioned, he knows that all life is a dream, and that fantastic illusions and feigned majesties like flowers wither and die. The Soldado 2⁰ tries to convince Segismundo of the reality of his proposal by pointing to the crowd outside eager and ready to obey the new ruler. Once before Segismundo had a similar experience only to find it was all a dream. Finally the Soldado 1⁰ argues that what happened previously was an omen of greater things to come. Segismundo agrees and is

14 Other instances of the working of the *desengaño* are found in verses 2085–86, 2314–15, 2342–43, 2365, 2667, 2977–86.

willing to dream, but with the prescience that he may reawaken
when he least expects it, and therefore

> *ha de ser*
> *con atención y consejo*
> *de que hemos de despertar*
> *deste gusto al mejor tiempo*
> *que llevándolo sabido,*
> *será el desengaño menos.*   (2360–65)

He admits that whatever power he obtains is only loaned to
him, and is to be returned to its owner God: *"es todo el poder
prestado / y ha de volverse a su dueño"* (2370–71).

Segismundo still has to battle with his animal nature as
he threatens to take up arms against his father, and bring about
his downfall. But he reasons that he may not be able to ac-
complish his objective, and hence should not speak about it.
Clotaldo rushes in and prostrates himself at Segismundo's feet
expecting death. But to the former's surprise, the prince meekly
confesses his gratitude to Clotaldo for his upbringing. According to St. Thomas, meekness is a virtue annexed to temperance
and checks the inordinate movements of the actions of anger.
This constitutes Segismundo's first victory over himself, and
shows that he is capable of perfecting himself in virtuous
living. The impact of ideas concerning moral conduct first
suggested to him by his tutor Clotaldo (2146–7), now becomes
manifest as Segismundo remarks:

> *Que estoy soñando, y que quiero*
> *obrar bien, pues no se pierde*
> *obrar bien, aun entre sueños.*[15] (2399–2401)

Clotaldo, troubled that Segismundo is threatening to wage
war on Basilio, refuses to become a rebel and once more expects
death. Incensed, Segismundo calls him a traitor and an ingrate.

15 See Bruce W. Wardropper, "The Unconscious Mind in Calderón's
El pintor de su deshonra," HR, xviii (1950), 286, where he says of *La
vida es sueño*: "The interpretation of the play as an examination of the
effect that actions performed in the earthly life have on the eternal life
is only one of a number of possible readings. If we reduce the range of
vision to exclude eternal life, the teaching is that unconscious thoughts
passing through the mind in sleep are significant in relation to the kind
of life a man leads, while conscious. The unconscious mental life has
moral implications for the conscious life."

But the recollection of the *desengaño* together with the exercise of the virtue of meekness cause the prince to check his irascible appetite:

> (*Mas ¡cielos!*
> *reportarme me conviene,*
> *que aun no sé si estoy despierto.*)   (2411–13)

Segismundo immediately admires Clotaldo's valor in the stand he has taken. The prince is now ready to reign regardless of whether he is awake or asleep, because *"obrar bien es lo que importa"* (2424). If Segismundo is asleep he will still rule well *"por ganar amigos / para cuando despertemos"* (2426–7). For, as St. Thomas wrote, ". . . among all worldly things there is nothing which seems worthy to be preferred to friendship. For friendship unites good men, preserves and promotes virtue." And according to Seneca "nothing . . . gives the mind so much pleasure as fond and faithful friendship (*"De Tranquillitate Animi,"* II, 237).

When Segismundo is on the field of battle surrounded by his soldiers, he feels bloated with an exaggerated pride so strong that he could conquer the firmament. Even Rome at the height of her glory would envy him now as he commands mighty armies. But for the third time the prince dominates himself, remembering that a *desengaño* might ensue. Experience, the mother of prudence, causes him to reason that

> *si ha de pesarme cuando esté despierto,*
> *de haberlo conseguido*
> *por haberlo perdido;*
> *pues mientras menos fuere,*
> *menos se sentirá si se pierde.*   (2667–71)

This reasoning then acts as a brake to his pride, which St. Thomas defines as "the desire to excel," and "the beginning of every sin." [16] And so resignedly Segismundo says:

> *Pero el vuelo abatamos,*
> *espíritu; no así desvanezcamos*
> *aqueste aplauso incierto.*   (2664–6)

A ruler, according to St. Thomas, should not seek the plaudits of a fickle public.

16 *Summa*, Iª–IIªᵉ, Q lxxxiv, a.4.

For in the whole range of human affairs nothing would seem to be more uncertain than the glory and honor of popular favor, since it depends upon human opinion, which is the most changeable thing on earth. . . . Furthermore, the desire of human glory destroys magnanimity of soul. For whoever seeks favor of men must consider their desires in all that he says and does; thus, because of his desire to please men he becomes the servant of individuals. It is this in fact which destroys the liberty of spirit which should be the greatest aspiration of the magnanimous man: while there is nothing which befits a prince who is elected to act with righteousness than this same magnanimity of soul.[17]

Rosaura now resumes the story she began in v. 277 and begs Segismundo to hear it. She implores him to prevent the marriage of Astolfo and Estrella, as it was Astolfo who had dishonored her. Segismundo knows now that he was not dreaming, since Rosaura saw and witnessed his former grandeur. With more scholastic rationalism he muses over a paradox:

> ¿tan parecidas
> a los sueños son las glorias,
> que las verdaderas son
> tenidas por mentirosas
> y las fingidas por ciertas?   (2938–42)

Segismundo wonders, if all earthly honors are brief and transient, why he should not seize the opportunity to take advantage of Rosaura:

> gocemos, pues, la ocasión:
> el amor las leyes rompa
> del valor y confianza
> con que a mis plantas se postra.   (2960–63)

Here Segismundo is subjected to the cruel temptation of lust which requires all his prudence and fortitude to overcome. He realizes that what he may now be dreaming may turn out to be a grief later. He is ultimately forced to concede that his reason has triumphed over his instinct: "*Mas ¡con mis razones propias / vuelvo a convencerme a mí!*" (2967–8). Segismundo clinches the argument, reasoning that he would be foolish to lose a divine glory for a temporary and fleeting earthly pleasure:

17 *De Reg.*, Chap. VII.

> *Pues si esto toca*
> *mi desengaño, si sé*
> *que es el gusto llama hermosa,*
> *que le convierte en cenizas*
> *cualquiera viento que sopla,*
> *acudamos a lo eterno;*
> *que es la fama vividora*
> *donde ni duermen las dichas,*
> *ni las grandezas reposan.*   (2977–83)

Segismundo is a prince, and as a ruler he must assume his moral responsibilities. As Rosaura is without honor, he is duty-bound to restore it to her: "*a un príncipe le toca / el dar honor que quitarle*" (2987–88). Thus Segismundo wins his fourth victory over himself by dominating his concupiscible appetite through continence, a virtue annexed to temperance. Here Calderón shows how the moral virtues render the movements of the appetitive powers conformable to their proper rule which is reason. The victory is none too soon as the prince concludes hastily and humanly: "*Huyamos de la ocasión, / que es muy fuerte*" (2992–3).

Basilio is disillusioned, for the rebels have won, and have acclaimed Segismundo as their ruler. After Clarín's death Basilio believes that all man's efforts against fate are of no avail. But Clotaldo reassuringly answers: "*Sí hay, que el prudente varón / vitoria del hado alcanza*" (3118–19). Basilio throws himself at his son's feet. Segismundo speaks sternly to his father, accusing him of turning his own son into a beast. Segismundo argues that even if he had been of a meek and docile nature, his upbringing would have sufficed to make him a brute. The lack of parental affection has raised against society the very monster Basilio sought to avoid. In other words he is criticizing his father's lack of prudence in the course of action he took, saying sarcastically: "*¡qué buen modo de estorbarlas!*" (3185). Utilizing scholastic rationalism once again, Segismundo presents three arguments to show Basilio's lack of prudence. If a man fears a wild beast, does he awaken it if it is sleeping? Or if he fears the sword, does he unsheathe it and point it at himself? Or if he fears death by drowning, does he plunge himself into a wild and churned-up sea? Fortune (or fate) is not conquered by injustice and vengeance, but rather it is the more incited.

Hence, he who wishes to overcome fate must do so *"con prudencia y con templanza"* (3219). Segismundo warns Basilio to let this strange event of a father prostrate at his son's feet, of a monarch overthrown, serve as an example. After all, how could Segismundo, who is less in years, valor, and wisdom than Basilio, conquer what was ordained by heaven? However much Basilio tried to alter the will of heaven, he could not do so.

Then Segismundo, showing great clemency, takes his father's hand and helps him to his feet. And since heaven has disillusioned the father in his erroneous manner of overcoming the prediction of the horoscope, Segismundo wins his fifth victory over himself, sublimating the brute aspect of his irascible appetite and in turn prostrates himself humbly at his father's feet. Calderón again seems to be following the precepts of St. Thomas:

> . . . when he [the ruler] contemplates that he has been appointed to this position in place of God, to exercise judgment in his kingdom, from another, he acquires the gentleness of clemency and mildness, when he considers as his own members, those individuals who are subject to his rule.[18]

Basilio, convinced by the noble action of his son, admits he is a prince. Segismundo, who hopes to go on to further victories, concludes that *"hoy ha de ser la más alta / vencerme a mí"* (3257–58). Then he orders Astolfo to marry Rosaura in order to restore her honor. And Segismundo marries Estrella so that she will not be disconsolate. He embraces Clotaldo, who has served Basilio so loyally. When the Soldado 1⁰ seeks a reward for starting the revolt that put Segismundo in power, the newly acclaimed prince prudently orders him to the tower: *"que el traidor no es menester / siendo la traición pasada"* (3300–01). This display of ingenuity causes all to remark: *"¡Qué discreto y qué prudente!"* (3304). And thus ends the play and Calderón's dramatization and personification of the virtues of prudence and temperance on a base of Thomistic-Aristotelianism, and to a lesser degree Senecan stoicism. Calderón conceives the ideal Christian prince as one who is guided by reason and not

18 *De Reg.*, Chap. XII.

by passion.[19] The prudent prince deliberates, argues, questions, and compares before taking action.

While the rational soul has the attributes of reason and will, Calderón follows the traditionalist view by placing reason above the will which had been regarded by one type of Renaissance man as the supreme instrument of virtue. Calderón begins the play by depicting Segismundo as an undesirable heir to the throne because of his rashness, cruelty, impetuosity, intemperance, and tyranny. His conduct is governed by his unrestrained passion. He sinks to the lowly category of the beast. An unsavory Machiavellian bias which repudiates the moral basis of political conduct and advocates expediency is detected in the actions of Segismundo. Basilio the king concludes that the prediction of cruelty and tyranny made by the horoscope is valid and returns his son to prison. On awakening Segismundo experiences a *desengaño* and a change of heart. The ability to apply reason to the control of his moral behavior—a latent gift, flashes of which appeared already in Act I—is sharpened and developed in the rest of the drama. Segismundo is subjected to a number of tests in which he is required to use his reason and discriminatory powers in choosing between right and wrong. We see the emergence of the ideal Christian prince whose conduct is based on Christian principles with the hope of eternal blessedness as the reward for his virtuous living. We see, too, the anti-Machiavellian tendency in the latter part of the play and the coalescence of Senecan philosophy and the cardinal virtues, especially prudence and temperance as explained by St. Thomas Aquinas in his *Summa Theologica* and the *De regimine principum*.[20] Man's happiness, and of course

19 *Summa*, II, 24, 2: "The passions of the soul, in so far as they are contrary to the order of reason, incline us to sin; but in so far as they are controlled by reason, they pertain to virtue."

20 Spanish political theorists of the sixteenth and seventeenth centuries emphasized *moral* values founded on Christian principles derived mainly from St. Thomas and the ancients, and applicable to all people, but especially to princes. Most of these writers inveighed bitterly against Machiavellianism because it denies the divine order of the universe, repudiated Christian moral principles and divorced politics from faith. A striking title among the many treatises is P. Claudio Clemente, *El Machiavelismo degollado por la Christiana sabiduría de España y Austria. Discurso Christiano-Político* (Alcalá, 1637).

the ruler's, derives from a virtuous life which is patterned, rationally, after nature, and whose ultimate source is God.

Calderón's hero has no regard for the cloistered virtues—unexercised and unbreathed. The perfect Christian prince must forge his own destiny by dominating himself and assuming his moral obligations. He must not withdraw from the world in hermetical isolation, but go forth to conquer it.[21]

21 Nowhere in Calderón's play is there any attempt to depict the ideal Christian prince as a perfect *caballero*, possessing all the qualities and talents of a model courtier, as is the case with D. Juan de Portugal in Lope's *El príncipe perfecto*. There in Act II, D. Juan seems to be one type of Renaissance gentleman endowed with those qualities and abilities most desired at court: physical strength and beauty, virtue, gentleness in speech, discretion in witticisms; an orator, linguist, friend of religion, skilful horseman, dancer, fencer and hunter; a devotee of bullfighting, musicals, dances, jousts, and feats of strength. But see E. M. Wilson and William J. Entwistle, "Calderón's *Príncipe constante:* Two Appreciations," MLR, xxxiv (1939), 207–222.

Part Three

El príncipe constante

7·The Figure of Fénix in Calderón's

El príncipe constante *

by Leo Spitzer

IN CONTRAST to earlier critics who have dealt only with the figure of Don Fernando, Wolfgang Kayser (*"Zur Struktur des* Standhaften Prinzen," in *Gestaltprobleme der Dichtung* [Bonn, 1957]) has the merit of recognizing the "Fernando-Fénix correlation" as an essential part of the drama and of subjecting it to a thorough investigation. The "secret correlation" or "partnership" of the Christian hero and the Moorish princess, he maintains, creates an *ordo simultaneorum* in contrast to the *ordo successivorum* (of the development of the drama around Fernando in several stages or "roles"): it creates an "atmosphere" (that of the world ordained by fate). Both protagonists are "incarnations of worldly perfection, he of chivalry, she of beauty." "A singular, private action does not develop around the two figures, yet a significant correlation stands out, which as an atmospheric content hangs over the whole drama. . . . This atmosphere remains ultimately incomprehensible, does not become so transparent that behind it a conceptual system

* *Editor's Note.* To economize on space I have with regret eliminated all footnotes, and excised a few illustrations and asides. Some excellent insights and much solid erudition have thereby been forfeited, as well as some characteristic scholarly debate. The specialist reader must turn to the original to get the full flavor of the late Professor Spitzer's interpretation of the play. My purpose in publishing even an abbreviated version of this article is to give those with little German an opportunity to sample Spitzer's reading of Calderón. For the translation I am indebted to another former colleague, Professor Emeritus Ernst Feise of the Johns Hopkins University, who is not responsible for errors committed by the editor. All quotations of *El príncipe constante* have been adjusted to Professor A. A. Parker's edition in the Cambridge Plain Texts series.

of correlations, an ideal sky of stars become visible." In the principal scene, the garden scene (II, 14), which is far from being a "lyric interlude," the two figures are exalted above all the others "through birth and perfect chivalry in the one case, through perfect beauty in the other, and both of them become progressively more consumed by grief." The male partner, the Christian, is shown rising above his suffering, the female, "in perpetual insecurity, threatened by and subjected to fate." "She, oppressed by melancholy and disturbed by an oracle, recognizes, when confronted with the Prince and the flowers, the essence of her grief." In III, 7 the two are brought together again, but with the unfortunate difference "that there exists between them no 'coherent action,' so that in Fernando's assertion that his value was superior to hers the relationship between the two . . . can only be heard in overtones." The lines of the two figures converge only in the final scene when Fénix is exchanged for the dead Fernando. Kayser then shows the development of the drama through the concatenation of the guiding line of the male hero with the line of a woman's fate—the structural principle of many of Calderón's dramas which have so far eluded classification through critical study (for example, Justina in El mágico prodigioso, Rosaura in La vida es sueño).

With a master of interpretation such as Kayser it is eo ipso to be expected that he should exceed his predecessors. But perhaps his expositions may require here and there a different shading or modification. In what follows I shall often have to accept Kayser's formulations, but often also to deviate from them. My divergent conception of the figure of Fénix can be summed up in two disagreements with Kayser. I consider this figure, first, not simply as an incarnation of earthly perfection, to wit, that of beauty; and, second, not as dramatically unrelated with that of the Constant Prince. Positively speaking, there is a nexus of action between the unequally perfect partners which is expressed in the great garden scene. This scene, as far as I can see, has not been fully interpreted hitherto.

Let us take in order those scenes in which the Moorish Princess appears. The drama begins in Fénix's garden with her servants' asking the Christian prisoners to sing for their mistress while she is dressing, so that she may derive pleasure from the

nostalgic songs. And at once—wonderful Calderón!—a criticism
made by the captives deeply elucidates Fénix's character: how
can music accompanied by the rattling of iron chains be pleas-
urable to her? Is the deepest human distress, whereby man
differs from beast, to serve as entertainment for the Princess?
"*Es / para divertir las penas / propias, mas no las ajenas.*" This,
then, is the first allusion to the melancholy of the Princess,
who seeks solace in the captives' songs, finds esthetic pleasure
in them without identifying herself with their pains—an essential trait of the Princess, as we shall see. Anticipating, we
may note now that she will not identify herself entirely with
the suffering of the captive Don Fernando later on. I interpret
the text of the captives' song differently from Kayser.

> *Al peso de los años*
> *lo eminente se rinde;*
> *que a lo fácil del tiempo*
> *no hay conquista difícil.*

Kayser thinks: "Fénix is the '*eminente,*' standing under the
sway of time, i.e. of transitoriness . . . but Fernando enters
that other realm, in which time and achievement become ef-
fortless; he represents constancy in faith." Surely over the years
those captives have thought of time and death, a theme which
permeates the whole play. But if in this song there is any allusion at all to the characters, "*lo eminente*" must be Fernando,
who will be overtaken by death, while "*lo fácil del tiempo*" must
refer to the youthful beauty of Fénix, for whom every conquest
is easy (of Muley, of Tarudante, and—perhaps—of Fernando).
Nowhere in the play do we see that Fernando "has it easy."

Now Fénix enters, praised by the servants as a beauty
putting nature to shame, as a second Aurora, and evidently
seen by the poet as identified with the seductive perfumes and
colors of the oriental garden. But Fénix's first utterance is her
demand for a mirror, a narcissistic gesture. Following a servant's
question "*¿Qué sientes?*" Fénix in her answer asserts the use-
lessness of her beauty since it brings her no joy. She distinguishes her "melancholy" from "sadness:" the latter would have
definite causes; the former would be a vague, perhaps illusory
feeling:

> *Sólo sé que sé sentir;*
> *lo que sé sentir no sé;*
> *que ilusión del alma fue.*

The indefinable sadness of the Princess seems to have its cause precisely in its indefinableness. Nature with her changing displays (the garden interchanges attributes with the sea and melancholy is present in the evening sunset) cannot heal her melancholia. Her mood is also known as a sort of sickness to her father, who now enters and shows her a picture of the handsome King Tarudante of Morocco, his ally, whom he has destined to be her husband.

Fénix apparently submits silently and humbly to the will of the King:

> *Si sabes que siempre has sido*
> *mi dueño, mi padre y rey,*
> *¿qué he de decir?*

But the asides which the poet puts in her mouth enlighten us about her true feelings: for her this marriage would be a death sentence. Does she love someone else? Actually she says *sotto voce:* "*¡Ay Muley! / ¡Grande ocasión has perdido!*" But she makes no protest, shows no emotion in favor of Muley, who is in love with her. And when, in the next scene, the choleric general Muley enters, he presents a comic picture as a result of the disparity between his shock at seeing the portrait of his rival in Fénix's hand and his forthright report to the king about the war situation. Prompted by his jealousy, Muley draws, as always, wrong conclusions about Fénix's feelings. In the next scene, alone with her, he accuses her of indifference and fickleness, since she has allowed his rival's picture to be forced on her, while Fénix shows herself offended by the unfounded accusation and justifies herself with her by now familiar oriental fatalism:

> Fénix: *¿Pude excusarlo?*
> Muley: *¿Pues no?*
> Fénix: *¿Cómo?*
> Muley: *Otra cosa fingir.*
> Fénix: *Pues ¿qué pude hacer?*
> Muley: *Morir;*
> *que por ti lo hiciera yo.*

Fénix:	*Fue fuerza.*
Muley:	*Más fue mudanza.*
Fénix:	*Fue violencia.*
Muley:	*No hay violencia.*

Muley guesses that his expected departure for war would cause
new inconstancy in the Princess. However, from her casual
remark (*"aunque mi deseo / licencia de amar te dio"*) we do
not gain the impression that Muley is the great love of her
life, rather that she allows herself to be loved by him. This impression is reinforced in scene 11, in which Muley tells Don
Fernando the story of his love. It was from the beginning a
childhood love, favored by the proximity of their houses:

> *Junto a mi casa vivía. . .*
> *porque más constante fuese*
> *este amor, más imposible*
> *de acabarse y de romperse.*

We note the irony with which the adjective, which is so often
accorded Don Fernando in the play as well as in the title, is
here applied to a relationship that gives every indication of
being inconstant and that arose merely through the accident
of their being neighbors. Muley himself rejects the comparison
of his love with a flash of lightning; he speaks rather of a feeling which first touches *"lo humilde, tierno y débil."* Amor has
wounded them both with *"arpones diferentes"*: that is, Muley
loved, Fénix did not, until Muley's tears at last were able to
soften *"la piedra del corazón."* Don Fernando releases Muley
after this story, saying he does so *"porque sé qué es amor / y
qué es tardanza en ausentes:"* he acts in chivalrous solidarity
with the lover so that Muley can hasten to his lady. It should
be noted that in this way Fernando, before he makes Fénix's
acquaintance or knows that Fénix is Muley's beloved, gives her
a present: he sends her the loving Muley as a slave for whom
she need not pay. His action foreshadows the possibility that
Fernando himself may, in a different sense, later become her
"slave."

The second act begins, like the first, with scenes focussing
on Fénix in a natural setting, only this time, as Kayser remarks,
not in the royal garden but in a strange mountain landscape.
Whereas in the first act an agreeable illusion reigned (garden

became sea, sea became garden), here Fénix tells of a frightening illusion, called expressly by Muley *"ese sueño, esa ilusión."* In the seductive beauty of a *locus amoenus* of nature, in which the Princess sought rest during a hunt, there appeared to her an old Moorish woman who resembled a skeleton hewn out of a tree. The woman took her hand and made her feel as if she had herself been changed into a tree trunk. The old hag prophesied to her: *"Esta hermosura / precio de un muerto ha de ser."* It is as if once lovely nature were renouncing all friendship with her favorite, preaching *desengaño* to beauty, trying to destroy her vital force and to remind her sensitive being of the wood of the coffin for which Fénix at the end of the play is to be exchanged as the *"precio de un muerto."*

We must digress here somewhat and discuss the concept of "price" or "ransom" (*precio, rescate*). Throughout the play these words recur in a great profusion of meanings in reference to the most diverse persons. Don Fernando refuses (I, 11) to accept a ransom (*precio*) for his liberation of Muley. Fernando's captivity has "cost" the death of the Portuguese King. The Prince's ransom (*precio*) is to be, according to the wishes of the Moorish King, the city of Ceuta; Fernando refuses this exchange (II, 7) on the grounds that a thousand living Christians would be sacrificed for one dead man. Yet in the end, Fernando at the moment of death not only demands from his followers the ransom of his corpse but from God interment under a Christian altar as a reward or price for his fight:

> que espero
> que, aunque hoy cautivo muero,
> rescatado he de gozar
> el sufragio del altar;
> que pues yo os he dado a vos
> tantas iglesias, mi Dios,
> alguna me habéis de dar.

Heaven has, so to speak, a duty to ransom him—a paradoxical conviction which stems from an absolute faith in God:

> obligado el cielo
> que vio tu fe, tu religión, tu celo, [tú is Don Alfonso]
> hoy tu causa defiende.

Librarme a mí *de esclavitud pretenae,*
porque, por raro ejemplo,
por tantos templos Dios me ofrece un templo. . . .
Llegues a Fez, no a coronarte agora,
sino a librar mi ocaso en el aurora. [librar *means* rescatar]

And the last words of Fernando, appearing as a specter, are:
"*Éste es el muro de Fez, / trata en él de mi* rescate." So in the
end, as a fulfillment of the hag's oracle, Fernando's corpse is
exchanged for the captive Fénix. Don Alfonso justifies this
exchange as complying with Don Fernando's wish:

> *Por su cadáver lo dijo,*
> *porque goce su cadáver*
> *por muchos templos un templo,*
> *y a él se ha de hacer el rescate.*
> *Rey de Fez, porque no pienses*
> *que muerto* Fernando vale
> menos que aquesta hermosura,
> *por él, cuando muerto yace,*
> te la trueco. *Envía, pues,*
> *la nieve por los cristales,*
> *el enero por los mayos,*
> *por las rosas los diamantes,*
> *y al fin, un* muerto infelice
> *por una divina imagen.*

Thereupon Fénix acknowledges the fulfillment of the oracle:

> *Precio soy de un hombre muerto;*
> *cumplió el cielo su homenaje.*

From this series of examples it becomes evident that the
expressions "price" and "ransom" represent "moral equiva-
lents." The question for Fernando was whether he was of equal
value with Ceuta; and the question for Fénix, whether her
beauty was of equal value with Fernando's constancy. Both
questions are answered in the negative: Ceuta is worth more
than Fernando, but because he dies in his steadfastness for this
true valuation, he becomes worth more than the mere beauty
of Fénix. Fernando recognizes this in one of the more important passages which occurs later in the sequence which I have
been observing, and which I shall have to discuss in detail in
its proper place:

Señora, es bien que sepáis,
aunque tan bella os juzgáis,
que más que yo no valéis,
y yo quizá valgo más.

This evaluation is emphasized at the end of the play through the actual exchange of Fernando's body not only for Fénix but also for her Moorish suitors, Tarudante and Muley. This final exchange—a visible emblem, as it were, on stage—was the reason why the tragedy of the protagonist's martyrdom off stage was extended. His body was necessary for the exchange, and in the face of death Don Fernando himself speaks of the ransom of his corpse as an obligation placed both on heaven and on the Christians in acknowledgment of the sacrifice of his soul. Behind the symbol of "price" is concealed an "equation of value," by means of which, in spite of Kayser, moral values are introduced into the action, and then made emblematically visible on the stage, so that Professor Wardropper is surely right when he terms our drama a cross between a *comedia* and an *auto sacramental:* it puts before us living characters who incarnate abstract forces.

Let us return to our presentation of Fénix's character. She has herself recognized the diminution of her own value, as expressed in the old Moor's oracle. The exact wording of this prediction was: *"Esta hermosura / precio de un muerto ha de ser."* But Fénix, betraying her humiliation, repeats it with the addition of the word *vil:* *"¡Ay de mí! que yo he de ser / precio vil de un hombre muerto."* Muley, like his Christian counterpart Don Enrique, is always wrong in his suppositions. Thus he interprets himself in the monologue which follows as the *"hombre muerto,"* since he would die for Fénix—which, however, does not happen. In II, 4 he speaks to Don Fernando about his love for Fénix. We see the Constant Prince deprecate the sufferings of his captivity in comparison with Muley's pangs of love, and we see the latter in a sly loquacity reveal the name of his beloved (which a secret lover should conceal), betraying her and yet not betraying her by using Fénix's name metaphorically. In a rather forced way Calderón makes one of the captives, speaking in the preceding scene to Don Fernando,

proclaim the name of the Phoenix as the eternally rejuvenated
bird: "*Siglos pequeños / son los del fénix, señor, / para que
vivas. . . .*" So, in II, 4 Muley in a long anaphorically inflated
passage could declare that his love was unique like the bird
called Phoenix:

> *Tan solo mi mal ha sido*
> *como solo mi dolor:*
> *porque el fénix y mi amor*
> *sin semejante han nacido.*
> *En ver, oir y callar*
> *fénix es mi pensamiento;*
> *fénix es mi sufrimiento. . . ,*

and so on for four more equations between his love and the
Phoenix. One should mark the egotistic tinge of this quite
ambiguous speech: his love, not really Fénix, is the Phoenix.

The next scene in which Fénix enters is played once more
in the beautiful garden with which we associate her. Don
Fernando, as a captive, has decided to live a real slave's life,
and, as it were, to mortify himself as a living corpse in order
to oppose his own *paciencia* to the *rigor* of the tyrannical King.
For this reason he is sent to hard labor in the garden, where
due to his changed looks—caused by his privations—he is not
recognized by his fellow-captives. The loyal Don Juan seeks
him in the garden, and finds him in a steadfast frame of mind
carrying two pails of water, presumably to water Fénix's flowers.
Meanwhile, Calderón's public has been waiting impatiently
for Fénix, the beautiful garden's mistress, to enter this place
where the humiliated Prince is practicing his heroism. Again,
just as in the first act, her servant girls enter first, and at her
command prepare esthetic enjoyments for her: this time a
basket of flowers is to be picked. Though the captives in the
first act were loath to obey the command to sing for Fénix,
Don Fernando volunteers to be the first to pick flowers for her:
"*Yo llevársele espero, / que en cuanto sea servir seré el primero.*"
In accordance with the technique of revealing the several phases
of Fernando's development through a series of pictures or roles
—a technique shown us by Kayser—the present picture, as just
described, is no longer of the captive Prince but of the slave.
And it is now his ambition to be the slave most eager to work:

his principle is "*no dejar hoy que hacer para mañana*," especially since "*nuestra suerte / . . . mañana ha de igualar la muerte.*" He speaks of his readiness to serve even if it should mean being the "first" to bring her flowers; he does not yet speak of "Fénix's service," as he will do in the great scene.

After Fernando has gone to pick the flowers, Fénix appears impatiently demanding the flowers which are to dissipate her melancholy. In her memory there still lingers the gruesome "dream" of the oracle, which appears to her to be an imminent fact. One of the servants, just like the captive in the first act, ventures a criticism: "*¿Y qué dejas para el muerto / si tú lo sientes así?*" Is it too daring to assume that the servant wishes to point out the egoism of this sadness? There is no room in Fénix's thoughts for the other person whose death must also somehow be a cause for regret. And now we are on the threshold of the great scene between Fénix and Fernando, since to her lamenting questions—

> ¡Precio de un muerto! ¿Quién vio
> tal pena? No hay gusto, no,
> a una infelice mujer.
> ¿Que al fin de un muerto he de ser?
> ¿Quién será este muerto?—

Fernando, returning with the flowers, utters that one fateful syllable: "*Yo.*" This prophesying of the end of the play is indeed a *coup de théâtre*, as Kayser calls it. Already older critics had emphasized that Calderón knew how to introduce "these forebodings of speech, apparently fortuitous oracles of the spirit . . . , into the common course of conversation, often in a marvelously pertinent way" (Schmidt in Krenkel's edition). But as well as the foreboding we must also understand the meaning of such words in the actual dramatic moment.

I do not hesitate to aver that whoever does not interpret the meaning of the "I" answer *in the scene itself* shuns the duty of explaining the whole scene and the structural position of the Fénix action. But I regret to say that all the critics whom I could consult in regard to the "Yo" form a *conspiration du silence*: Immermann, Wilson, Entwistle, Sloman, Ortigoza, Kayser, Wardropper say nothing about it. How can Fernando designate himself as the dead body meant in the oracle, the dead body to whom Fénix belongs? That he is a "dead man" we understand from what has gone before: he has died as Prince and is as a slave destined to die. But the answer "Yo" still contains another statement, the answer to Fénix's question: "*¿Que al fin de un muerto he de ser?*" This question is not comprehensible in itself: the Moorish woman spoke only of a "price for a dead man," not of "belonging to a dead man." Fénix's shaken spirit has evidently drawn the conclusion that a beauty which is only the equivalent of a corpse will not attract a living person, cannot belong to a living person. Since we cannot assume that Fernando has heard only the last question, and not the preceding question too, his "Yo" is an answer also to the latter: he intimates therefore to Fénix that she belongs to him even though he is a dead man or one consecrated to death. The "Yo" is the tragic declaration of a dead man's love, coming as it were from beyond life, hence so powerful, so lapidary, so monosyllabic, so mysterious a revelation for the Princess as well as for us. Only a full measure of passionate feeling can justify such a neglect of all social forms—of first greeting, of slow approach—and such an assured, loud answer to the passive self-questioning of the Princess, who is such an essential "thou." The "Yo" betrays an inner relationship with the Princess and at the same time an acceptance of their fate of eternal separation in death. How in the face of death has this attraction to her sprung up? The Prince has not been represented from the beginning as an ascetic saint: he knows what love is ("*sé qué es amor*"); he has seen Fénix in the garden and recognized her beauty, a fact we hear about only in the third act. He has also recognized that if he were not in the shadow of death he would belong to her. For this reason—not only to fulfill his "slave's duty"—he offered to be the first to pick flowers for her. And the gesture of bringing flowers he accompanies with an assurance of his "service of love" for Fénix: "*Yo pues, Fénix, que deseo* / servirte humilde, *traía* / *flores.* . . ."

While Fernando addresses Fénix by name, and using the familiar form, Fénix calls him Fernando only later in the question: "*¿No eres Fernando?*"—a question which presupposes acquaintance. It is hard for her to recognize in his present garb and looks the Prince whom she has evidently seen before in his

sunlike beauty. The erstwhile Fernando must have attracted
her as she has him. Thus they converse with each other like
people who are intimately connected and instinctively know
they are: "*¡Ay cielos! ¿qué es lo que veo? / . . . de una
suerte / me admira el oirte y el verte.*" It is compassion that
Fénix utters here, as the same expression is used by Muley earlier
in addressing the compassionate Fernando:

> *Movido de piedad,*
> *de oirme, español, y verme,*
> *preguntado me has la causa*
> *de mis suspiros ardientes.*

Whereas Fernando, speaking to the captives, has illustrated
the radical change that has taken place in him through the
image of the theatrical presentation of time ("*Que el tiempo
estas miserias representa*"), he now uses, speaking to the Princess, the image, or "hieroglyphs," of the fast wilting flowers.
It is impossible to think that the Prince would give such a
personally tinged symbolization of his own fate to a lady to
whom he was bound only by *courtoisie* or *gallanterie*. Only in
the event of a deeper connection is such essential utterance
conceivable. On the other hand, while in a real declaration of
love the proffered flowers are a symbol of life (of love, of the
beloved), they are in this case a symbol of death (of the
lover), a macabre token of love:

> [Yo] *traía*
> *flores, de la suerte mía*
> *geroglíficos, señora,*
> *pues nacieron con la aurora,*
> *y murieron con el día.*

Fernando expresses through a tender allusion, through the
flowers, the thought that not only his life but their mutual
attraction, scarcely unfolded, are already sacrificed to death.
Fénix, however, otherwise shadowed by fate, does not wish to
yield to this thought. She looks at the marigold, the *maravilla*,
in this bouquet and, playing with its name, emphasizes that
the blooming of this flower represents a miracle, just as—we
may assume—their attraction to one another is a miracle: "A
la maravilla dio / ese nombre al descubrilla." Fénix clings in

this moment of intimate association to the matutinal blooming of the flower and of love. Don Fernando's reply—again symbolic —demands an extended commentary which no critic gives us: "*¿Qué flor, di, no es maravilla / cuando te la sirvo yo?*" One could think of the superficial sense: "Every flower, not just the one called miracle flower, is a marvel;" but then the personal tone of "*cuando te la sirvo yo*" would be lost. On the other hand, are we to believe that Fernando would give such a banal answer as "Every flower becomes a miracle when I bring it?" The sense must be that it is a miracle when Fernando, although destined to die, renders homage to her in bringing flowers lovingly. And Fénix understands the phrase in the way we propose:

> Es verdad. Di, ¿quién causó
> esta novedad?
>
> Fernando: Mi suerte.

Thus: it is true that it is a miracle when you, even though so sadly changed, bring me flowers. The word *novedad*, referring to Fernando's decline, is proof of Fénix's previous acquaintance with him. She has understood the dead man's wooing. So far the allusive conversation through flowers, through "*di*" on the lips of both partners, contains a tone of closeness and intimacy. Now, however, the symbol is dropped, and there ensues a dialogue in hemistychomythies, which in spite of the stylization involved in this technique is the most beautiful example of simple, terse, loving, essential human speech that a poet could have invented:

> Fernando: Mi suerte.
> Fénix: ¿Tan rigurosa es?
> Fernando: Tan fuerte.
> Fénix: Pena das.
> Fernando: Pues no te asombre.
> Fénix: ¿Por qué?
> Fernando: Porque nace el hombre
> sujeto a fortuna y muerte.

The most important line here is: "*Pena das.—Pues no te asombre.*" Fénix feels another's woe in herself for the first time, and Don Fernando feels the impulse to calm the other in her sympathetic suffering. As lovers, Prince and Princess are very close to each other. Fénix's excited questions *"¿Quién te puso así? ¿Quien lo hizo?"* are variations on *"¿Quién causó esta novedad?"*—questions which breathe resentment against the suspected originator of Fernando's suffering: her father and her King. She receives from Fernando the answer she expects: *"El Rey."* Remarkably well informed concerning the latest development, she then asks: *"¿Pues no te ha estimado hoy?"* and receives the reply: *"Y también me ha aborrecido."* This quick change in the father's mood within a single day, from respect to hatred, itself an example of Moorish *inconstancia*, gives Fénix the occasion to sound for the first time the motif of the stars. This symbolic reference to the inconstancy of fate will appear from now on entwined with the flower theme: *"¿Un día posible ha sido / a desunir dos estrellas?"* The two stars which go their different ways on one day are Fénix's father and Don Fernando. But on one day the flowers Fernando brought also die. And so Fénix may also mean by the two separating stars herself and Fernando, for the scene will shortly depict the couple's separation following their intimate encounter.

In any case each of the two partners, to speak in a Wagnerian way, now has a *Leitmotif*, or better, in Calderón's sense, his own emblem, Fernando the flowers, Fénix the stars. In the symmetrically constructed scene each will be permitted to describe his motif in a sonnet, in a kind of antiphony or *tenso* which circumscribes in oriental allegory two world views without allowing the contrast to become personal. Both emblems are concerned with the mutability of life, and yet neither character can recognize the emblem of the other. On Fernando's part this becomes clear in the line which precedes his sonnet about the flowers: *"Para presumir por ellas [las estrellas] / las flores habrán venido."* In other words, Fernando sees the mutability of human fate symbolized rather by flowers than by stars. Fundamentally, we might say, Don Fernando and Fénix are equally fatalistic; but Fernando wishes to regard human destiny, like that of the flowers, as determined by nature and preordained, whereas Fénix takes more account of the changeable and the unforseeable, the influence of the stars. In this way the Christian and Islamic world views are symbolized: here, acquiescence in a fate which the Christian considers God-given; there, submission to a moody, incalculable Kismet. Fernando can speak with greater calm than Fénix since he has come to terms with this world. Fénix speaks in the midst of a revolt against a fate which, incomprehensible as it is, is at this very moment happening to her. Between the two symmetric sonnets we hear a dialogue which takes its coloring from Fénix's passionateness and Fernando's constancy. In Fernando's flower sonnet the Princess has perceived the macabre accent which signifies the death of the beloved as well as of her own love. Fernando sees "these flowers" which he has brought to Fénix as hieroglyphs of his fate. But Fénix recognizes in them her own fate, and she will have none of it. She scolds Fernando for having conjured up such pictures in her mind:

> Horror y miedo me has dado,
> ni oirte ni verte quiero;
> sé el desdichado primero
> de quien huye un desdichado.

Though the two were joined for a moment in grief and sympathy, they are now far removed from each other. That participation in another's misfortune has changed into an inhuman fleeing of one unfortunate from another unfortunate. Surprise at Fernando's change has turned to loathing in the beautiful, beauty-seeking Princess. She can only act esthetically and so egotistically ("*Ni oirte ni verte quiero*"), and at the same time she feels the change as an ineluctable turn of fate. While Don Fernando used to emphasize the consoling element in fate's mutability—

> Sufrid con ella [la prudencia] el rigor
> del tiempo y de la fortuna:
> deidad bárbara, importuna
> hoy cadáver y ayer flor,
> no permanece jamás,
> y así os mudará de estado.—

Fénix has been seized by the Moorish *miedo*. We remember that Fernando finds "*miedos vanos*" suitable to Moors, not to Christians. To his brother, who superstitiously believes in omens, he says:

> *Estos agüeros viles, miedos vanos,*
> *para los moros vienen que los crean,*
> *no para que los duden los cristianos. . . .*
> *El castigo de Dios justo es temerle:*
> *éste no viene envuelto en miedos vanos.*

Kayser certainly saw clearly that the two partners were united in grief, that the male stood above suffering, that the female appeared in "perpetual insecurity, threatened and subjected to fate." But this latter attitude itself needs a further motivation; it cannot simply be taken for granted. Are we to think that Calderón contrasts in his play Fernando's insistently expressed constancy with a feminine beauty who is for some inexplicable reason, and at all times, melancholy, or, as we would say, psychically disturbed? Why is Fénix melancholy? Why does she take no pleasure in her own beauty? Evidently because she lacks something that Fernando has, because her beauty is egotistic and cannot forget itself. For this reason she feels her deliverance to fate and thus is the exact opposite of Don Fernando who, self-sacrificing and altruistic, is constant in the face of fate. Now, to be sure, when an attraction to the Prince seems to seize her, she can rise to fear and pity, but not to his constancy and self-restraint. Without self-control she tears up in anger the flowers which have been presented to her as a hieroglyph of the fate of the beloved. For this is indeed the emblematic gesture which accompanies her words when Don Fernando wishes to deflect her attention from himself to the gift of flowers:

Fernando:	*¿Y las flores?*
Fénix:	*Si has hallado*
	geroglíficos en ellas,
	deshacellas y rompellas
	sólo sabrán mis rigores.

She vents her feelings upon the innocent flowers, which Fernando at once picks up. Why? Because she transmutes the flower symbol into the Moorish belief in stars:

Fernando:	*¿Qué culpa tienen las flores?*
Fénix:	*Parecerse a las estrellas.*
Fernando:	*¿Ya no las quieres?*
Fénix:	*Ninguna*
	estimo en su rosicler.

With the "*¿Ya no las quieres?*" the inconstancy of the
Moorish Princess is characterized in contrast to the constancy
of Don Fernando. For Fénix the flowers equal the stars which
exert their incalculable effect upon human fate: one emblem
merges with the other. Fénix explains her bondage to fate as the
destiny of woman, by changing Fernando's earlier saying "*Nace
el hombre / sujeto a fortuna y muerte*" into "*Nace la mujer /
sujeta a muerte y fortuna.*" This means not just that the feminine sex is generally weaker than the male or even that the
Mohammedan woman is more dependent on the man than is
the Christian woman; it means also something in terms of
Fénix's personal attachment to Fernando: his fate is that of her
love. We gauge from the general maxim how deeply she as a
woman is involved in the fate of the beloved. At this moment
the two still see the same emblem, the flowers, but their interpretations of it differ considerably. Fénix says: "*Y en esta
estrella importuna / tasada mi vida vi.*" She looks upon the
flower, the *maravilla*, and sees in it the star of her own fate.
Fernando has earlier used the word *importuna* in reference to
Fortune, the "*deidad bárbara.*" The Calderonian metamorpho-
sis of natural objects has here been adapted to the character of
the Moorish Princess. Not in vain does Don Fernando reject
this substitution. He asks how she can compare flowers with
stars. By way of reply Fénix in her *tenso* sonnet blends flowers
and stars in Islamic fashion, confusing emblems with objects.
Speaking in exact parallel to Don Fernando's sonnet on the
flowers, she evidently looks towards heaven and points to the
stars:

> Esos *rasgos de luz*, esas *centellas* . . .
> *flores nocturnas son* . . . ,
> *pues si un día es el siglo de las flores,*
> *una noche es la edad de las estrellas.*

With the melancholy perspective of the ephemeral in both
cosmos and fate the scene has reached its end, dramatically
symbolizing the melancholy nature of the change from the
momentary propinquity to the fateful separation of two human
beings. The beauty of the scene lies in the lyric contest between
two emblems, into which is simultaneously incorporated the
dramatic exposition of two human fates: perfect drama and

perfect lyric are seldom so beautifully interwoven. After the lyric climax of her sonnet Fénix leaves, and we know that the lovers have separated forever.

It will be objected that Calderón in this scene did not provide clear evidence to back up my hypothesis of a meeting and separation of lovers, that my imagination has constructed an affective relationship between the hero and the heroine. Aside from the fact that several passages do not seem to me to be meaningful without such a hypothesis I cannot imagine in the theatre such an abstract confrontation of man and woman as "representatives" of two world views or "forms of suffering," as Kayser would have it, unless some erotic bond unites them. Neither the experienced playwright Calderón nor his Mediterranean audiences would have approved a purely theoretic discussion between representatives of the two sexes. On the stage the collective unconscious in all its dynamics prevails much sooner than in any other genre: there above all, man is man, and woman is woman. Precisely this consideration that a spiritual hero, as the sole protagonist, would be monotonous for his intensely credulous public prompted Calderón to introduce a love interest in other dramas. The immediate source of our play, Lope's *La fortuna adversa*, also contains a love scene, though it is an overwhelmingly aggressive one between an amorous queen and a spiritual prince. Treating the situation more organically Calderón avoided coarse suggestive allusions and raised his love scene to a highly spiritual and poetic level. The motif of a love between a Christian knight and a Saracen princess had been a familiar theme since medieval times. Calderón gave this theme, as well as the opening sentimental-Moor theme, which Wardropper has expounded, an entirely new twist: he let this love affair be merely glimpsed on the horizon at the moment when fate has already spoken and the Christian knight must follow his true vocation. Before the scene with Fénix we saw Fernando bear the intensification of his suffering with equanimity; after it he feels the temptation to let himself be freed by the faithful Muley. In all three scenes his *constancia* is victorious. At the end of the second act he can justly repeat: "*seré un príncipe constante / en la esclavitud de Fez.*" The central garden scene brings another, no doubt necessary, temptation to Fernando: what would a constant prince be who had not proved himself in the temptation of love? The ineffable beauty of this scene, which all the critics have felt, consists in its otherworldly tone and the lyircal breath of melancholy which distinguishes this love scene (which is nothing of the sort) from all analogous ones. And precisely from the unreal quality of the love scene proceeds that delicate allusive stylization which enabled critics to overlook the existence of the love motif.

In the next act the strange inefficiency of the two Moors, Muley and Fénix, is revealed. Both intercede with the King of Fez to alleviate the tortures meted out to Fernando. Because the distrustful King has surrounded Don Fernando with guards, Muley has been unable to carry out his plan to free the royal prisoner. He now appeals directly to his King, but without success. Fénix too in an exactly parallel scene receives a blunt refusal from her father. Moreover, this scene is interrupted by the arrival of her suitor Tarudante and the Portuguese King Alfonso. But this time, at least, Fénix has dared to pass beyond her previous egocentricity. When it is announced that the King of Morocco's ambassador (in reality Tarudante himself) seeks an audience, both Fénix and Muley acquiesce with their hereditary fatalism. Fénix assumes that she is already being fetched by her royal suitor, Muley that he has *en un día* lost his love and his friend. And it must be admitted that Muley is sorely tested when he is appointed Fénix's guardian by the King of Fez—for the duration of the war and until such time as Tarudante shall marry her. Tarudante is treated by Fénix with the same detached politeness that she had used earlier towards Muley.

The final separation of Fernando and Fénix is sealed by Act III, Scene 7. In his role as Job on the dunghill Fernando, like a common beggar, implores the King of Fez, then Tarudante, and finally Fénix for pity. In all three cases his voluntary self-abasement has no success. The scene with Fénix is quite short, but psychologically sharply formulated and therefore impressive, since we perceive the Prince's suffering behind the clear expression of his disillusionment with Fénix. As we have seen, Kayser finds fault with this scene in that there is "no substantial coherent action" between the two partners, and in that Fernando was represented as forsaken, so that "only in overtones" would the inner union be suggested. I however think that the union which was already being melancholically dissolved in the garden scene here completely and suddenly breaks apart; this development of the action is predicated on the harsh illumination which Fernando gains concerning the beautiful but selfish personality of Fénix. It is significant that Fernando, who in the garden scene has addressed Fénix as *tú* and *señora*, here employs *vos* and *señora*: from the start, then, a cooling of feelings, a ceremonial conversation.

After Tarudante has left Fernando to himself with the words "*¡Qué desventura!*" Don Fernando speaks to Fénix:

> *Si es alma de la hermosura*
> *esa divina deidad,*
> *vos, señora, me amparad*
> *con el Rey.*

Fénix: *¡Qué gran dolor!*
Fernando: *¿Aun no me miráis?*
Fénix: *¡Qué horror!*
Fernando: *Hacéis bien; que vuestros ojos*
                   no son para ver enojos.
Fénix: *¡Qué lástima! ¡Qué pavor!*
Fernando: *Pues aunque no me miréis*
                   y ausentaros intentéis,
                   señora, es bien que sepáis,
                   aunque tan bella os juzgáis,
                   que más que yo no valéis,
                   y yo quizá valgo más.
Fénix: *Horror con tu voz me das,*
                   y con tu aliento me hieres.
                   ¡Déjame, hombre! ¿Qué me quieres?
                   Que no puedo sentir más.

In this scene Fernando subjects Fénix to a hard test. He probes to see whether her body's beauty is one with her soul's; but she fails the test. She does what she has hinted at in the garden scene, though at that time she was reproaching Fernando. She, an unfortunate woman, flees from the unfortunate man, becoming as it were "*el desdichado primero que huye a un desdichado.*" The wording of Fernando's challenge ("*si es alma de la hermosura / esa divina deidad*") seems to confirm my interpretation that Fernando was attracted to the physical, "divine" beauty. We hear the reason for his love, which became clear to us in the garden scene, only now, at the moment when he realizes that her body's beauty is not complemented by her soul's. And in this scene it becomes evident that Fénix herself cannot go beyond the physically esthetic. To the extent that Fernando's sufferings increase, Fénix's physical abhorrence grows. The figure *"ni verte ni oirte quiero"* gives way, in effect, to the sentiment: "I can't bear to hear (*'tu voz'*) or smell (*'tu aliento'*) this abject figure of suffering." Don Fernando therefore draws the conclusion that Fénix is less valuable than he— a prefiguration of the end of the play, when Fénix *plus* Tarudante are objects of barter for Fernando's dead body. As in the garden scene, we not only come face to face with a mere interplay of values, but find both heroes speaking in a tone which makes them believable as human beings. Fernando, otherwise so serene in his constancy, this time speaks as if in bitter disillusionment and personal irritation, rather like a lover whose eyes have been opened: "you do not even look at me!" How could Fernando, if there had been no previous personal relationship, have had the right to demand that the Princess look at him? His anger even causes him to doubt her beauty and to make a drastic formulation of her loveless nature. Never before has the Prince spoken so directly, so offensively. And, on the other hand, we hear in Fénix's speech the nervous tension of a woman who, incapable of further feeling, senses that she has reached the limit of her being and finds it necessary almost in exasperation to shake off an importunate suitor. Observe her irritable *tú* and *hombre* in reaction to the *vos* and *señora* of Fernando: *"¡Déjame, hombre! ¿Qué me quieres? / Que no puedo sentir más."* And the painful parting could not be more clearly audible than through the last word *más* in the two end verses of the *quintillas*: *"y yo quizá valgo más . . . Que no puedo sentir más."* The male partner expresses himself positively, the female negatively. Calderón forces the simplest words into a meaningful, almost emblematic, antithesis. As in the garden scene so here Calderón contents himself with the simplest, most matter-of-fact words devoid of Calderonian pomp: one human being is taking leave of another. As the extended lyrical

and conceptist garden scene produced a declaration of love
"from beyond life," so this laconic and inexorable scene produces the leave-taking of a lover who cannot take with him into
eternity a beautiful picture of the beloved. The Constant Prince,
so near the grave, must recognize the *desengaño* which lies in
the "*divina deidad de la hermosura.*" The harsh tones which
ring out through this scene give us retrospectively a proper understanding of the softer ones used in the garden scene.

The selfishness of Fénix, however, is not yet at an end.
After the defeat of the Moors in the face of her father's fatalistic despair—he wishes to kill himself and his daughter—we
witness a furious outburst on Fénix's part: she cannot understand how he can sacrifice *her* to his despair. The Princess, at
other times so humble and quiet, finds flaming words when her
own life is at stake, words which directly parody her earlier
humble ones. Compare, in Act I,

> Señor,
> *si sabes que siempre has sido*
> *mi dueño, mi padre y rey,*
> *¿qué he de decir?*

with

> *Siendo Rey, has sido fiera;*
> *siendo padre, fuiste áspid;*
> *siendo juez, eres verdugo:*
> *ni eres Rey, ni juez, ni padre* (Act III).

And of course such furious self-assertion contrasts with Don
Fernando's constant readiness to die. The two lines of development diverge even more strongly after Fernando's death.

Even though Fénix goes into a moral decline, her beauty
remains unaltered. In this, the last scene in which Fénix speaks,
she is extolled as a beauty by Mohammedans as well as by
Christians. Her father wishes to immolate her with the words:
"*Da la muerte a Fénix bella,*" while the Christian Alfonso
proposes the exchange with enthusiastic, conceptist words,
which, while they confirm Fernando's earlier "comparison of
values," only a "divine beauty" could command:

> *Envía, pues,*
> *la nieve por los cristales,*

> *el enero por los mayos,*
> *por las rosas los diamantes,*
> *y al fin, un muerto infelice*
> *por una divina imagen.*

No doubt the solemnly funereal, gruesomely beautiful description of the *rigor mortis* of the corpse (snow, January cold, diamantine hardness) is just as artificial as the divine picture of the living woman (dewy freshness, roses, the new growth of spring). Both examples of linguistic pomp illustrate what Hugo Friedrich (quoted by Kayser) has said of Calderón's language in general: "The restlessness of the linguistic pomp seems to shine out over a void and is itself based on the illusion of emptiness which is concealed in beauty." In our passage, however, especially noteworthy are the last two verses, which in their simple stylization seem to reveal a more elementary feeling on the part of the poet than one might expect from his ever alert didacticism: "*y al fin, un muerto infelice / por una divina imagen.*" How, then, if the linguistic pomp as well as the "comparison of values" have taught us to prefer worth to emptiness, can Calderón end with the contrasting of an unfortunate dead man and a *divine image* of beauty? It is as though grief over the death of what is transitory were at the last moment ruining the plan of the moralist Calderón. Kayser is right both when he writes "melancholy hovers like an aura around the figure of Fénix" and when he asserts that our drama is "tinged with a painful love of worldliness." But still, the sudden break in style and feeling in the last two lines surprises us: perhaps we should read "*muerto infelice*" and "*divina imagen*" as if they were enclosed in quotation marks: "a so-called unfortunate dead man," "a so-called divine image."

We hear of Fénix for the last time in the speech in which King Alfonso begs the King of Fez to give Fénix's hand to her constant lover out of respect for the friendship Muley had shown to Don Fernando. Sloman says rightly: "The relationship of Muley and Fénix . . . is one of a series of misunderstandings coldly patched up in the last scene by the single stipulation of Alfonso." Why does Calderón betray this sudden coldness toward the divine image of beauty? Fénix is really pushed around like a piece on a dramatic chessboard as though she were regarded with contempt: *desengaño* has disenchanted her before our eyes. At least she is not married to Tarudante, whom she dislikes; but her will does not count in the end. The reason for the marriage is not Muley's love for her, but his relationship with the Constant Prince. She, who could not love, has no right to a will of her own or to a real life.

If my interpretation proves to be right, a "singular, private action" would connect the two main characters, and the "Fénix-Fernando correlation" would not create "an ultimately incomprehensible atmosphere," behind which no "conceptual system of correlations" was visible. Fénix, the divine beauty, who cannot love unselfishly, and Fernando, the Constant Prince who in self-abnegation sacrifices himself to his cause, have in the garden scene been for one moment two stars, whose courses approached each other only to be separated forever ("*en un día desunidas*"). As a result, the female partner, as it were, shrinks before us to nothingness, while Fernando, favored by heaven, celebrates a personally moral and nationally religious triumph. Around the two partners is wafted a singular poetic atmosphere which however, as always with Calderón, can be formulated in sharp intellectual terms. The necessity, which Calderón felt in other dramas as well, to complete a male hero's line of development with the help of a female figure probably results from the poet's emblematically visual talent, which creates people as representatives of opposing values in a sensually visible, almost graphic, dramatization.

8 · Calderón's *El príncipe constante,* a Tragedy?

by Arnold G. Reichenberger

El príncipe constante is the dramatization of the story of a nobleman who became a saint by virtue of his constancy, founded on Christian faith.

In the first Act, Prince Fernando, the protagonist, is established as the epitome of the Christian knight, whose actions are guided by two qualities: on the secular level his nobility, on the spiritual level his constancy. He frees his prisoner Muley because *"hombre noble soy y no más"* (I, 825). When himself is captured by the Moorish king he identifies himself simply as a *"caballero"* (I, 906). His constancy, faith, and Christian optimism, his dominant qualities, are driven home by contrast with his easily despairing brother Enrique on the one hand and on the other, and in a more subtle way, by contrast with the *melancolía* of the beautiful Moorish princess Fénix. When the Portuguese army is surrounded by the enemy, Fernando's courage remains undaunted: *"Morir como buenos / con ánimo constante"* and *"por la fe muramos,"* is his counsel (I, 862–870). Resisting the victorious King of Fez would be *"desesperación"* (I, 922). His own conduct is guided by the same principle which he recommends to his royal brother: to act as a *"príncipe cristiano"* (I, 952).

The second Act brings what is from the worldly point of view a rapid deterioration of Fernando's position. At first an honored prisoner on a social level equal to that of the Moorish king, he becomes a *cautivo* like all the others when, with his impassioned speech—occurring properly in the center of the

161

play—he rejects the offer to be exchanged for the Christian city of Ceuta:

> ¿Quién soy yo? ¿Soy más que un hombre?
> ....De nobleza
> no es capaz el que es esclavo (II, 391–395).

In battle he had lost his *ser*, that is to say his nobility, and died a civil death: *"perdí el ser, luego morí"* (II, 402), but he finds a new mission: to uphold the Catholic faith as *"príncipe constante entre desdichas y penas"* (II, 441–442). He accepts slavery almost eagerly not only because he recognizes the secular laws which make the prisoner of war a slave, but even more so because slavery is a short-cut on the way to his *"última posada,"* death (II, 475–478). Now the battle between the king's *rigor* and the prince's *paciencia* begins. While others, Christians and Moors alike, pity him and themselves, Fernando is sustained both by his code as a nobleman who does not complain and by his faith in heaven. Secular and religious values are merged:

> . . . No ha de quejarse desa suerte
> un noble. ¿Quién del cielo desconfía?
> La prudencia, el valor, la bizarría
> se ha de mostrar ahora (II, 605–608).

Fernando resists the temptation to flee at the expense of his Moorish friend's honor: *"No acetaré / la vida porque tu honor / conmigo seguro esté"* (II, 891–893). At the end of Act II, Fernando proclaims: *"Seré un príncipe constante / en la esclavitud de Fez"* (II, 926–927).

The third Act adds physical death to civil death, but also brings redemption. As the king remarks (III, 98–105), Fernando's pitiful lot is entirely of his own choosing: *"Si por ser cruel y fiel / a su fe, sufre castigo . . . , él es cruel consigo, / que yo no lo soy con él."* Fernando is reduced to a living corpse, beset by hunger and illness, a horrible sight to all. Even his last wish to die *"por la fe . . . dar / la vida en defensa justa / de la fe"* (III, 524–530) is denied to him by the *rigor* of the king. Yet, *"firme he de estar en mi fe"* (III, 562). Finally, Fernando's life is snuffed out by his long suffering (after III, 649).

Yet, in the end, both the Portuguese arms and Christian faith triumph on both levels, the secular and the religious. Fernando's spirit leads the Portuguese army to victory. His dead body is exchanged for the living *hermosura* of captive Fénix, thereby symbolically expressing the superiority of spiritual values over the worldly ones. Fernando receives a Christian burial, Ceuta is kept in Christian hands. The Portuguese national honor, which suffered defeat in Act I, is restored through victory in Act III. Even in the light secondary plot, Muley and Fénix will be happily united in marriage.

The world order, upset and threatened in the course of the dramatic action by frightening *cambios de la fortuna*, both personal and national, has been restored. There are no unanswered questions left at the end of the play.

El príncipe constante lacks the one essential quality for tragedy, catastrophe at the end. Fernando is a flawless character who lives unflinchingly by a code of hierarchically arranged values, both secular and religious. His death, chosen by himself in the exercise of his *libre albedrío*, is the logical conclusion of his Christian constancy. His re-appearance as a spirit after death brings on the triumph of right. Fernando is a martyr and a saint, but not a tragic hero.

Tragedy must leave us stirred by the awe-inspiring incomprehensibility of the human situation, our emotions uplifted by the dignity by which the tragic hero bears his destiny imposed upon him against his will, coupled with a more or less consciously felt revolt against the blind cruelty of uncontrollable forces. Our emotions are divided: Aristotle's fear and pity. *El príncipe constante* leaves us at one with ourselves and with the ordained order of the world, both human and divine. *El príncipe constante* is an exemplary Christian martyr play, the play of the

> divino *príncipe constante* (III, 854),
> *príncipe en la fe constante* (III, 888).[1]

1 The foregoing interpretation was read at the meeting of the Comediantes on December 27, 1958, held in connection with the annual MLA convention, to open the discussion of the question "*El príncipe constante*, a tragedy?" Professor Ortigoza presented the opposite view, arguing that the play *is* "a tragedy in the sense in which the Golden Age understood the term." See the "Minutes," by Helen Sears, *BCom*, XI (1959), 6–7.

Part Four
Other Plays

9 · Calderón's Strange Mercy Play

by Edwin Honig

THE SPANISH REPUTATION for pride—fierce, glorious, and absurd—
goes back at least as far as the Cid. Starting as an obscure
soldier-squire, the epic hero is tricked and banished by powerful
enemies among the nobility, vengefully returns, becomes a rich
conqueror, sees his enemies punished, and his daughters married to kings. This type of Christian warrior, whose ideals are
rooted in a mixed heritage of Visigothic and Moorish honor,
later conquers the New World, spreading his peculiarly anachronistic version of militant Catholicism, at once zealously
mystical and egregiously imperialistic. When we come upon
him again in Don Quixote, with all his ideals chastened by
defeat, his persistent absurdity wrings a momentous Pyrrhic
victory from his misadventures. Paradoxically in this way he
revives the standard of Spanish pride so successfully that he
becomes a sort of secular saint—the counterpart to the only
other Spanish saint whose *order* endures, Ignatius Loyola.

In Spanish Golden Age drama something else happens
to heroic pride. Methodized and internalized, it becomes the
conscientious resource of heroes who feel themselves estranged
from society yet act strictly according to its unwritten, vengeful
code of honor. The honor code lends itself to the intolerably
burdened conscience, the embattled condition of outraged pride,
a state of personal fear mirroring society's fear of contamination
and the assault against its autocratic rule. The burdened conscience resorts to a desperate ultrarational dialectic, a kind of
private Holy Inquisition (viz. the stocktaking soliloquies and
dialogues in the honor plays), a legalistic tourney justifying the
precise foul means involved in regaining lost personal honor.
The medicine of hypocrisy is often used to bring about the

catharsis, the shedding of the burden in murder, whereby the social law is preserved and the individual is sacrificed. Even where an alternative is offered in a series of frenzied aggressive acts justified by religious devotion and supernatural mercy, the redeeming action seems almost as hypocritical, self-defensive, and criminally directed as the vengeance principle it is meant to combat. The hero engaged in either cause is similarly induced by disguised sexual passion to perform acts of violence and sadism as grim as the traditional *auto da fé*.

The honor play became a convention before Calderón, mainly because it gave the dramatist a sure-fire formula to capture popular audiences. In a dramatic handbook of the period, Lope de Vega wrote, "Incidents concerning honor are preferable because they move all people forcefully." When as a new playwright in the 1620s Calderón picked up the formula, he made it serve unexpected ends. In his plays honor is more than a thematic convenience or an exemplification of a code; it becomes the chief implement of design, shaping, infusing with life and dramatic necessity the very substance of his plays. The reason for this is that Calderón, more than any other dramatist of his time, is temperamentally disposed to view the world and his art allegorically. His secular plays show a more and more symbolic orientation in their typological use of character and situation, leading toward the form of the *auto*, the sacramental morality, with which he was almost exclusively concerned in the last thirty years of his career.

To the allegorist the world is a permanent battleground for the strategic maneuvers of body and soul, best typified in the *Psychomachia* of Prudentius, the early Spanish-Latin poet. The literary allegorist gives first importance to this theme, exploiting it with the whole armory of his artistic contrivances until it becomes inextricable from the work itself. Calderón turned the honor code into a complex dramaturgical machine entirely directed to serving as an allegorical purveyor of his theme. To anyone aware of the multiple effects, the condensations of meaning, and the urgent tone of anxiety which such a form produces, the language and craftsmanship of Calderón's plays immediately appear to be full of allegorical devices. One cannot in any case disregard the devices, for they are used with uncommon persistence. And when such uses are probed they reveal something wholly different from the chilling artifices, monstrous rhetoric, and casuistic apology they are often taken for. They point to a triumph of sensibility over severely limited materials and the effects of a relentless, largely forbidding, ideology. It is only when these matters are mistakenly viewed by realistic criteria that Calderón's work collapses into absurdity.

In Calderón's definitive honor play, *Secret Vengeance for Secret Insult* (1635), honor's surrogate is the king and its instrument is Don Lope, "membered to the body" of the state. For the most part, the dramatic action is significantly internalized through Lope's soliloquies. The legalistic development of the theme is worked out appropriately in secret, through definitions of his state of mind, implemented by his conscientious strategy. Symbolic counterparts to this action appear in the critically realistic speeches of his servant Manrique, in the recurrent elemental symbolism throughout the play, and through the various inset actions and witnessings which other characters introduce. Dramatically we are aware of a constant balancing and symmetry of processes; the play's highly schematized structure, based on the allegorical treatment of theme, makes for sharp but discrete doubling effects, like sounds counterposed to echoes and images counterposed to mirrored reflections.

In *Devotion to the Cross* (1633),[1] where the honor theme is eclipsed by an incest situation and transcended by supernatural mercy, there is a blurring of dramatic action, an impression of structural imbalance and of a thematic resolution which shocks belief. One reason for this difference between the plays is that the action of thought in *Devotion* is largely externalized; there is no nice thematic complementariness set up between auxiliary characters and the principal agents. And because the allegory is revealed through what the main characters do, the course of action must be taken as a continuous analogue to the archetypal situation of man's fall and redemption. Though the play is structurally ragged and esthetically less satisfying than *Secret Vengeance*, it is more moving. Like *Hamlet* or *Doctor*

---

1 All translations from *Devotion to the Cross* are from *Calderón: Four Plays* (New York: Hill and Wang, Inc., 1961), edited, with an introduction, by Edwin Honig. Reprinted by permission of the publisher.

Faustus the play's dramaturgic failure is somehow overcome by its resonant tone of outrage and the depths of implication at its center. The gross melodrama enforces a pathetic, and strategically delayed, action of self-realization, and this is achieved by a flouting of the very credibility the play insists upon in order to make its point.

For us the play is problematic; for Calderón's contemporaries it was little more than a religious thriller, a lesson in heavenly clemency steeped in blood and spiced with incest. But our problem with it is not how to swallow the melodrama with its religious message in one gulp, which is what troubled nineteenth-century critics of the play. For Albert Camus, who adapted *Devotion* in French, neither the dramatic tenor nor the morality was anachronistic when he remarked:

> Grace transfiguring the worst of criminals, goodness wakened by excessive evil are for us, believers and non-believers alike, familiar themes. But it was three centuries before Bernanos that Calderón in the *Devotion* provocatively illustrated the statement that "Grace is everything," which still tempts the modern conscience in answer to the nonbeliever's "Nothing is just."

To go further: the larger problem of belief depends upon how we understand the implications of honor and incest in the play. What, we may ask, has honor to do with incest and, if there is a real connection, does this account for the resonances we feel in the play as well as the shock of poetic justice underlying the thaumaturgic actions at the end? Unless we frame the problem this way we must stop with a literal reading of the play, and a literal reading of *Devotion* leads to a tangle of absurdities.

Lisardo has challenged his friend Eusebio to a duel for daring to court Julia, Lisardo's sister, without asking permission of Curcio, their father. Eusebio, as Lisardo tells him, would not qualify as her suitor anyway since he is presumably not of noble blood. So Lisardo must now redress the blight on the family honor brought about by Eusebio's rash suit, and Julia must be made to end her days in a convent. Eusebio tells Lisardo the story of his strange birth at the foot of a cross and the charmed life he has led; then, vowing to have Julia at any price, he mortally wounds his antagonist. But in answer to the dying Lisardo's plea to be shriven, Eusebio carries him off to a monastery. Following this, Eusebio enters Curcio's house secretly, speaks with Julia, hides when her father appears and, after the body of Lisardo is brought in and Curcio leaves, Eusebio emerges and carries on an impassioned dialogue with her over Lisardo's corpse; then at Julia's bidding he escapes, promising never to see her again.

In Act Two Eusebio is a refugee from justice and the leader of a band of highwaymen, notorious for their crimes in the mountain passes and nearby villages. Eusebio spares the life of a traveling priest, Alberto, and exacts a promise from him to be shriven before dying. Next, he breaks into Julia's convent, where he is about to rape her when he discovers she bears the same sign of the cross on her breast which he bears on his. He will have nothing to do with her now, and escapes. She leaves the convent to search for him, although he does not know this. Meanwhile Curcio, directed by the law to capture Eusebio dead or alive, leads a group of peasants and soldiers through the mountain. There he reveals the story, partly hinted at in the first act, of his mistrust and jealousy of his wife Rosmira. We learn of the ruse by which he brought her to the mountains when she was pregnant, and of his attempt to kill her there. We also learn that he had left Rosmira for dead at the foot of the cross, where she had given birth to twins; on returning home he found her, miraculously transported there, with the infant Julia, the other child having been lost.

In Act Three Julia, disguised as a man, is captured and brought before Eusebio. Left alone with him, she first attempts to kill him, then is persuaded to tell her story, which turns out to be a fantastic tale of multiple murders she has committed since leaving the convent. She is interrupted by the report of Curcio's arrival. When Eusebio and Curcio meet both are momentarily immobilized by a feeling of mutual sympathy. They fight briefly without swords and are interrupted by Curcio's men, who chase Eusebio; they slash at him until he topples from the cliff and falls dying at the foot of the same cross where he was born. Discovered there by Curcio, he is acknowledged as a long-lost son, Julia's twin, and dies. Meanwhile the approach of Alberto, the priest, causes the dead

Eusebio to revive and call out. The priest confesses him and Eusebio gives up the ghost in a scene witnessed by Curcio and his group, as well as the disguised Julia and the highwaymen. Revealing herself now, Julia publicly confesses her crimes, but when her father advances to strike her, she reaches for the cross, which ascends heavenward and bears her away with the dead Eusebio.

Most critics have been annoyed by the play's hypocrisy, its crude religious propaganda, its perverse morality which pardons the devout but unsympathetic criminal. Among the few contrary opinions are William Entwistle's view of the play as "a representable idea" and A. A. Parker's insistence that it be read in terms of the unity of its theme. Actually, only when the play is read allegorically does it become intelligible despite its strange immorality.

Through Eusebio, its chief character, *Devotion* represents the figurative fall and redemption of mankind. As a figure for the fallen Adam, Eusebio is redeemed by the Cross ("tree divine"), which bears him heavenward, and thus fulfills his "secret cause"—a prefiguration, as Adam in the Bible prefigures Christ. At infancy he is abandoned (assumed to be "lost") at the foot of the cross where, we learn later, his mother fell under the hand of his jealous father. Having no identity, Eusebio takes the cross as a totemic object which corresponds to the talisman etched on his breast like a birthmark. This makes him a candidate for salvation, as it does Julia his twin, who is similarly marked. As Eve may be said to have been Adam's twin, and as both were victims of the tree of the knowledge of good and evil, so Eusebio and Julia share a common destiny, part of which is to be restored through grace by the Cross, the tree of eternal life. The implication of incest, which underlies the act of original sin in Genesis, is here metaphysically, if not sacramentally, material to Calderón's allegory. The reason for this is that Eusebio must learn who he is, which he can do only by discovering and rejoining Julia, his other half. But to do so he must relive symbolically the primal scene in the garden, whose analogue in the play is the convent where Julia, as "the bride of Christ," is immured.

Another analogue suggested here is that of the body and

the soul, the twin or complementary entities. The soul (Eusebio) seeks to be restored to the body (Julia) from which it has been separated. When Eusebio finds Julia in the convent and is about to re-enact the primal deed, he dimly senses in her talismanic sign some heavenly purpose linking her to his secret cause. This foreboding makes him reject her, much as a figure of the new Adam, forewarned of his cause, would reject the old sexual crime—incest, original sin. Yet he must suffer Adam's fall literally as well as symbolically; and this occurs when Eusebio falls from the ladder by the convent wall. In her turn Julia, the fallen body and rejected spouse, is separated by means of the same wall and ladder from re-entering the garden-convent. In ignorance of her destiny, she follows Eusebio and tries to destroy him. The crimes she commits on the way are, like Eusebio's earlier crimes, committed in blind outrage at having been separated from her other half.

In the worldly terms represented by the shepherds, Eusebio's and Julia's cause is criminally absurd. But since at the play's end, worldly discretion and justice are both foiled by the twins' heavenly ascension, it seems clear that it is the spiritual significance of the action, symbolically represented, which interested Calderón.

A Christian hero, Eusebio, like the heroes of all myths, is at the start unaware of his origin, though supremely conscious of some unrevealed fate he has been designated to fulfill. While still ignorant of when and how his fate will be revealed, and because he cannot know if his duel with Lisardo will end disastrously, he tells the story of his life, ticking off each miraculous episode as if to indicate his triumphs over merely earthbound, mortal forces. To Lisardo's grim reminder of Eusebio's inferior blood, Eusebio retorts, "Inherited nobility / is not superior to / nobility that's been acquired." He can say this because he knows he has a patent to act in ways that transcend a nobleman's prerogatives; his "escutcheon" is "inherited from this Cross." He has been tested and has triumphed before; he will triumph again: in the wilderness of the mountain, in the garden-convent, and finally—to his eternal reward when he dies—at the foot of the same cross where he was born. To that cross he is to speak later as Adam might have spoken to God,

remembering the paradise tree: "Forgive me for the injury /
of that first crime against you." And again like Adam with
foreknowledge of his sin, he will say, "I do not blame /
my father for denying me / a cradle. He must have sensed / the
evil that was in me." Eusebio's invocation to the cross at the
end is shot through with transfigured consciousness:

> Oh Tree, where Heaven chose to hang
> the one true fruit to ransom man
> for his first forbidden mouthful!
> Oh flower of paradise regained!
> Rainbow light that spanned the Flood
> and thus pledged peace to all mankind!
> Oh fruitful vine; the harp of yet
> another David; and the tablets
> of another Moses:
> Here I am, a sinner seeking grace.

Eusebio has been transformed from the human agent of his
crimes into a symbolic force voicing the redemptive hope of all
mankind. In this way he defeats the exactions of earthly penal-
ties, and incidentally overcomes the harsh, tyrannical laws of
honor represented by Curcio, the father who survives his wife
and all his children.

Indeed, what about the honor theme which is so abruptly
transcended at the end of the play by divine law? The question
of honor not only bulks large throughout the play but is also
curiously altered in the light of Eusebio's cause. Further in-
quiry tells us something about the unconscious motivations
supporting the honor code as shown in the implicit incest-re-
lationship lividly darting forth from the root situation of the
play. For as they affect human motives, the impulsions and
repulsions of the characters, the conventions of honor relate
to certain basic though unspecified taboos concerning the sexual
assault of male against female in the same family. But we must
begin with the first recorded sexual relationship, in Genesis,
and then go on to the society represented in Calderón's plays.

In effect the Genesis story demonstrates an archetypal incest situation inherent in man's disobedience, his fall from
God's grace, and his knowledge of good and evil. Taken as a
paradigm for man's earthly condition, the sexual crime called

original sin derives from a transgression against divine command, a transgression that brings with it the knowledge of guilt.
Instigated by Eve, man rebels against a paternal authority,
Jehovah, who punishes her accordingly: "I will greatly multiply
thy sorrow and thy conception; in sorrow thou shalt bring forth
children; and thy desire shall be to thy husband, and he shall
rule over thee." Later in Genesis (V, 2), one finds, "Male and
female created he them; and blessed them, and called their
name Adam, in the day when they were created." The creation
of man and woman out of one body, the division of interests
indicated between male and female, the transgression against
authority, the sorrow of sex and childbearing, and the dominance of Adam over Eve are set down as almost simultaneous
events and become an archetypal situation.[2]

It may be assumed, then, that Eve's transgression is con-
genital and innate: as woman, she will always rebel against
the authoritarian principles. Eve, "the mother of all living,"
will be a divisive force in fallen society, just as she was in
paradise. One way to counteract her innate rebelliousness is to
idealize her, as the Middle Ages did: first, symbolically, by ele-
vating the Virgin Mary as an object of worship; secondly, by
lodging the image of woman as a venerated but scarcely at-
tainable love object in the tradition of courtly love. Another
way is to bind her, as the prize and victim of transgression, to
a code of honor—a role descending from the courtly tradition

2 I have summarized elsewhere J. J. Bachofen's view of such a situation:
"Archetypal situations of this sort apparently involve the dynamic interplay of two broad, antagonistic principles. One might say the conflict between these principles is nearly pervasive enough to affect every emotion
and every move a person makes or thinks of making. Together these principles engender the dichotomies of art evolving out of authoritarian religion,
and relate to the biases of artistic expression we call classical or romantic,
rational or enthusiastic. One principle is the dominance of woman and the
natural virtues imputed to her, which are culturally shaped into the matriarchal ideals of love, equality, peace, mercy, fecundity, the reassuring peri-
odicity of nature, human freedom, brotherhood, and the world as an earthly
paradise. In opposition is the powerful and now triumphant principle of
male authority, which encompasses all the virtues of civilized life: law,
conscience, justice, military heroism; the concepts of hierarchy, primogeni-
ture, and individualism; and the material conquest over nature." (*Dark
Conceit: the Making of Allegory* [Evanston: Northwestern University Press,
1959], p. 35.)

and modified by the needs of an authoritarian society, typical of seventeenth-century Spain.

The peculiarly tight, claustrophobic condition of the honor code appears to derive from an already tense, anxiety-ridden view, featured in myth and religion, of woman's unreconciled position between transgressor and idol. In addition, this view is overlaid by the historical and social exigencies of an imperial Spain warring against Protestantism as it had for centuries warred against Islam. In this struggle the impossible myth of Spanish Christian purity and pure-blooded (*castizo*) descent would have to be sustained against the millennial evidence of intermarriage with Berbers, Moslems, and Jews, not to mention cultural assimilation with other peoples of Western and Mediterranean Europe, going back to the early Phoenicians. The avowal that one is an "old Christian Catholic," repeated so often in Renaissance Spanish literature, becomes a self-defensive cry; vainglorious and perversely aggressive, it reminds one of Nazi Germany's self-conscious aryanism. And so where the invasion of one's honor is sexually directed, an attack on one's personal pure-bloodedness, with social and religious implications, is also immediately assumed.

In the autocratic society of Calderón's plays, every family seems to be a Spain-in-little seeking to preserve itself against the real or imagined, but always chronic, invasions of lawless forces from the outside. That the laws of honor are inhuman and tyrannical—a protest constantly being voiced by Calderón's heroes—does not interfere with their being fulfilled. And as they are being fulfilled, often in strictest secrecy, we are struck by the incredible, tragic strength of will involved in acting upon an impossible ideal according to an impossible sense of justice.

The fear of incest and the fear of sexual assault become one and the same thing; particularly notable in *Devotion to the Cross*, the same fear is evident in most of Calderón's honor plays. In addition, the incest barrier is complemented by the religious barrier between different faiths as well as by the social barrier between classes; and behind such barriers lurks the constant fear of contamination. Life under these circumstances is seen as warfare, catastrophe, and fatality, in which the vaguest hint of misdemeanor is as culpable as any number of overt murders. Where authoritarian justice rules, whether theocratic or monarchic, to think or to be tempted as a human being (the hero in *Secret Vengeance* exclaims, "How is it one thinks or speaks at all?") is as dangerous as to put one's thoughts and temptations into action. What makes the honor code so strange to us is that it is a reduction (often to absurdity) of an imperialistic legal structure, from its embodiment in ecclesiastical and state authority to an individual psychological problem, without any mitigation of its impersonal emphasis. What would justify legal punishment by state or church—the impersonal need to preserve the community against assaults by criminal or heretic—becomes bizarre when voiced as a rationale by human beings following the letter of the honor code. They act as though they had set some gigantic, superhuman machine in motion, which is just what they have done. What makes for further bizarreness is the unconscious irony with which they speak in rationalizing their human pride as the cause of justice while being ignorant that they themselves are part of the machine and that their voice is actually the voice of the machine. The pride they boast of concerns the acts and strategies of will —their skill, their cunning; what they do not know is that such pride is simply the fuel that makes the honor machine run. Human pride, then, frequently becomes a sign not of personal satisfaction but of the impersonal glorification of the legal structure; and the act which the human agents engineer in its name becomes a personal *auto da fé*, a self-punishing sacrifice in the name of a super-personal faith.

That this makes for dramatic irony in Calderón's plays may be seen in the various views, ranging from satiric to sacramental, with which the central character's situation is regarded by other characters as well as the opposing views he has of it himself. The dramatic irony is further evident in the rapid glimpse we get of the hero's fate at the end of the play, where he appears at best a Pyrrhic victor, exhausted, wrung out by the machine, and hardly distinguishable from his victim. Dramatic irony is highly schematized in Calderón's plays, being part of, if not indeed the instrument for creating, a larger moral irony. It is interesting to see how the ironic form shapes the honor-bound figure of Curcio in *Devotion*.

An aspect of the moral irony made explicit here is that the avenger complains against the tyrannical laws of honor, though they are the only laws he can follow in exacting his revenge. But an even more pronounced irony is that the object of Curcio's revenge, Eusebio, is redeemed at the end by a higher law than that of honor, so that the matter is literally taken out of Curcio's hands. Since the action of the play is allegorical, we can no more read this final turn of events realistically than we can any other part of the play. The literal meaning is apparent: Curcio is not avenged, and in not being avenged, the course of honor which he has pursued throughout is defeated. How then are we to take his defeat and, by clear analogy, since he is its implement, the defeat of honor? The obvious answer is that honor has been superseded by a miracle; the intervention of divine powers indicates that Eusebio is not to be punished, but having entered into a state of grace is, on the contrary, given his heavenly reward along with Julia. Curcio's last speech —his final remarks to the audience are simply conventional and do not count—is clearly a revenger's furious threat addressed to Julia, an intended victim: "I shall kill you with my own two hands, / and have you die as violently / as you have lived." She pleads to the Cross, and as Curcio "is about to strike her," she embraces it and so is lifted heavenward with Eusebio. Curcio could not have been more plainly foiled, and to say that his vengeance, including his authority for seeking it, has been superseded by divine intervention, does not seem a full or satisfactory answer. For apparently Curcio was mistaken—just as badly mistaken here, when about to kill his daughter, as he was earlier when striking at his innocent wife, who was similarly rescued by the Cross. The deeper moral irony, then, is that the laws of honor, so assiduously upheld by Curcio, are indeed defeated and their justification, as enacted by their avenger here, is shown to be reprehensible on the highest possible authority.

Is honor here defeated or merely superseded? To seek a fuller answer to the question, one must rephrase it to accord with Curcio's allegorical role in the play. In what way is Curcio, the surrogate of honor and an omnipotent figure in the community, responsible for the fate which his family suffers? First, and most generally, it is evident that by accusing his wife of infidelity and seeking to kill her on admittedly groundless evidence, Curcio touches off a series of actions which ends with the death of his three children and his wife. Secondly, it is made clear that Curcio is temperamentally handicapped: he is prodigal, rash, desperate, and overweeningly proud. Some of these attributes are inherited and reinforced to his own detriment by his own children, in a way suggestive of King Lear. Lisardo's brief appearance before he is killed by Eusebio seems at least partly intended to characterize his father:

> My father
> was a profligate who rapidly
> consumed the great estate
> his family had left him.
> In so doing, he was heedless
> of the straitened circumstances
> to which his children were reduced.
> And yet, although necessity
> may beggar one's nobility,
> it does not lessen in the least
> the obligations one is born with.

Following his inherited obligation, Lisardo must challenge Eusebio for lacking the noble qualifications to court his sister Julia. Lisardo's pronouncement concerning his sister, considering it is addressed to her lover who is also his friend, seems precipitous and mechanical, as though echoing a catechism learnt from his father:

> An impoverished gentleman
> who finds his fortune does not meet
> the requirements of his rank
> must see to it his maiden daughter,
> rather than pollute his blood
> by marriage, is taken off
> in safety to a convent.
> In all this, poverty's the culprit.
> Accordingly, tomorrow, my sister
> Julia will quickly take the veil,
> whether she wishes to or not.

Julia's subsequent report confirms the fact of her brother's anxious nature. Lisardo's face pales, drained by suspicion; he prevaricates—"snatched the key / impulsively, and angrily / unlocked the drawer," to discover the evidence of Eusebio's courtship; then, "without a single word, oh God? / he rushed out to find my father. / Then inside his room behind locked doors, / the two of them spoke loud and long— / to seal my fate. . . ." Lisardo is hardly distinguished from his father, whose purpose he is serving before he is killed. Later, when Julia questions Curcio's decision to put her into a convent, his voice seems simply a magnification of Lisardo's catechism. "Right or wrong, my will / is all you need to know." "My decision will suffice, and that / has been resolved. The matter's closed." "Rebel, hold your tongue! Are you mad? / I'll twist your braids around your neck, / or else I'll rip that tongue of yours / out of your mouth with my own hands / before it cuts me to the quick again." Curcio immediately identifies Julia's rebellion with her dead mother's, now impulsively finding "proof" where later he admits no evidence existed.

> So at last I have the proof
> of what I long suspected:
> that your mother was dishonorable,
> a woman who deceived me.
> So you attack your father's honor,
> whose luster, birth, nobility
> the sun itself can never equal
> with all its radiance and light.

It is apparent from this moment on that Curcio, hiding his defects behind the shield of honor, is steering a course which must victimize Julia as surely as he has victimized his elder son Lisardo and wife Rosmira. Though victimized as well, Eusebio listens to a higher law in his worship of the Cross. It would be possible to show similarly that Curcio's defects of despair, pride, and simple-minded credulity also influence the course of events. And though the exemplification of such personal defects would suffice to support the action in realistic terms, this is not what we get in *Devotion to the Cross*. What we get instead is allegorical action, action by analogy, by symbolic counterpart. By such action Curcio figures dominantly as a type of vengeful Jahveh, the thunder god in Genesis, the creator and punisher of the incestuous pair who exceeded the commandment and attained to a knowledge of good and evil—as in their separate ways Eusebio and Julia do. In the Bible the vengeful God is superseded by a sacrificed human God, who comes as Christ and redeems the Adamic sin. The code of honor, one might say, is similarly transcended in *Devotion*. It is superseded and defeated as a partial truth, but without being destroyed or removed—as the Old Testament is superseded by the New.

The attraction and repulsion which lead Eusebio towards and away from Julia, and which induce her to act in complementary movements, have been discussed in terms of the Adam and Eve analogy and the body-soul analogy. Similarly, a movement from repulsion to attraction is evident in the relationship between Curcio and Eusebio, and the effect is concentrated wholly in Act Three. Two of Curcio's speeches summarize this shift: "his chilling blood cries out / to me so timidly. And if/ his blood were not my own in part, / it would not beckon me, / nor would I hear it cry." "How I hated him / alive; now how I grieve his death!" As soon as father and son confront one another, there is mutual affinity between them, though they do not know they are related. It is so intense that Eusebio refuses to use his sword to fight Curcio. When they struggle barehanded, the sense of their combat is dreamlike—a scene reminiscent of a more famous father-son contention in Calderón's *Life is a Dream*. Eusebio, who is unwilling to surrender to the law, will nevertheless give himself up to Curcio, out of "respect." And Curcio, though he has long hunted Eusebio, suddenly offers to let him escape. Eusebio refuses, and when Curcio's men arrive, the father intervenes; to his men's astonishment he suggests the alternative of a legal trial: "I'll be / your advocate before the law." But it is too late; the honor machine has already moved closer to its inexorable goal: Eusebio is mortally wounded by Curcio's men at the foot of the cross.

In his despair Curcio recognizes the inefficacy of the honor machine and admits a guilt he can no longer hide from himself. The mystery of the twin birth at the cross is a mystery which he, as the surrogate of honor and fallen pride, is not prepared to contend with. Mercy is not a principle which autocratic honor accepts. We witness Curcio's gradually increasing helplessness, a condition which the avenging thunder god of Genesis might experience in confronting the imminent redemption of his "son," Adam, gradually transfigured into Christ. Overwhelmed by the clemency of the Cross, Curcio further astonishes his men by telling them to "Take up this broken body / of Eusebio's, and lay it / mournfully aside till there is time / to build an honorable / sepulcher from which his ashen gaze / may contemplate my tears." To this request they reply with the outraged disbelief of men who have similarly become cogs in the honor machine.

Tirso:	What? How can you think of burying a man in holy ground who died beyond the pale of Church and God?
Blas:	For anyone like that, a grave here in the wilderness is good enough!
Curcio:	Oh, villainous revenge! Are you still so outraged you must strike at him beyond the grave?
	[Exit Curcio, weeping.]

But there is still the final and clinching irony to account for. If Curcio admits the defeat of honor before the miracle of heavenly clemency, how can he suddenly revert to the vengeance principle at the end when he tries to destroy Julia? Curcio unwittingly instigates this turn and countermovement by recognizing the mercy principle; his recognition calls forth Julia's confession.

Curcio:	My dearest son! You were not so wretched or forsaken after all, when in your tragic death you merit so much glory. Now if only Julia would recognize her crime.
Julia:	God help me! What is this I hear, what ominous revelation? Can it be that I who was Eusebio's lover was his sister too? Then let my father and the whole wide world, let everybody know about my crimes. My perversions hound and overwhelm me, but I shall be the first to shout them out.

> Let every man alive be told
> that I am Julia, Julia
> the criminal, and of all
> the infamous women ever born,
> the worst. Henceforth my penances
> will be as public as the sins
> I have confessed. I go now to beg
> forgiveness of the world for the vile
> example I have given it,
> and pray that God forgive
> the crime of all my life.

Here Curcio erupts and attempts to kill her, at which she pledges her word to the Cross to "atone beneath your sign / and be born again to a new life," and the Cross bears her away to heaven. If we momentarily overlook this heavy melodramatic turn, Calderón's serious allegorical purpose will emerge. Desperate and defeated though he is, Curcio still incarnates the vengeance principle—a principle which survives in him, even after he has been chastened by the higher law. In this he is like Eusebio, who represents the mercy principle and must survive his own death and revive in order to be shriven. Because he embodies the honor code, Curcio must strike out as he does, spontaneously, against Julia's offense and dishonor. And her offense in this instance is precisely her public confession of guilt instigated by Curcio's wishful remark. For according to the code, the public admission that one's honor has been wronged compounds the wrong that has already been committed against it. And so Julia's public declaration not only constitutes the last blow against her father's crumbling defenses but also makes explicit the cruel inoperativeness of the honor code when faced with any personal human cry for clemency. Julia's assertion that she will make her penances public is intolerable to honor and inadmissible to a code which categorically denies foreigveness. By implication there is no forgiveness on earth but only in heaven.

If as an honor figure Curcio cannot extend mercy, he is likewise incapable, as a figure for the Genesis thunder god, of offering reconciliation to Julia. And in the final exchange between the two, we are also reminded that Julia's "crime of all my life" like Eve's "crime" is not forgivable in terms of the old dispensation in Genesis, where the sexual act is incestuous and the original crime of the creation underlies the discovery of good and evil. Significantly, it is when she learns of the incestuous relationship with Eusebio that Julia makes her public declaration. As a type of Eve, Julia is the quintessential criminal ("of all / the infamous women ever born, / the worst"), universally damned by authoritarian law. Only the figure of a sacrificed god, according to the new dispensation, can redeem her, as Eusebio does at the end. We see then that honor is a form of the old, merciless, unregenerated, earthbound, dehumanized, patriarchal law, which is ultimately self-defeating. It prevails to the end, and presumably will continue to exist on earth opposing the merciful, regenerative, humane, and matriarchal law of heaven, symbolized in the Cross which has vanquished it.

At the conclusion of the play, where the Cross triumphs so resolutely, so providentially, and so patently as a *deus ex machina*, we are inclined to minimize its connection with the rest of the drama. Yet its function throughout is not only essential to the theme but also integral to the action. One might say that the final appearance of the Cross culminates many symbolic manifestations, from the beginning, of an extraordinarily complex role. And that role, in fact, is to serve dramatically as a complementary mechanism, a machine working in countermotion to the honor machine.

We first hear of the Cross early in the first act in Eusebio's lengthy recital of the events of his life, while holding off Lisardo. Eusebio's story is eager, rapt, proud, enthusiastic. He has been the subject of strange, benevolent miracles; he rapidly imparts his sense of wonder and mystery at these happenings— and is never so confident again. The effect of the speech, more notable for the feeling it releases than for its literal sense, is to introduce a sensation of power and authority into a tense situation. The tension leading to an impasse is exemplified in the opening scene of the play by the peasants Gil and Menga, vainly trying to drag their stalled donkey out of the mud. When Lisardo and Eusebio arrive, the impasse is augured in their pale, silent, distraught appearance. Gil describes them: "My, how pale / they look, and in the open fields / so early in the morning! / I'm sure they must have eaten mud / to look so constipated." Whenever the Cross is introduced subsequently, the effect is similarly to dispel an impasse, initiate a contrary action, or metaphorically to lend a new dimension to the scene. Eusebio's Cross "that towered over me at birth, / and whose imprint is now pressed / upon my breast" is a talismanic object which he serves and which actively serves him, symbolic of his paternity, a charismatic "symbol of some secret cause, / unrevealed as yet." And its "secret cause" gradually begins to emerge in a series of significant actions.

Lisardo's dying plea "by the Cross Christ died on" deflects Eusebio's sword and makes him carry the fallen man away to be shriven, an action which later aids in Eusebio's own redemption. When Lisardo's corpse lies between the divided lovers, Julia and Eusebio, there is a curious dramatic effect which the theatricality of the scene emphasizes. Curcio's two living children seem here to form the horizontal appendages of a cruciform figure whose vertical stalk is the dead Lisardo. As the pair speak across the corpse we realize that it is the only time when the three children are joined together in the play. Joined, but also divided by the visible presence of the dead brother. That one power of the Cross is to join and another is to separate will appear significantly again.

At the beginning of Act Two, Alberto, the priest, is saved when Eusebio's bullet is stopped by the holy book the priest carries in his tunic. The metaphor Eusebio uses underlies the merciful power of the Cross to deflect the course of violence: "How well that flaming shot / obeyed your text by turning / stubborn lead softer than wax!" By this token Eusebio releases the priest who will reappear only once, in the third act, to confess him. The next reference to the Cross occurs in Curcio's soliloquy describing the miracle which saved his wife after she protested her innocence at the foot of the Cross, where he thought he had killed her. There the twins Eusebio and Julia were born, though, as we learn later, Eusebio was left behind when Rosmira was rescued by divine intervention and brought home with Julia. Subsequently, when Eusebio forces his way into the convent to violate Julia, he discovers that she too bears the imprint of the Cross on her breast, and fearfully withdraws.

Here the Cross serves to prevent the incestuous act, and in doing so separates the Adamic from the Christ figure in Eusebio. Julia and Eusebio are not meant to repeat the paradisiacal crime under the Eden tree; they must now be separated from one another. They are only destined to be joined in an act of heavenly redemption at the Cross where they were born.

As we observed, when Eusebio falls from the ladder leaning against the convent wall, he symbolically enacts Adam's fall. Of this fact he seems dimly aware on rising: "Oh Cross Divine, this I promise you / and take this solemn vow / with strict attention to each word: / wherever I may find you, / I shall fall upon my knees / and pray devoutly, with all my heart." Julia, too, vaguely senses that her destiny is to follow Eusebio's "fall" by way of the ladder, though she is not impelled by heavenly signs nor aware, as he is, of the Cross's "secret cause." At this point she may simply be following the Genesis prescription—"and thy desire shall be to thy husband, and he shall rule over thee"—when she says, "This is where he fell; then I / must fall there too and follow him." Or perhaps she is feeding her desire with a later rationalization: "Does not my creed tell me / that once I give assent in thought / I thereby commit the crime?" Yet when she continues in this vein, we see that she has clearly identified her destiny with Eusebio's, though she may not know what that destiny is.

> Did not Eusebio scale
> these convent walls for me?
> And did I not feel pleased
> to see him run such risks
> for my sake? Then why am I afraid?
> What scruple holds me back?
> If I leave now I do the very thing
> Eusebio did when he entered;
> and just as I was pleased with him,
> he'll be pleased to see me too,
> considering the risks I've taken
> for his sake. Now I have assented,
> I must take the blame. And if
> the sin itself be so tremendous,
> will enjoying it be any
> less so? Since I have assented
> and am fallen from the hand of God. . . .

In modern terms the covert incest motive may be fused here
with the affinity science has noted between closely related
persons, particularly twins, causing similar behavior patterns
because of similarities between their neuro-electrical activities.
But in Christian terms it is clear that once Julia "falls" (i.e.
descends the ladder), she is seized by the chilling evil of the
symbolic act: "I find that my esteem for mankind, / honor,
and my God is nothing / but an arid waste. Like an angel /
flung from Heaven in my demonic / fall I feel no stirring of / repentance."

With this admission she becomes Eve, the transgressor in
Eden and cohort of the fallen angel, the eternal rebel against
the patriarchal order of society. Her rebellion is an assault
against man's contempt, the authoritarian abuse of her fruitful
power to love and to heal the divisive prohibitions which sacrifice individual men to its order:

> I am alone, in my confusion
> and perplexity. Ingrate, are these
> your promises to me? Is this
> the sum of what you called your love's mad
> passion, or is it my love's madness?
> How you persisted in your suit—
> now by threats, now by promises,
> now as lover, now as tyrant,
> till I at last submitted to you.
> But no sooner had you become
> master of your pleasure
> and my sorrow than you fled
> before you had possessed me.
> Now in escaping you have
> vanquished me entirely.
> Merciful Heaven, I am lost
> and dead! Why does nature provide
> the world with poisons when the venom
> of contempt can kill so swiftly?
> So his contempt will kill me,
> since to make the torment worse
> I must follow him who scorns me.
> When has love been so perverse before? . . .
> Such is woman's nature that
> against her inclination
> she withholds that pleasure
> which she most delights to give.

The capacity to sin is no different from the capacity to hurt and be hurt, perversely, against one's inclination. But to tell one's hurt, confess one's sin and be forgiven is to triumph over the corruptions of evil enforced by social law. As Julia says, this forgiveness can be extended by the restorative power of providence:

> faith teaches
> there is nothing which the clemency
> of Heaven cannot touch or reach:
> all the sparkling constellations,
> all the sands of all the oceans,
> every atom, every mote upon
> the air, and all these joined together,
> are as nothing to the sins
> which the good Lord God can pardon.

Contempt, scorn, division, separation, hopelessness, despair— these are the goads to crime and destructiveness. And this is what Julia recognizes when the ladder leading back to the convent is withdrawn:

> Ah, but I begin to understand
> the depths of my misfortune.
> This is a sign my way is barred,
> and thus when I would strive
> to creep back, a penitent,
> I am shown my cause is hopeless.
> Mercy is refused me.
> Now a woman doubly scorned,
> I shall perpetrate such
> desperate deeds even Heaven
> will be astounded, and the world
> will shudder at them till
> my perfidy outrages all time
> to come, and the deepest pits
> of hell shall stand agape
> with horror at my crimes.

Understood symbolically, according to the dialectic of fall and redemption, male and female principles, the subversion of humanity by the authoritarian necessity of honor, Julia's intentions and subsequent crimes are not the ludicrous things they appear to be when viewed according to cause-and-effect realism. They are dramatic epiphanies proceeding from closely related lines of thought, feeling, and action rising from the implications of the thematic "devotion to the cross." It is only the misuse of symbolic meaning which is ludicrous. Calderón makes this clear immediately following Julia's speech, at the start of Act Three.

Gil enters "covered with crosses; a very large one is sewn on his breast." The situation is reversed: a man is now following a woman's "bidding," as Gil says with regard to Menga, adding,

> I go. . .
> scouring the mountainside for firewood,
> and for my own protection
> I've concocted this stratagem.
> They say Eusebio loves crosses.
> Well, here I am, armed from head to foot
> with them.

But Gil's cross is not charismatic. He sees Eusebio, hides in a bush and is immediately stuck with thorns. Eusebio at this point is brooding over the meaning of the Cross inscribed on Julia's breast: "I was driven, by the impulse of a higher power / whose cause prevailed against my will, / forbidding me to trespass on / the Cross—the Cross that I respect . . . . / Oh Julia, the two of us were born / subject to that sign, and thus I fear / the portents of a mystery / which only God can understand." And the scene where he discovers Gil is oddly discordant, mixing serious and comic elements to such effect that Eusebio's cause appears ludicrous.

Gil [aside]:   I can't stand it any longer;
              I'm stung all over!
Eusebio: There is
              someone in the bushes. Who's there?
Gil [aside]:   Well, here's where I get tangled
              in my snare.
Eusebio [aside]: A man tied to a tree,
              and wearing a cross on his breast!
              I must be true to my word and kneel.
Gil: Why do you kneel, Eusebio?
              Are you saying your prayers, or what?
              First you tie me up, then you pray
              to me. I don't understand.
Eusebio: Who are you?
Gil: Gil. Don't you remember?

Ever since you tied me up here
with that message, I've been yelling out
my lungs but, just my luck,
nobody's yet come by to free me.

Eusebio: But this is not the place
I left you.

Gil: That's true, sir.
The fact is, when I realized that
no one was passing by, I moved on,
still tied, from one tree to the next,
until I reached this spot.
And that's the only reason
why it seems so strange to you.

[Eusebio frees him.]

Eusebio [aside]: This simpleton may be of use
to me in my misfortune.
—Gil, I took a liking to you
when we met the other time.
So now let us be friends.

Gil: Fair enough,
and since we're friends I'll never
go back home but follow you instead.
And we'll be highwaymen together.
They say the life's ideal—not a stitch
of work from one year to the next.

Gil's mention of "the other time" refers to the occasion
in Act Two when Eusebio found Gil and Menga in the mountains, had them tied to tree-trunks, and left them with a crucial
message for Curcio—a message Gil fails to deliver. The message
has to do with something which Curcio does not yet know,
and by its means Eusebio would attempt to reconcile himself
with Lisardo's father and absolve himself from the charge of
murder. Eusebio does not know that Gil did not deliver the
message, nor is it certain that if Gil had done so the effect
would be to alter the course of events up to this point. But
Gil's appearance immediately after Julia's speech at the end of
Act Two, the absurd story he tells Eusebio about progressing
"still tied, from one tree to the next," and Eusebio's own
curiously quixotic reaction to Gil's cross are all, at first glance,
puzzling and disconcerting details. For Gil's antics are bathetic
to the same degree that Eusebio's devoutness is ludicrous, so
that both seem to be defects of taste and dramatic emphasis.

Considered symbolically, however, the scene is anything but bathetic or implausible; on the contrary, it comes as a sharp, immediate reminder of the opposing claims of honor and mercy, of vengeance and devotion, the very theme developed in the play's movements and countermovements we have been tracing. In effect Calderón is reminding us that Eusebio's devotion is a cause squarely opposed to Curcio's vengeance, and that the one has its provenance in a heavenly mystery symbolized by the Cross as the other has in the code of honor. Troubled by the symbol on Julia's breast, Eusebio is caught off-guard when Gil's presence interrupts his thoughts. He does not know it is Gil; all he sees is the cross on Gil's breast, to which he automatically responds by kneeling respectfully, according to his vow. It is the symbol and not the man he responds to. The act immediately makes him out to be a fool—not the crazy fool Gil takes him for, but the "fool in Christ," the devoted servant of the Cross. Gil, of course, has correctly guessed that wearing the cross will protect him from Eusebio, just as it saved Alberto, the priest, at the beginning of Act Two. What Gil does not understand is the objective power and principle of the Cross; and we may see in his being entangled in the briers until Eusebio frees him an exemplum of this mistaken view. The absurd story he tells about moving "still tied, from one tree to the next" is an extension of his mistaken view because it supposes that Eusebio, though dangerous, is merely simple-minded. But the effect of Gil's story is to identify him and to bring Eusebio's attention away from the symbol in order to recognize "the simpleton" who is wearing it. Eusebio awakes to his own situation, his self-defensive strife against Curcio's pursuit of vengeance, in which Gil "may be of use" to him as one who knows the mountainous terrain. On the other hand, all Gil can conclude about Eusebio's offer of friendship is that the other's addiction to crosses somehow involves the charmed life of brigandry—"not a stitch / of work from one year to the next." The fact is, however, that Eusebio's situation is narrowing and, as later events show, he is ridden by anxiety and by the burden of his cause. He is fast approaching his own end, which will entail the complete revelation of heaven's secret symbolized by the Cross. But while waiting for the mystery to unfold, he must contend with Curcio's vengeance. As a result, he acts feverishly, half terrified, half audacious, as a man aware of some impending catastrophe would act.

This is notable in his response to Julia, who has reappeared dressed as a man, and who after attempting to kill him has told the story of her crimes. He says:

> I listen to you fascinated,
> enchanted by your voice,
> bewitched by everything you say,
> although the sight of you
> fills me with dread. . . .
>   I fear Heaven's
> retribution looming over me. . . .
> I live in such horror of that Cross,
> I must avoid you.

His anxiety is also apparent in the orders he gives his men, and later in his hand-to-hand encounter with his father.

> I do not know what reverence
> the sight of you instills in me.
> But I know your suffering awes me
> more than your sword . . .
> and truth to tell, the only
> victory I seek is to fall
> upon my knees and beg you
> to forgive me.

And so it is almost with relief that he receives the mortal wound at the hands of Curcio's men. He can at last yield to his father and die; but also—and this he does not know—he is to be resurrected in order to receive absolution at the foot of the cross where he was born. In this way his destiny is fulfilled, his secret cause revealed, his life career run full cycle. But there is also the posthumous miracle of his heavenly ascension which includes the sanction of Julia. Besides proving Julia's earlier declaration that "there is nothing which the clemency / of Heaven cannot touch or reach," this last miracle reclaims her from the perversely male-dominated role of revenger ("the symbol / of terrifying vengeance") in which the honor machine had cast her. There is perhaps a conclusive irony in this last turn: that the monolithic, all-pervasive engine of the honor machine on earth can only be transcended by the more powerful, absolutist machine of heavenly mercy.

10 · Honor in El alcalde de Zalamea

by C. A. Jones

Los casos de la honra son mejores,
porque mueven con fuerza a toda gente.

When Lope de Vega wrote this in his *Arte nuevo de hacer comedias en este tiempo,* of 1609, he had already had ample opportunity of proving it by his own success in several plays, including *Los comendadores de Córdoba,* with its story of the gruesome vengeance of the Alderman Fernán Alfonso. In that work he gave a definition of honour which might well apply to most of the Golden Age plays in which it appears:

> *Honra es aquélla que consiste en otro;*
> *ningún hombre es honrado por sí mismo;*
> *que del otro recibe la honra un hombre;*
> *ser virtuoso hombre y tener méritos,*
> *no es ser honrado; pero dar las causas*
> *para que los que tratan les den honra.*[1]

But this honour, however useful as a dramatic motive, was not entirely satisfactory to Lope. In his short story *La más prudente venganza,* he suggested the futility of vengeance for lost honour;[2] in *La Dorotea* it occurred to him that jealousy might be the most reasonable motive for killing a wife, and not offended honour;[3] in the *autos sacramentales* worldly honour is

---

1 Lope de Vega, *Obras,* ed. M. Menéndez y Pelayo, XI, 290b.
2 "Y he sido de parecer siempre que no se lava bien la mancha de la honra del agraviado con la sangre del que le ofendió, porque lo que fue no puede dejar de ser; y es desatino creer que se quita, porque se mata al ofensor, la ofensa del ofendido; lo que hay en esto es, que el agraviado se queda con su agravio y el otro muerto, satisfaciendo los deseos de la venganza, pero no las calidades de la honra, que para ser perfecta no ha de ser ofendida." BAE, XXXVIII, 34a.
3 "Julio: Díjole Armenio a Ciro que no mataban los maridos a sus

frequently condemned, even while, as B. W. Wardropper has pointed out, Lope retained for it a sneaking regard.[4] In the *comedias* themselves, Lope sometimes refused to confine honour to the narrow sense of a nobleman's reputation, as for instance in *Fuente Ovejuna*; and in *Los comendadores de Córdoba* the Veinticuatro protests against the tyranny of honour which forces him to his cruel vengeance.[5]

With Lope's death, in 1635, Calderón became the most important dramatist of Spain, and in the same year he produced his two most striking honour dramas, *El médico de su honra* and *A secreto agravio secreta venganza*, where he portrayed husbands who were fanatically attached to honour, a tyrant whose laws demanded of them the sacrifice of the wives whom they loved, on the merest suspicion of dishonour. In spite of the exaltation they feel at the thought of duty done, they protest bitterly against the *pundonor* and the action it forced upon them;[6] moreover, as Professor Entwistle pointed out, there is at least a hint that they are somewhat abnormal types. Don Gutierre Alfonso de Solís, of *El médico de su honra*, is so jealous of his honour that even before marriage he has left Doña Leonor, the woman to whom he was betrothed, on the very slightest suspicion; Don Lope de Almeida, in *A secreto agravio secreta venganza*, is a noble Portuguese, an old man married to a young wife, who at the same time that he rejoices in his good luck in winning her, feels insecure in his position and excessively fearful of losing his honour.[7] It seems that,

---

mujeres cuando las hallaban con los adúlteros, por la culpa de la ofensa, sino por la rabia de que les hubiesen quitado el amor y puéstole en otros. Ludovico: ¡Extraño pensamiento! Y que mirado bien debe de ser el primer movimiento para matarlas. . . ." Op. cit., III, 4.

4 "Honor in the Sacramental Plays of Valdivielso and Lope de Vega," MLN, LXVI (1951), 81–88.

5 E.g., *"¡Ay, honra, al fin sofística inventora / de tantas ceremonias y locuras!"* Op. cit., in *Obras*, XI, 291a.

6 E.g., *"D. Gutierre: . . . ¿Qué injusta ley condena / que muera el inocente y que padezca . . . ?"* *El médico de su honra*, in *Obras*, ed. Astrana Marín (Madrid, 1945), p. 200b. Cf. *"D. Lope: . . . ¡Ay, honor, mucho me debes! / Júntate a cuentas conmigo. / ¿Qué quejas tienes de mí? / ¿En qué, dime, te he ofendido? / Al heredado valor,"* etc. *A secreto agravio*, ibid., p. 307b.

7 Cf. W. J. Entwistle, *"Honra y duelo,"* RJ, III (1950), 404–420.

however effectively Calderón used the honour theme in these plays, he accepted the usual conception of honour with reservations.

About 1642 Calderón produced *El alcalde de Zalamea*. The critics have always found this play difficult to classify in the dramatist's repertoire. In the closing lines of the play, it is described as an *historia verdadera*, and some, like Ernest Mérimée, have chosen to include it among the historical dramas; [8] others, including Valbuena, have taken their cue from the scenes of military life and called it a *comedia costumbrista*.[9] But it is easy to show that Calderón has taken considerable liberties with history, in many instances following the earlier play of the same name attributed to Lope; moreover, there is much in the play which is of a higher order than the *costumbrista elements*, and Pedro Crespo, Don Lope de Figueroa, and Isabel, at least, are obviously idealized types, though as a whole convincing human beings. For this reason, to call the play a comedy of character is to ignore many improbabilities in these figures, and moreover to invent a *genre* which is practically unknown in the Golden Age. Finally, there are obvious differences between *El alcalde de Zalamea* and the honour plays. The case is not here one of conjugal honour, nor is it that of the cloak and sword comedy.

Yet honour is obviously of great importance in *El alcalde*, though it is so radically different from the tyrant of the first dramas. "*El honor*," says Pedro Crespo, the chief character, "*es patrimonio del alma, y el alma sólo es de Dios*," [10] The old tyrant is there, too, but he comes off second best in the contest with the kind of honour which is dependent on neither king nor birth. It seems to me that in this play Calderón uses the idea of true honour and contrasts it with the conventional honour of Lope and of some of his own earlier plays, which had not altogether satisfied him.

Honour had been used by Lope and by Calderón to create

8 Cf. *Précis d'histoire de la littérature espagnole* (Paris, 1922), pp. 417–421. In the text Mérimée refers to the class as "*ce genre semi-historique*."

9 Cf. A. Valbuena Prat, *Calderón* (Barcelona, 1941).

10 Op. cit., in *Obras*, ed. Astrana Marín, p. 521a.

196   ESSAYS ON THE THEATRE OF CALDERÓN

exciting situations, above all by placing it in jeopardy through
an attack on its most responsible and yet most vulnerable guardian, woman. If the woman were unmarried, she must save the
family honour by marriage to the gallant who had threatened
it, or otherwise by retiring to a convent if her dishonour were
unknown; or, in an extreme case, she must be put to death,
along with the gallant. If the woman were married, her husband
was responsible for killing her lover and herself, and only if the
lover were of royal blood did he escape. Honour was reputation,
and to save reputation, valued more highly than life, a bloody
vengeance was the only solution.

In *El alcalde de Zalamea* honour was defined as something
more than reputation. Pedro Crespo was a *villano*, a rich farmer,
but not a noble, and therefore not entitled to the honour of an
aristocrat or an officer. According to the Captain Don Álvaro,
who abducted Crespo's daughter Isabel, the *villano* had no
honour to lose; [11] according to Pedro Crespo, however, not only
did he possess honour, but this honour had been damaged by
the violation of Isabel. He claimed, as any noble might have
done, that life without this honour held no further value for
him: "*¿Qué importará, si está muerto / mi honor, el quedar
yo vivo?*" [12]

What steps, then, could he, a *villano*, take in order
to secure satisfaction of his honour? The first step, it appeared, was to find the gallant and attempt to make him marry
the offended girl. This failed, and since according to the conventional view of honour he could not attack a noble, not being
noble himself, his only action could be against Isabel. If her
dishonour were unknown, she might be sent to a convent;
otherwise she must be killed.

But Pedro Crespo asserted that he would kill not only
a captain but even the general of the army in defence of
honour.[13] It is doubtful whether, if he had done so, Calderón's
audiences would have tolerated the play. Yet to allow the offence
would also be to court unpopularity from the public. The solution lay ready to hand in the earlier play attributed to Lope de
Vega. There Pedro Crespo was Mayor of Zalamea almost from

11 "*¿Qué opinión tiene un villano?*" *Obras*, p. 519b.
12 *Obras*, p. 530b.
13 Cf. *Obras*, p. 520b.

the beginning. Calderón chose to delay the appointment until a moment when it would be much more effective. At first it appears as an obstacle to Crespo's vengeance, but on further consideration he sees that it is the means of achieving it. However, before acting as mayor, Pedro Crespo, in one of the play's most moving scenes, goes down on his knees and appeals as a man to the Captain to marry his daughter, offering him all his wealth as her dowry. Don Álvaro haughtily refuses his offer, and Pedro Crespo takes up his rod of office and prepares to act in his official capacity. As mayor he is responsible for keeping the peace and securing justice in Zalamea. The Captain's action is manifestly a breach of the peace and of justice, whoever his victim may be; and so Pedro Crespo takes it upon himself to execute vengeance against Don Álvaro, who is garrotted by the public executioner.

Don Lope de Figueroa, when he hears that one of his officers has been imprisoned by a local mayor, is furious, and vows that the latter shall be made to suffer. He does not alter his decision when he finds that the mayor is his old friend Pedro Crespo. But Crespo is saved by the timely appearance of King Philip II, who happens to be passing through Zalamea on the way to Portugal. He inquires into the action of Pedro Crespo, and agrees that it was just. But Crespo has still committed two technical offences: first, he has executed justice outside his own civil province; and secondly he has garrotted the Captain, who as a noble should have been beheaded. Crespo's answer to the first charge is that since the King's justice is one body, it is a matter of little importance which member acts in defence of the whole; while the second charge meets with the ingenious and amusing defence that, since the nobles of Zalamea are well behaved, the executioner has never learned the art of beheading, and has had to make do with a method he did know. Philip accepts these answers, approves Pedro Crespo's action, and makes him Mayor of Zalamea for life. Justice has been done, and incidentally honour has been saved.

Isabel, at the end of the play, goes off to a convent. When she had been violated she assumed that her father would want to put her to death, and for this reason she hesitated to release him when she found him tied to a tree, where he had been left by the soldiers, until she had explained her innocence. But

Pedro Crespo did not want to put her to death. To do so would not have saved his honour, and there was still hope that a marriage would save the day. Presumably because she was innocent the honour which she enjoyed was not taken away, as it would have been if honour merely meant reputation, and retirement to a convent was deemed sufficient to satisfy the demands of the audience.

If Calderón in this play is setting honour as *patrimonio del alma* (that is, the attribute of any human soul and not that of a particular social class) against formal aristocratic honour, and showing the superiority of the former, many of the changes which Calderón made from the earlier play can be explained. Apart from the postponement of Pedro Crespo's appointment as Mayor of Zalamea, these are chiefly connected with the treatment of character.

In the earlier *Alcalde de Zalamea* Pedro Crespo had two daughters, who were seduced by two captains with little difficulty or protest. When they were subsequently abandoned by the captains, there was little cause for sympathy for them in their unhappy plight. Calderón has reduced the two daughters to one, the dignified, idealized Isabel, and she is abducted and raped by one captain. On the other hand, Calderón has added the characters of Juan Crespo, and of Don Mendo, the foolish *hidalgo* with his servant Mendo, and has amplified and ennobled the characters of Pedro Crespo and of Don Lope de Figueroa.

Calderón often chose to embody the themes or central ideas of his plays in a character, surrounded by others who threw this main character, and hence the theme or central idea itself, into relief, sometimes by contrast, sometimes by an illustration on a different level. So Eusebio, in *La devoción de la Cruz*, illustrates the theme that devotion to the Cross is a means of salvation; the *gracioso* Gil covers himself with little wooden crosses to protect himself from the wrath of his master, and by showing how ridiculous a mere material acceptance of the Cross can be, gives a further illustration of the spiritual theme.[14]

14 Cf. E. M. Wilson and W. J. Entwistle, "Calderón's *Príncipe constante*: Two Appreciations," MLR, XXXIV (1939), 207–222.

In *El alcalde de Zalamea* Pedro Crespo represents the kind of honour which is *patrimonio del alma*, while Don Lope de Figueroa embodies the formal, aristocratic concept. Juan Crespo and the Captain show the two contrasted concepts in a less perfect manner. Juan, in the face of his sister's dishonour, attacks Don Álvaro and, failing to wound him mortally, is just about to turn to Isabel, being prevented by her father from killing her, only just in time. As a *villano* Juan has no right to attack an officer, and while his father is alive he has no right to assume responsibility for his sister; so, to avoid a breach of the law of honour and of justice, Pedro Crespo shuts up his son in prison until he himself has had an opportunity to act. Don Álvaro shares the privileges of the noble and of the officer, but fails to realize, as Don Lope does realize, that he has duties as well as privileges, and that respect is due to one's fellow human beings, even if technically they are not men possessing honour. The honour of Don Mendo, described as a type of Don Quixote, is a caricature of the formal, aristocratic kind, and he makes it an excuse for his cowardice and irresponsibility. La Chispa and Rebolledo, two vivid minor characters invented by Calderón, provide us with further interesting sidelights on honour, for the camp follower thinks it an honour to stay by the side of her soldier friend, who also considers himself as a man bound by honour to pay his debts.

It has been maintained that *El alcalde de Zalamea* is the only play of Calderón in which he has departed from his usual norm and invented great characters, and critics have often considered for this reason that it is his finest work.[15] This seems to imply that Calderón was always aiming at the creation of characters, and that only here did he achieve his aim. This view seems to be a mistaken one.[16] It is true that Pedro Crespo and Don Lope de Figueroa stand out in one's memory as few of Calderón's characters do, but I am inclined to think that this is largely an accident. Moreover, they are not altogether probable characters, being highly idealized, while the parallelism of

15 E.g. A. Valbuena Prat, *Calderón*, pp. 81–84.
16 Cf. E. M. Wilson, "*La vida es sueño*," *Revista de la Universidad de Buenos Aires*, Tercera Época, Año IV, 3 & 4 (1946), 61–78.

their attitudes and speeches in certain scenes of the play is a little too forced to be entirely convincing.[17]

The fact that Pedro Crespo and Don Lope de Figueroa are much more highly developed characters than we usually find in Calderón may be due chiefly to the unusual conflict which exists between them as representatives of two different concepts of honour. Conflicts in Calderón are generally between two demands on a single personality, such as those of love and honour. This kind of conflict tends to make the person who faces it into an abstraction or a monster. On the other hand, a conflict between two personalities, representing two different points of view, is likely to lead to their development through mutual influence into more complete human beings.

According to Munárriz, the first writer in modern times to treat Spanish dramatic honour critically, the only defect of Calderón's honour plays in their depiction of life is the fact that they did not place alongside the honour-ridden noble one who was sane and discreet and who would show the injustice of the noble inspired by these deplorable Gothic laws.[18] Perhaps in *El alcalde de Zalamea* Calderón was attempting to show a man who, if not technically noble, was truly honourable, and at the same time sane and discreet, a man who would show the limitations of formal honour.

Pedro Crespo is a yeoman farmer, a man of wealth enjoying a certain independence and dignity in society. He is, we should now say, an honourable man. He is indignant at the attentions of the ridiculous *hidalgo* Don Mendo to his daughter, and he advises his son to avoid gambling debts which he is unable to pay. He is loyal to his king. But he despises *honor postizo* and refuses to buy a patent of nobility which would enable him to avoid the necessity of receiving troops in his house. In all these things Pedro Crespo is an admirable person, and his dignity is nowhere greater than when he kneels before Don Álvaro and begs him to marry his daughter in exchange for his wealth and

17 Cf. Dámaso Alonso and Carlos Bousoño, "La correlación en la estructura del teatro calderoniano," in *Seis calas en la expresión literaria española* (Madrid, 1951), pp. 115–186.

18 L. Munárriz, *"Adiciones"* to H. Blair, *Lecciones sobre la retórica y las bellas artes* (3rd ed., Madrid, 1817), IV, 307.

even the service of himself and his son. Not only is Pedro Crespo a dignified and honourable man; he is successful, sensible, tender-hearted, and prudent. He enjoys the respect of his fellow citizens, marked in their election of him as mayor, an election confirmed for life by King Philip II.

Maccoll made the remark that there is marvellous subtlety in the way in which Calderón suggests that the Captain is, despite his pride of birth, an essentially mean wretch.[19] Calderón was not, of course, anxious to show that the aristocratic or military concept of honour was worthless. He may have protested against the tyranny of conventional honour in the heroic dramas, but he would scarcely have said that this honour had no value at all. And even if the husbands in the honour plays were abnormal or rash, even if their actions made them seem monsters, there was something admirable about them nevertheless. In *El alcalde de Zalamea*, Calderón has not left us with Don Álvaro as the sole, or even the best representative of formal honour. For this part he has chosen the historical figure of Don Lope de Figueroa; and it is perhaps significant that Don Lope only just falls short of the dignity of Pedro Crespo, though we remain with the impression that Pedro Crespo was right. As Don Lope says in their first encounter, in answer to Pedro Crespo's definition of honour as *patrimonio del alma:* "¡Vive Cristo, que parece / que vais teniendo razón!"[20]

Honour, at one time a force of fundamental value in human life, the inspirer of all distinguished and unselfish conduct, as Menéndez Pidal has suggested,[21] had become in many Golden Age plays, and even to some extent in life itself, a tyrant and a monster, limited to the sense of a noble's reputation, and subject to the most detailed and extravagant laws. As such it was a very effective dramatic motive, but even Lope, who knew its value as such, could not help realizing that it was a distortion. Calderón followed Lope in using it as the subject of his most striking plays, but he was perhaps even more aware of the limitations of this narrow view of honour. Even in its most exag-

19 N. Maccoll, *Select Plays of Calderón* (London, 1888), p. 260.
20 *Obras*, p. 521b.
21 R. Menéndez Pidal, "*Del honor en el teatro español*," in *De Cervantes y Lope de Vega* (3rd ed., Buenos Aires, 1945), p. 159.

gerated application in the heroic dramas, conventional honour had something fine about it, but there was something more to honour than that. Honour need not be limited to the nobility, nor be bound up with birth or with office. It was something of universal human value, which the *villano* could possess as well as the noble, and which the noble could lack as well as the peasant. It was left to the *villano* Pedro Crespo to define and demonstrate this more ample view of honour in *El alcalde de Zalamea*:

> . . . *el honor*
> *es patrimonio del alma,*
> *y el alma sólo es de Dios.*

11 · *El pintor de su deshonra* and the Neo-Aristotelian Theory of Tragedy

by A. Irvine Watson

AS P. N. DUNN has recently pointed out in this journal, there has been of late a tendency amongst scholars to depart from more traditional attitudes towards Calderón's honour plays.[1] These *calderonistas* no longer see the author of *El médico de su honra,* *A secreto agravio secreta venganza* and *El pintor de su deshonra* as an "advocate of revenge," nor do they believe him to have been "an unquestioning accepter of accepted social attitudes." They believe rather that Calderón was hostile to those aspects of the code of honour, such as the cruel honour-vengeance, which could not be reconciled with Christian ethics.[2] They maintain that Calderón's dislike of the unchristian facets of the code can be seen not only in plays such as *El alcalde de Zalamea* and *La devoción de la cruz,* but also in the notorious wife-murder plays. They have shown us how, in Dunn's words: "Calderón uses character and situation so as to make demands on the moral awareness of his audience, and lead it to a critical attitude towards the code of honour" (p. 79).

This critical reorientation (to my mind, an enlightened one) commands such a wide measure of support from British scholars (it is less popular in Spain) that the time would seem

1 "Honour and the Christian Background in Calderón," *BHS,* XXXVII (1960), 75–105.

2 See A. A. Parker, *"Santos y bandoleros en el teatro español del Siglo de Oro,"* Arbor (1949) and *The Approach to the Spanish Drama of the Golden Age,* Diamante series, No. 6 (London, 1957); E. M. Wilson, *"La discreción de Don Lope de Almeida,"* Clavileño, No. 9 (1951) and "Gerald Brenan's Calderón," *BCom,* VI, i(1952); A. E. Sloman, *The Dramatic Craftsmanship of Calderón* (Oxford, 1958), pp. 18–58.

ripe to re-examine one of the questions which has often troubled students of the wife-murder plays. Are they tragedies or not? Menéndez y Pelayo sensed their tragic quality and included all three in his list of *Dramas trágicos* by Calderón, but he was unfortunately so shocked by what appeared to him to be their immorality that he failed to follow up his intuition. He did however provide us in passing with what I believe to be a fruitful approach to these plays: "*En suma: Calderón, protestando, contra esta ceguedad moral* (i.e. the honour-vengeance), *la pone en escena porque entra en ella poesía y ventajas estéticas para hacer un drama trágico.*"[3] (Menéndez y Pelayo was referring here to A *secreto agravio* . . ., but his remark could equally well apply to either of the other two plays.) British *calderonistas* seem to share the approach advanced somewhat half-heartedly by the nineteenth-century scholar; thus Professors Wilson and Sloman describe *El médico de su honra* as a tragedy, and Professor Parker has interpreted *El pintor de su deshonra* as a special kind of tragedy evolved by Calderón.[4] Yet, on the other hand, we have Gerald Brenan who believes that *El médico* "is not a tragedy at all, so far at least as the chief character is concerned, but on the contrary a drama offering a moral example," not to mention Professor MacCurdy who would banish Calderón's honour-plays from the tragic canon altogether.[5] In view of this divergence of opinion it might seem worth while to relate the wife-murder plays to contemporary tragic theory, especially as this never seems to have been done in any detail. This may seem a peculiarly appropriate moment for such an exercise, since the Spanish neo-Aristotelian theorists have recently earned the attention of Margarete Newels, Alfredo Hermenegildo and Sanford Shepard.[6]

3 *Calderón y su teatro* (Buenos Aires, 1946), p. 232.

4 "Towards a definition of Calderonian tragedy," BHS, XXXIX (1962), 222–37. Professor Parker kindly allowed me to see a copy of this paper prior to publication.

5 G. Brenan, *The Literature of the Spanish People* (2nd ed.) (Cambridge, 1953), p. 284; R. MacCurdy, *Francisco de Rojas Zorrilla and the Tragedy* (Albuquerque, 1958), p. 21. Brenan sees A *secreto agravio secreta venganza* as "not so much a bungled tragedy on the theme of jealousy as a problem play" (p. 285).

6 Margarete Newels, *Die dramatischen Gattungen in den Poetiken des Siglo de Oro* (Wiesbaden, 1959); Alfredo Hermenegildo, *Los trágicos*

There can be little doubt that Calderón read one or more of the commentaries on Aristotle's *Poetics* which were published in Spain between 1596 and 1633, and he may well have had some knowledge of the works of Italian neo-Aristotelian theorists. López Pinciano's *Filosofía antigua poética* (1596), Francisco Cascales's *Tablas poéticas* (1617) and even González de Salas's *Nueva idea de la tragedia antigua* (1633) all precede the earliest of the three wife-murder plays in date,[7] and it would seem almost certain that a dramatist of Calderón's scholarship would have had some knowledge of them. But whether he had read the theorists of his day or not, it would at least seem worth while to compare their recipes for the concoction of tragedy to Calderón's practice in perhaps the most controversial of his plays. In so doing, I have no desire to prove that Calderón had read the theorists (although I have little doubt that he had). He could equally well have found his guide in earlier Golden Age plays (e.g. *El caballero de Olmedo*) which themselves owe something to neo-Aristotelian theory.

Aristotle, it will be remembered, divided the tragic fable or plot into two parts which he called the Complication and the Dénouement. "By Complication I mean all from the beginning of the story to the point just before the change in the

españoles del siglo XVI (Madrid, 1961); Sanford Shepard, *El Pinciano y las teorías literarias del Siglo de Oro* (Madrid, 1962). Neo-Aristotelian theories of tragedy are expounded in detail by these scholars, but as none of them has sought to relate this body of theory to Calderón's practice, my own brief summary of the neo-Aristotelians' precepts for tragedy will, I hope, be found useful. Shepard remarks in passing that the death of Mariene in *El mayor monstruo los celos* is in accord with the Aristotelian pattern (p. 102).

7 It is possible that Calderón's *El médico de su honra* was performed in 1629, i.e., before the publication of González de Salas' book, but there is no conclusive proof of this. The play may have been presented at the Royal Palace in 1635, but even this is not certain. It was printed in Calderón's *Segunda Parte* (1637). *A secreto agravio secreta venganza* was performed in 1636 and there is a MS copy of the play dated 1635. It was also printed in the *Segunda Parte*. *El pintor de su deshonra* would appear to have been written in the sixteen-forties, probably not long after Calderón's return from Catalonia. The *princeps* of this play is believed to be the text in Vol. 42 of *Comedias de diferentes autores* (Zaragoza, 1650). See N. D. Shergold and J. E. Varey, "Some early Calderón dates," *BHS*, XXXVIII (1961), 274–86; E. W. Hesse, "The publication of Calderón's plays in the seventeenth century," *PQ*, XXVII (1948), 37–51.

hero's fortunes; by Dénouement, all from the beginning of the change to the end." [8] The three Spanish neo-Aristotelians accept this division of the plot into *conexión* and *solución*, and Cascales advises the writer of tragedy to pay careful attention to the balance between them:

> . . . el Poeta a de prescrivirse, y assignarse una metad, o termino hasta donde vaya en crecimiento la Fabula. Que para dezillo breve es quando se trueca la fortuna de la persona fatal [i.e. protagonist] de felicidad en miseria, o al contrario.[9]

Although Cascales holds here that the *mutación* or *mudanza* may be either from happiness to misery or from misery to happiness, he agrees elsewhere in his *Tablas poéticas* with Aristotle's view that the purest tragic plot is one in which the protagonist's fortunes suffer a change for the worse, and both López Pinciano and González de Salas come to the same conclusion. Cascales and González de Salas also subscribe to Aristotle's belief that the perfect plot should have a single and not a double issue, or, in other words, that the dramatist should concentrate on the downfall of one person, without introducing any corresponding rise in the fortunes of another:

> . . . ay Fabula simple, y doble: simple, quando de un alto, y excelente grado se viene a una gran miseria, y este es el mas verdadero, y Tragico caso de todos. . . . Llamase doble aquella Tragedia donde ay mudança de infelicidad en felicidad, no en una persona, sino en diversas, quando un vando principal de la Tragedia de prosperidad cae en miseria, y otro de miseria en prosperidad . . . (Cascales, 326).

If, then, Calderón had consulted the Spanish theorists on the subject of tragedy he would have found that they followed Aristotle in recommending a plot in which the tragic hero passes from happiness to extreme adversity and in which the issue is a single rather than a double one. In the words of González de Salas: ". . . *la mejor Constitucion es la que consta de la mudança unica de alguno, i que esta sea de la felicidad a la infelicidad, i no al contrario.*" [10]

---

8 *The Poetics*, ed. I. Bywater (Oxford, 1909), p. 51.
9 Francisco Cascales, *Tablas poéticas* (Murcia, 1617), p. 335.
10 González de Salas, *Nueva idea de la tragedia antigua* (Madrid, 1633), p. 46.

The Spanish *preceptistas* were by no means unaware of what Aristotle meant by the word catharsis. In the discussion on this subject which arises in the *Filosofía antigua poética*, Pinciano (who appears as one of the interlocutors), expresses surprise that pity needs to be purged, since he has always heard that it is a virtue. Fadrique agrees with him that inability to feel compassion is a fault, but that, on the other hand, an excess of pity can be very harmful. Hugo sees immediately what Fadrique is driving at:

> Sí señor, Hugo dijo, que el Rey muy tierno, y el juez muy muelle . . . harán una política y una economía muy tierna, muelle y blanda. . . . Entero y no muy compasivo conviene sea el hombre; y esta entereza se gana con la tragedia. . . .[11]

The *entereza* to which Hugo refers is, of course, the happy mean or *punto de discreción* lying at the centre of the two vicious extremes of cruelty and over-leniency or sentimentality. Tragedy can help the spectator to achieve this healthy emotional condition by showing him the suffering of a human being who is worthy of his compassion. If he can appreciate the tragic predicament of a Lear, say, or an Othello, he will be less likely to weep unrestrainedly over some minor misfortune such as the death of a favourite pet. González de Salas had something of this sort in mind when he wrote:

> . . . habituandose el animo a aquellas passiones de Miedo, i de Lastima, frequentadas en la Representacion Tragica, vendran forçosamente a ser menos offensivas. i despues quando succedan occasiones proprias a los mortales, de experimentar aquellas passiones en sus infelices successos, las sentiran menos sin duda, medicado ia el sentimiento con el Uso, i con el Exemplo de otras semejantes infelicidades, o de las que fueron maiores (p. 17).[12]

All three Spanish commentators realized that "tragedy controls the emotions by directing them to the right objects in the right way," [13] and they only differed from Aristotle in regarding ca-

11 López Pinciano, *Filosofía antigua poética* (*Valladolid*, 1894), p. 321.
12 There is an interesting article by E. C. Riley in which he discusses the possible influence of the Spanish neo-Aristotelian theorists: "The dramatic theories of González de Salas," *HR*, XIX (1951), 183–203.
13 Humphry House, *Aristotle's Poetics* (London, 1956), p. 109.

tharsis as more of a didactic than an aesthetic process. They concentrated on the usefulness for the individual and hence for society of regulating the passions, and in this way they fitted Aristotle's theory neatly into the Horatian and Golden Age ideal of *enseñar deleitando*.

During the discussion in the *Filosofía antigua poética* to which I have already referred the all-important distinction is drawn between the *tragedia patética* and the *tragedia morata*. Attention has already been drawn to this passage by Raymond MacCurdy,[14] but I believe it to be of such fundamental importance for students of Golden Age drama that I hope I may be forgiven for reproducing it at length:

> Será mejor la tragedia que, siendo compuesta de agniciones y peripecias fuere patética, porque el deleyte viene a la tragedia de la compassión del oyente, y no le podrá tener si el agente no parece estar muy apasionado; por la qual causa deven las tragedias mudarse de felicidad en infelicidad, que el fin de la soltura de la fábula es el que más mueve. La segunda especie, dicha morata o bien acostumbrada, aunque es de más utilidad, no de tanto deleyte trágico, porque la persona que tiene la acción en las partes principales, o es buena o mala; si es buena la persona, para ser morata la acción y que enseñe buenas costumbres, ha de passar de infelicidad a felicidad, y passando assí, carece la acción del fin espantoso y misericordioso; carece, al fin, de la compassión, la qual es tan importante a la tragedia, como vemos en su definición; y si es la persona mala, para ser morata y bien acostumbrada la fábula, al contrario, passará de felicidad en infelicidad, la qual acción traerá deleyte con la venganza y con la justicia mas no con la conmiseración tan necessaria a la patética. . . . Es, pues, la mejor tragedia la patética, porque más cumple con la obligación del mover a conmiseración, y si tiene el fin desastrado y miserable, es la mejor.

Perhaps the most important thing to notice here is that in a so-called *tragedia morata* (it is, of course, not really a tragedy at all) we see either a virtuous protagonist rewarded or a wicked one punished. In other words the yardstick of poetic justice can be aptly applied to this type of play. (I use the term "poetic justice" in a more limited sense than Professor Parker; I take it to mean "ideal justice in the distribution of rewards and punish-

14 Op. cit., p. 13.

ments in works of literature.") Most serious Golden Age plays fall into this *morato* category, but I would suggest that we should always be on the alert for the occasional *tragedia patética* in which the dramatist is concerned less with punishing his hero's wickedness or rewarding his virtue than he is with arousing the tragic emotions in his audience. If the protagonist of a play suffers greater misfortune than he strictly deserves, then the tragic emotions are likely to be stirred and we may find that we are dealing with a *tragedia patética*.

My purpose here is to suggest that Calderón's wife-murder plays and, in particular, *El pintor de su deshonra* need to be regarded in the light of the above distinction. If we are to reach the correct conclusion as to whether these works are *tragedias patéticas* or not, we must first establish whether their protagonists meet with suffering beyond their deserts, and, if this is the case, whether Calderón makes us feel pity for any or all of them. If they are *tragedias patéticas* we shall not expect to see the tragic heroes rewarded or punished as they deserve since, if poetic justice be satisfied, the tragic emotions will be, *ipso facto*, frustrated.

The Spanish neo-Aristotelians agree with Aristotle that the tragic hero should be neither wholly virtuous nor wholly wicked. If he be wholly wicked the spectator will enjoy his suffering, but there will be no pity for him: "*porque aunque el ver esto es agradable al hombre, no empero de allí resultarán el Miedo pretendido de la Tragedia, ni la Misericordia*" (González de Salas, 43). If, on the other hand, he be wholly virtuous, the audience will be shocked by his inexplicable suffering, and the cathartic process thus impeded. As Hugo puts it in the *Filosofía antigua poética*: "... *ser un bueno perseguido hasta el fin enoja al oyente; y, aguada la conmiseración con el enojo, queda aguado el deleite de la acción*" (p. 323). The three Spanish theorists all subscribe to Aristotle's restriction of the tragic hero to what González de Salas calls the *indiferente* class. He should be a personage of middling virtue, (he should be as virtuous as the plot permits), who is to some degree responsible for his own downfall, in order that the audience's sense of justice (as distinct from poetic justice) may not be outraged. As Cascales explained to his seventeenth-century readers:

> . . . *las personas que son en parte buenas y en parte malas, son*
> *aptas para mover a misericordia, y miedo, y es porque le parece*
> *al oyente que aunque el que padece, merece pena, pero no*
> *tanta, ni tan grave; y esta justicia mezclada con el rigor, y*
> *gravedad de la pena, induze aquel horror, y compassion que es*
> *necessario en la tragedia* . . . (p. 316).

or as Humphry House has more recently so admirably expressed
the same idea:

> Ideally according to justice, the two scales of goodness and
> badness and of pleasure and pain should be in harmony, so
> that the good have pleasure and the bad pain. Tragedy il-
> lustrates a dislocation of this harmony: for it is of the essence
> of the situation which calls forth pity, that the misfortune and
> suffering are undeserved.[15]

But if the tragic hero suffers more than he deserves, in
what way does he deserve to suffer at all? López Pinciano, following Aristotle, holds that he should be *"de tal condición que*
por algún error haya caido en alguna desventura y miseria
especial; y ya que no sea caida por error, a lo menos cuanto a
sus costumbres no merezca la muerte" (p. 323). We notice here
that López Pinciano has rendered *hamartia* as *error*, but he does
not go on to say exactly what he means by this somewhat ambiguous word. What sort of mistake does the tragic hero make?
Does it consist of an error of judgement or is it a form of moral
error? This vital question brings us to the heart of the matter.

As Ingram Bywater and Humphry House amongst others
have pointed out, *hamartia* in the Aristotelian sense of the term
has nothing to do with moral error. It is a mistake or error of
judgement and it originates not in vice or depravity, but usually
in ignorance of same material fact or circumstance. "This ignorance" (in Bywater's words) "takes the deed out of the class of
voluntary acts and enables one to forgive or even pity the
doer." [16] Aristotle, as is well-known, had Oedipus's tragic mistake in mind as a perfect example of *hamartia* and as Bywater
reminds us: "The Sophoclean Oedipus is a man of hasty temper,
but his *hamartia* was not in that, but in the great mistake he
made, when he became unwittingly the slayer of his own father."

15 Op. cit., p. 102.
16 Op. cit., p. 215.

It was perhaps inevitable that, in interpreting Aristotle to a Christian society, most of the sixteenth- and seventeenth-century theorists should have interpreted the mistake made by the tragic hero as a form of moral error. This is particularly noticeable in the case of the Spanish commentators. As we have seen, López Pinciano was not too explicit on this point, but fortunately Cascales dealt with it very thoroughly and provided his contemporaries with an excellent recipe for the kind of tragic hero acceptable to a seventeenth-century Spanish audience. The tragic hero, according to Cascales, should be *"aquel que padece por algún pecado hecho sin malicia, por imprudencia, y por algún error humano"* (p. 318). Cascales, then, does not hesitate to use the word *pecado* to describe the hero's mistake, but he immediately introduces important qualifications. He refers his reader to the passage in Aristotle's *Ethics* where all human acts are divided into two groups: voluntary acts and involuntary acts. Having established this division (which he could equally well have found in St. Thomas Aquinas), Cascales concludes that voluntary errors are unsuitable in a tragic hero (*"voluntaria es quando maliciosamente, y por culpa mia incurri en la miseria que padezco,"* p. 319) and that even a certain kind of involuntary error will fail to rouse the tragic emotions. This latter is what Cascales calls *"acción violenta (quando uno haze una cosa mas de fuerça que de grado")*, and as an example he cites the hypothetical situation of a man who is told by a tyrant that he will die unless he kills his own father.

Cascales, having ruled out as his tragic hero both the man who deliberately errs and the man who is compelled by superior strength to act as he does, arrives at his recipe:

> *Resta pues que sea aquella accion propria del tragico, adonde por ignorancia padezco algún gran trabajo. . . . Haze la cosa por ignorancia, quien imprudentemente, y sin saber que aquello que haze es malo, lo haze* (p. 319).

González de Salas, although uncharacteristically he treats this important matter in less detail, comes to the same conclusion —that the tragic hero must sin unwittingly. The *indiferentes* who are suitable as tragic heroes *"son los que inadvertidamente cometen algún delicto, porque no son buenos, pues peccan; ni malos, habiendo pecado con ignorancia"* (p. 44).

To sum up: Calderón could have gathered from the Spanish neo-Aristotelian theorists the following basic recipe for the concoction of a tragedy:

(a) The purest kind of tragedy depicts the fall of one person from a state of happiness to a state of misery.

(b) The tragic hero should be neither wholly good nor wholly bad, but he should be as virtuous as the plot permits.

(c) He should make some mistake which contributes to his downfall, but if the mistake takes the form of a mortal error, it must be involuntary so that the spectator may sympathize with him in his subsequent misfortune and thus feel pity for him.

Only by following this recipe, according to the theorists, could the tragic emotions be aroused and tragedy therefore perform its true function.

But to what extent may Calderón be said to have conformed to these rules, consciously or unconsciously, in his wife-murder plays? I propose now to discuss one of them, *El pintor de su deshonra*, in the hope that I may succeed in substantiating my belief that it is a kind of *tragedia patética*; if I fail in this purpose I hope that the exercise will at least help to throw a little further light on this excellent play.

The spectator's or the reader's immediate impression of Don Juan Roca in the first scene of *El pintor de su deshonra* is that he is a truly happy man. Calderón leaves us in no doubt about this. As the play opens, Juan has just returned to his friend Don Luis's house in Gaeta, after collecting his beautiful young bride from Naples. He had thought the young cousin, whom he had chosen as his bride, attractive from the portrait of her which had been sent to him at his home in Barcelona, but now that he has seen the girl in the flesh he has fallen in love with her. The bride's father, Don Pedro, and other relatives and friends are accompanying her to Gaeta to see her off to her new home in Spain, and Juan has come on ahead of the wedding party to share his happiness with his loyal friend of so many years' standing:

D. Juan: Yo me siento
tan alegre, tan ufano,
tan venturoso, tan vano,

> que no podrá el pensamiento
> encareceros jamás
> las venturas que poseo,
> porque el pensamiento creo,
> que aun ha de quedarse atrás. (p. 966) [17]

Don Juan's good fortune and happiness (*"tan alegre"*; *"tan venturoso"*), which he has every right to enjoy, is of course vitiated by a note of presumption (*"tan ufano"*; *"tan vano"*) which will make him deaf to the reality of his situation. He is so pleased with himself that he fails to realize the mistake he is making in marrying someone so much younger than himself. His contentment knows no bounds when Luis insists that the wedding party should be his guests whilst they await the arrival of the galleon which will carry the couple to Barcelona. Juan certainly has cause to feel happy for he can congratulate himself on having both a beautiful young wife and a true friend.

As we see Juan radiating happiness in this first scene and later in the first act, we may perhaps wonder what Calderón is about. It is only later in the play that we realize that he has placed his protagonist on the very peak of good fortune in order that his downfall may be the more effective later in the action.[18] Don Juan Roca, with tragic lack of perception, remains totally unaware of the mistake he is making, although the audience is left in no doubt by the *gracioso* (who performs the function of a Greek chorus here) that bride and groom are unsuited to each other. Juanete illustrates this by means of an anecdote about a courtier who invited a guest to a picnic by the river at which he served chicken which was cold when it should have been hot, and wine which was warm when it should have been chilled. The guest promptly immersed his chicken in his wine and explained that by this means he hoped either to cool the wine or warm the chicken. The *gracioso* then interprets this parable for the benefit of Don Luis and his daughter (Juan is not present), and of course for the spectator:

17 All references are to the Valbuena Briones edition (Madrid: Aguilar, 1959), vol. I.

18 Calderón's dramatic technique is very similar in the first act of his *A secreto agravio* . . . , where Don Lope de Almeida also congratulates himself on the beautiful young wife he has found and the friend that he has kept.

> *Lo mismo me ha sucedido*
> *en la boda, pues me han dado*
> *moza novia y desposado*
> *no mozo: con que habrá sido*
> *fuerza juntarlos al fiel,*
> *porque él cano, ella doncella,*
> *o él la refresque a ella,*
> *o ella le caliente a él.*   (p. 968)

Don Juan's error lies above all in faulty timing. In his conversation with Don Luis in the first scene we learn that the somewhat elderly bridegroom had devoted his more youthful years, when his mind should presumably have turned to thoughts of marriage, to painting and reading. Luis used often to reprove him for this, but he showed no inclination to take a wife, and continued with his artistic pursuits, gaining some proficiency in the art of painting. His belated decision to marry is more an error of judgement (*hamartia*) than a moral error; if there is anything of moral error in it, there can be no doubt that Juan errs in all innocence and without the slightest trace of malice. He believes that he is carrying out his social duty by marrying, and explains to Luis that he is acceding to the wishes of relatives and friends who have urged him to marry, and that furthermore he thinks it advisable to found a *mayorazgo* for his heir in order that his wealth may remain in the family:

> *Pues siendo todo eso así,*
> *ya rendido a la atención*
> *de mis deudos, o a que fuera*
> *lástima que se perdiera,*
> *faltándome sucesión,*
> *un mayorazgo que creo*
> *que es ilustre y principal*
> *y no de poco caudal,*
> *correspondí a su deseo.*   (p. 967) [19]

It is significant too that Luis, although he has tried to persuade his friend to marry in earlier days, does not reprove him now for marrying Serafina, and even compliments him on his excellent choice.

---

[19] Curiously enough, almost exactly the same situation occurs in Calderón's *Las tres justicias en una* where the elderly Don Lope de Urrea has married a young girl of under fifteen for precisely the same reasons.

Don Juan, then, is completely unaware of the tragic mistake he has made. At the end of the first act he is still as sublimely happy as ever, little realizing that he has sown the seed of a major disaster. Unlike the audience, he has no knowledge that Luis's son, Álvaro (who has reappeared after having been assumed drowned at sea), is his wife's former lover. Nor can he know that this unscrupulous young man has no intention of respecting the marriage sacrament. He has shown a moment's concern on hearing that Serafina had fainted whilst he was away at the port, but he has no idea of the real cause of her collapse, and hence no reason to feel suspicious. The gathering clouds are hidden from the tragic hero as Calderón holds back the *mudanza* until the appropriate moment in the play.

Calderón begins his second act with a further illustration of his protagonist's tragic lack of perception. Juan and Serafina are now married and living in Barcelona, and we witness a domestic scene in which he attempts to paint a portrait of her. He finds that he is unable to reproduce such beauty, but instead of blaming his own limited ability as a painter he holds Serafina's beauty responsible for his failure. Juanete helps the audience to understand the significance of this scene with another of his anecdotes. He tells how a man awoke one morning having lost his sense of hearing during the night and how, seeing that those around him were moving their lips but that he could hear nothing, he came to the conclusion that everybody had begun to speak a new silent language:

> *Volvían a hablarle bien,*
> *y él decía: "¡Hay tal! ¡Que den*
> *hoy en hablar quedo todos!"*
> *sin persuadirse a que fuese*
> *suyo el defecto. Tú así*
> *presumes que no está en ti*
> *la culpa; y aunque te pese,*
> *es tuya, y no la conoces,*
> *pues das, sordo, en la locura*
> *de no entender la hermosura*
> *que el mundo te dice a voces.*   (p. 979)

Juanete's story is a perfect illustration of his master's deafness to his own faults or, in other words, his tragic lack of perception,

and this latter is further exemplified by Juan's failure to take any
notice of the *gracioso*'s words. "*¡Qué locura!*" is his only comment. He pays just as little heed to Juanete's next anecdote
about a woman who accused her confessor of breaking the seal
of the confessional because he had called her husband "cuckold"
in an argument. As Juanete says, it is sometimes possible for
a wife to know more about her husband than he knows himself.
This exemplary tale might have made another man of Don
Juan's years with such a young and beautiful wife open his eyes
a little wider, but Juan continues to wear blinkers. All he can
find to say is "*¡Oh, qué tema tan cansado!*" (p. 979).

At this stage of the action Álvaro arrives in Barcelona disguised as a sailor. He waits until he is sure that Juan is out,
and then knocks at the door of his house. Serafina does everything she can to get rid of her unwelcome visitor without seeing
him, but he slips into the house uninvited and resumes his attack on her firmly entrenched sense of virtue. (B. W. Wardropper's analysis of this scene, which he interprets as evidence
of Serafina's guilt, is based on a mis-reading of the text.) [20]
With Juan's sudden and unexpected arrival back home the
scene is now set for the *mudanza*. He has returned to tell Serafina that his relations and friends are to offer a special Carnival
banquet in her honour on the following day, and that he would
like her to choose a new dress or costume for the occasion. Juan's
kindness and generosity to his wife in this scene are particularly
important in that they are qualities which help the spectator
to sympathize with him and feel pity for him in the later stages
of the play. Álvaro has to be hidden and, in a typical *capa y
espada* scene, Juan's suspicions are aroused for the first time.
Up to this moment he has been a happy man who has been able
to be frank and open in every way, but now he utters his first
aside in the play: "(*¡Válgame el cielo!*) / *¡Hombre aquí!*" (p.
982) and with these words the *mudanza* has been reached. We

20 B. W. Wardropper, "The Unconscious Mind in Calderón's *El pintor
de su deshonra*," *HR*, XVIII (1950), 296. The author's general conclusion that "unconscious desire in the subliminal parts of her mind thwarts
her [Serafina's] moral will" seems to me the exact opposite of the truth.
Serafina is a rock of virtue from the moment that she enters the married
state.

are almost exactly half-way through the second act and Don Juan's tragic downfall has begun.

Humphry House has remarked that "tragic pity is felt only for the good: and it is therefore not a patronising feeling or sentimental feeling by which we look down on the sufferer: we continue to look up at him" (p. 102). This is precisely the feeling which we have for Juan as we watch his consternation in the *capa y espada* scene, followed by his suffering at the Carnival celebrations where Álvaro continues his assault on Serafina. Calderón has seen to it that we should continue to admire Juan, despite his potentially humiliating situation, by showing us earlier in the action that he is kind and generous in his personal relationships and highly responsible in his social behaviour. And now, in order to increase this respect for his tragic hero, the dramatist exemplifies his great courage in the scene in which Don Diego de Cardona's *quinta* catches fire. Juan not only rescues his wife from the flames, handing her over to be safeguarded by a group of sailors (amongst whom is the ubiquitous Álvaro), on the beach, but he rushes back into the *quinta* to help save the other guests:

> Amigos,
> si esta ruina, esta desgracia
> piadosos os ha traído
> [para socorrer] a tanta
> gente como aquí perece,
> la más noble, la más alta
> será que aquesta hermosura
> tengáis un instante en guarda,
> en tanto que vuelvo yo
> a costa de vida y alma
> a su socorro; que son
> los que mi favor aguardan,
> deudos, parientes y amigos.   (p. 988)

At this moment, when the spectator's admiration for Juan has reached its peak, Calderón deals his hero the harshest blow of all. On his return to the beach he discovers that Serafina has been abducted by the treacherous Álvaro. This cruel blow is more than he can stand, and he succumbs completely to wrath and jealousy, rushing half-crazed into the sea. This lack of self-control, although it represents a flaw in Juan's moral character, would in no way alienate the audience from him. On the contrary, it would help them to identify themselves more closely with him than before, since they themselves might behave equally imprudently and with some justification in similar circumstances. Like the tragic hero recommended by the Spanish neo-Aristotelian theorists, Don Juan is not wholly good. He is as virtuous as the plot permits, but he is not morally perfect, and by creating him in this mould Calderón has ensured that the cathartic emotions will be experienced by those who behold his suffering.

At the beginning of Act III Don Luis reads a letter from a friend in Barcelona in which he tells how Juan has vanished from his home, soon after the abduction of his wife. Luis is deeply grieved at his friend's misfortune and he exonerates him from blame in what are perhaps the most important words in the play if my interpretation of it is correct:

> ¡Oh, válgame Dios, a cuántas
> desdichas y sobresaltos
> nace sujeto el honor
> del más noble, el más honrado!
> Aquí el serlo lo disculpe,
> pues a los ojos humanos,
> por más que ésta sea desdicha,
> no deja de ser agravio.   (p. 990)

Herein lies the tragic conflict at the heart of the play. What is in fact a tragic misfortune (*desdicha*) for Juan is held by society to be an insult to his honour (*agravio*) which must needs be avenged if he is to hold up his head in society again. By leaving home in search of his wife and her abductor and with the intention of killing them, Juan is displaying his customary sense of social responsibility. He will do what society requires of him, but in so doing he will become the tragic victim of a cruel social aberration.

Juan appears in Act III dressed as a poor painter, in sharp contrast to the fine clothes he has worn in the preceding acts. He succeeds in getting some paintings commissioned by the Prince of Ursino and comes to see him, only to find that the Prince has left for an afternoon's hunting. Left alone, Juan draws attention to the change in his fortunes exemplified by his new costume: "*¿Qué es lo que pasa por mí, / fortuna deshecha mía?*" (p. 995) and goes on to inveigh against the code of honour which has obliged him to leave home with his mind set on a bloody vengeance:

> *¿Cómo bárbaro consiente*
> *el mundo este infame rito?*
> *Donde no hay culpa ¿hay delito?* (p. 995)

He considers himself to be completely blameless for his misfortunes, and he is almost justified in reaching this conclusion. But not quite; he has contributed to his own downfall, as Juanete's apt little anecdotes have shown, and now he is placing himself in a morally untenable position by obeying a code which he has shown to be unjust. Juan's mistake here is that he fails to *apurar la verdad* (to use a favourite phrase of Calderón's); he realizes that the code of honour is unjust in that it punishes not only the guilty, but also the innocent, yet he fails to draw the logical conclusion from this that he should obey God's law rather than a code of behaviour which his own misfortune has proved unjust. His obedience to the code is the result of his over-developed sense of social responsibility; he fails to realise that Man's law, in insisting on the honour-vengeance, runs counter to God's law of forgiveness. Yet although he errs, he does so unwittingly and without malice, and thus he measures up to Cascales' and González de Salas' definitions of the tragic hero. The spectator pities him in his misfortune, because although he sins he does so out of ignorance.

Soon the Prince reappears and asks Juan whether he has completed any of the paintings he has commissioned. Juan replies that he has finished his representation of the story of Hercules, Deyanira and the centaur Nessus. It is not surprising that Juan should have chosen this classical myth as the subject for his painting, for it offered a striking parallel to his own situation. He has depicted Hercules, consumed with jealousy and pursuing the abducting centaur. In the background can be seen the sacrificial pyre on which Hercules threw himself and Juan has decided on the following title or *mote* for his work: "*Quien tuvo celos primero, muera abrasado después*" (p.

996). What are we to make of this title? Is *"muera abrasado"* a
mere metaphor or are we to take it that Juan will suffer the
same fate as Hercules and die as a result of his consuming passion of jealousy? I do not think so. Juan does not die at the end
of the play, and there is no suggestion in the text (unless we interpret the title of his painting as such) that he will die other
than in the fulness of time. My own view is that Calderón
introduced this reference to Hercules's violent death as a contrast rather than as a parallel to his protagonist's fate. *El pintor
de su deshonra* is in many ways a re-working in a contemporary
setting of the Hercules/Deyanira/Nessus myth,[21] but the dénouement of Calderón's story is different because he was a
Christian creating Christian characters for a Christian audience.
Don Juan does not deserve to die other than an honourable
death. He suffers more than enough in the course of the play's
action.

The Prince's next job for his artist is of a more dangerous
nature; he asks him to paint, unseen, a portrait of the woman
(Serafina) with whom he (the Prince) has fallen in love. Ar-
rangements are made to conceal the painter in an inner room
of the hunting-lodge where Álvaro has taken the unfortunate
girl. As Juan follows the caretaker of the lodge to this strategic
position he makes a particularly interesting remark, since it
may be said to point to the attitude of mind which helps to
bring about his downfall: *"Guiad vos; que obedecer / me toca,
no hacer examen"* (p. 999). Juan obeys too easily and questions too little, but we pity him since he suffers far more than
he deserves thanks to the criminal irresponsibility of Álvaro
and the demands of a cruel code. He is willing to risk his life
in securing the portrait required by the Prince, because he has
already suffered so much:

> Mal, señor, mi valor sabes;
> que no acobardan peligros
> a quien no matan pesares.   (p. 999)

21 Calderón had already dramatized this myth in Act III of his *Los
tres mayores prodigios* of 1636. Deyanira's remarks in this play on the folly
of a husband killing his innocent wife out of fear for his reputation are of
particular interest. (Calderón, *Obras completas*, ed. cit. I, 1676.)

But Juan has still further to fall from the peak of happiness on which he felt so secure in Act I. When he recognizes that the woman he has been commissioned to paint is his own wife, and realizes for the first time that her abductor is the son of his best friend, he falls prey to a fit of jealousy and rage and shoots both Serafina, who is innocent, and Álvaro, who is guilty. With the honour-vengeance complete and his wife dying in her father's arms, Don Juan emerges as a truly tragic figure. The only words that he can find to utter are: "*Ahora más que me maten; / que ya no estimo la vida*" (p. 1001). With his life in ruins and his beloved wife dead, he no longer has anything left to live for, and he calls on Don Luis and Don Pedro to kill him for taking the lives of their children; but at this moment the Prince intercedes:

> *Ninguno intente injuriarle;*
> *que empeñado en defenderle*
> *estoy. . . . Esas puertas abre.* (p. 1001)

The Prince's overt reason for interceding on Juan's behalf is that the latter is in his employ and thus entitled to his protection, but it seems to me that he has another deeper motive: he sympathizes, like Calderón himself, with the wronged husband and knows that he does not deserve to die. Yet ironically enough the two fathers have no desire to kill the murderer of their offspring, since they believe him to have done no more than his social duty: "D. Luis: *quien venga su honor no ofende.*" Menéndez y Pelayo was shocked, it would seem, by the attitude of the fathers in this last scene of the play, and he went on from there to assume an immoral attitude in Calderón himself, but there is, of course, no reason to believe that Calderón shared the views of Don Luis or Don Pedro. They merely represent the voice of a society which believes in the value of the honour-vengeance as a deterrent to would-be adulterers. Calderón's own view was, I suggest, that Don Juan did what society demanded of him, but that he sinned by killing his wife and, to a lesser extent, her lover. Don Juan Roca is the tragic victim not only of Álvaro, but also of a society which still clings to a barbaric and totally un-Christian code of behaviour. He is far more sinned against than sinning, and the only Christian solution is for him to be allowed to live out the rest of his shattered life without further punishment.

To sum up: whether Calderón was conscious of it or not, it would certainly seem that he shared some of the views put forward by neo-Aristotelian theorists on the best way to write a tragedy. Don Juan is the sort of intermediate personage mentioned by Aristotle and his commentators as suitable for the part of tragic hero. He is as virtuous as the plot permits: kind, generous, brave, a good husband, a good friend and a man with an acute sense of social responsibility. Yet he is not a paragon of virtue, as is made evident by his two attacks of uncontrolled jealousy and rage. Thus we can both admire him and at the same time experience the cathartic emotions (which rely on our being able to identify ourselves with him) when he begins to suffer. He contributes both by *hamartia* and by involuntary moral error to his own downfall and we sympathize with his hopeless plight at the end of the play, a plight which is in itself an indictment of the honour-vengeance. For what has strict adherence to the code of honour achieved? It is true that Álvaro deserves to die; he sins voluntarily and maliciously and Juan may be seen as the instrument of divine justice in bringing about his death. But, on the other hand, the innocent Serafina has also been sacrificed, and her husband, although he can once more hold up his head amongst his fellows, no longer wants to do so. This is the tragic irony of Don Juan Roca's situation at the end of the play.

In the course of this paper, in which I have tried to show that Don Juan is a tragic hero in the neo-Aristotelian mould, the reader will have noticed that I have assumed throughout that the husband is the protagonist of the play. I do not think there can be any doubt that this is the case. *El pintor de su deshonra* is Juan's story and the other characters revolve around him. Furthermore, neither Serafina nor Álvaro qualifies as a tragic hero in the neo-Aristotelian sense since the former is morally perfect from the moment of her marriage onwards and the latter is an obstinate and malicious sinner. Serafina is too good to qualify as a tragic heroine and Álvaro is too bad to justify the title of tragic hero. The death of the former is totally unmerited and the death of the latter is richly deserved and in conformity with the law of poetic justice.

Yet if we agree that Juan is the tragic hero of the play and that *El pintor de su deshonra* has the essential characteristics of a *tragedia patética*, it may only be described as such with one important reservation. Calderón wrote his play in accordance with the conventions of Golden Age drama, and his mingling of tragedy and comedy would have met with the disapproval of Cascales and, to a lesser extent, López Pinciano. (González de Salas had something to say in favour of tragicomedy). But if he included ingredients other than those recommended by the theorists, he did so with the inspired touch of a master-chef. He followed contemporary theatrical convention by writing in a part for a *gracioso*, but he blended this character so subtly into the tragic mixture that he in no way obtrudes. On the contrary, he is made to perform the vital function of leading the spectator towards a correct assessment of Don Juan Roca's degree of responsibility for the tragic misfortune which overtakes him.[22]

22 I am indebted to Professors E. M. Wilson, A. A. Parker and A. E. Sloman and to Mr. J. W. Sage for reading my typescript and offering advice, comments and criticism. None of these is of course in any way responsible for the views expressed here. Professor Wilson kindly allowed me to read the analysis of *El pintor de su deshonra* which he has written as part of a book on Calderonian drama. Whereas his work takes the form of a critical study of the play as a whole, I have merely sought to relate it to neo-Aristotelian theory.

Select Bibliography

SELECT BIBILOGRAPHY

ENGLISH TRANSLATIONS

F. Birch and J. B. Trend, tr., *Life's a Dream* (Cambridge, 1925).

Roy Campbell, tr., *The Surgeon of His Honour* (Madison, 1960).

————, "Life Is A Dream" and "Love After Death," in Eric Bentley, ed., *The Classic Theatre*, Vol. III: Six Spanish Plays (Garden City: Doubleday Anchor Books, 1959).

Edward Fitzgerald, tr., *Eight Dramas of Calderón, Freely Translated* (New York: Dolphin Books, n.d.). This "Shakespearean" translation, readily available in several editions, takes such liberties with Calderón's texts that it is heatedly disavowed by *calderonistas*.

Edwin Honig, tr., *Calderón: Four Plays* (New York: Mermaid Dramabooks, 1961).

Kenneth Muir, tr., "A House With Two Doors Is Difficult to Guard," *TDR*, VIII, No. 1 (1963), 157–217.

The following list of recent studies on Calderón's drama excludes works which do not pretend to be, in one way or another, critical. Asterisks indicate that an article has been reprinted in this book.

CALDERÓN'S DRAMATIC ART AND POETIC LANGUAGE

A. L. Constandse, *Le Baroque espagnol et Calderón de la Barca* (Amsterdam, 1951).

Max Oppenheimer, Jr., "The Baroque Impasse in the Calderonian Drama," *PMLA*, LXV (1950), 1146–65.

A. A. Parker, *The Allegorical Drama of Calderón: An Introduction to the Autos Sacramentales* (Oxford, 1943).

————, "Towards a Definition of Calderonian Tragedy," *BHS*, XXXIX (1962), 222–237.

J. Sage, "Calderón y la música teatral," *BH*, LVIII (1956), 275–300.

Micheline Sauvage, *Calderon* (Paris, 1959).

A. E. Sloman, *The Dramatic Craftsmanship of Calderón* (Oxford, 1958).

——, "Calderón and Falconry: A Note on Dramatic Language," *RPh*, VI (1953), 299–304.

Ángel Valbuena Prat, *Calderón. Su personalidad, su arte dramática, su estilo y sus obras* (Barcelona, 1941).

E. M. Wilson, "The Four Elements in the Imagery of Calderón," *MLR*, XXXI (1936), 34–47.

HONOR

* P. N. Dunn, "Honour and the Christian Background in Calderón," *BHS*, XXXVII (1960), 75–105.

——, " 'Patrimonio del alma,' " *BHS*, XLI (1964), 78–85.

Edwin Honig, "The Seizures of Honor in Calderón," *KR*, XXIII (1961), 426–447.

E. M. Wilson, "Gerald Brenan's Calderón," *BCom*, VI, i (1952).

CALDERÓN AND RELIGION

Father Martin Jarrett-Kerr, "Calderón and the Imperialism of Belief," in his *Studies in Literature and Belief* (London, 1954), pp. 38–63.

* A. A. Parker, "The Theology of the Devil in the Drama of Calderón," *The Aquinas Society of London: Aquinas Paper No. 32* (London, 1958).

CALDERÓN AND ART

Ernst Robert Curtius, "Calderón und die Malerei," *RF*, L (1936), 89–136.

Eunice Joiner Gates, "Calderón's Interest in Art," *PQ*, XL (1961), 53–67.

Everett W. Hesse, "Calderón and Velázquez," *Hispania*, XXXV (1952), 74–82.

EL ALCALDE DE ZALAMEA

* C. A. Jones, "Honor in *El alcalde de Zalamea*," *MLR*, L (1955), 444–449.

Sturgis E. Leavitt, "Pedro Crespo and the Captain in Calderón's *Alcalde de Zalamea*," *Hispania*, xxxviii (1955), 430–431.

LA DEVOCIÓN DE LA CRUZ

W. J. Entwistle, "Calderón's *La devoción de la Cruz*," *BH*, L (1948), 472–482.
* Edwin Honig, "Calderón's Strange Mercy Play," *MR*, iii (1961), 80–107.

EL MÁGICO PRODIGIOSO

W. J. Entwistle, "Justina's Temptation: An Approach to the Understanding of Calderón," *MLR*, xl (1945), 180–189.
Bruce W. Wardropper, "The Interplay of Wisdom and Saintliness in *El mágico prodigioso*," *HR*, xi (1943), 116–124.

EL MÉDICO DE SU HONRA

A. D. Kossoff, "*El médico de su honra* and *La amiga de Bernal Francés*," *HR*, xxiv (1956), 66–70.
A. E. Sloman, "Calderón's *El médico* and *La amiga de Bernal Francés*," *BHS*, xxxiv (1957), 168–169.
A. Soons, "The Convergence of Doctrine and Symbol in *El médico de su honra*," *RF*, lxxii (1960), 370–380.
Bruce W. Wardropper, "Poetry and Drama in Calderón's *El médico de su honra*," *RR*, xlix (1958), 3–11.
A. Irvine Watson, "Peter the Cruel or Peter the Just?" *RJ*, xiv (1963), 322–346.

EL PINTOR DE SU DESHONRA

Bruce W. Wardropper, "The Unconscious Mind in Calderón's *El pintor de su deshonra*," *HR*, xviii (1950), 285–301.
* A. Irvine Watson, "*El pintor de su deshonra* and the Neo-Aristotelian Theory of Tragedy," *BHS*, xl (1963), 17–34.

EL PRÍNCIPE CONSTANTE

Y. Gulsoy and Jack H. Parker, "El príncipe constante: *Drama barroco de la contrarreforma*," *Hispano*, No. 9 (1960), 15–23.

Wolfgang Kayser, "*Zur Struktur der* Standhaften Prinzen *von Calderón*," in *Gestaltprobleme der Dichtung*, hrsg. von Richard Alewyn et al (Bonn, 1957).

Carlos Ortigoza Vieyra, *Los móviles de la comedia:* El príncipe constante *de Calderón de la Barca* (México, 1957).

* Arnold G. Reichenberger, "Calderón's El príncipe constante, a Tragedy?," *MLN*, LXXV (1960), 668–670.

A. E. Sloman, *The Sources of Calderón's* El príncipe constante (Oxford, 1950).

* Leo Spitzer, "*Die Figur der Fénix in Calderón's* Standhaftem Prinzen," *RJ*, x (1959), 305–335.

Bruce W. Wardropper, "Christian and Moor in Calderón's *El príncipe constante*," *MLR*, LIII (1958), 512–520.

William M. Whitby, "Calderón's *El príncipe constante:* Fénix's role in the Ransom of Fernando's Body," *BCom*, VIII, No. 2 (1956), 1–4.

E. M. Wilson and W. J. Entwistle, "Calderón's *Príncipe constante:* Two Appreciations," *MLR*, XXXIV (1939), 207–222.

LA VIDA ES SUEÑO

Milton A. Buchanan, "The Presidential Address: Calderón's *Life is a Dream*," *PMLA*, XLVII (1932), 1303–21.

Joaquín Casalduero, "*Sentido y forma de* La vida es sueño," *CCLC*, No. 51 (1961), 3–13; reprinted in his *Estudios sobre el teatro español* (Madrid, 1962), pp. 161–184.

P. N. Dunn, "The Horoscope Motif in *La vida es sueño*," *Atlante*, I, No. 4 (1953), 187–201.

* Everett W. Hesse, "*La concepción calderoniana del príncipe perfecto en* La vida es sueño," *Clavileño*, IV, No. 20 (1953), 4–12.

Edwin Honig, "Reading What's in *La vida es sueño*," *TA*, xx (1963), 63–71.

Leopoldo Eulogio Palacios, "*La vida es sueño*," *Finisterre*, II (1948), 5–52; reprinted in his *Don Quijote y La vida es sueño* (Madrid, 1960); translated into French as "La Vie est un songe: *essai sur le sens philosophique du drame de Calderón*," *Laval Théologique et Philosophique*, VII (1951), 123–149.

Michele Federico Sciacca, "*Verdad y sueño de* La Vida es

sueño, *de Calderón de la Barca*," *Clavileño*, ɪ, No. 2 (1950), 1–9.

* A. E. Sloman, "The Structure of Calderón's *La vida es sueño*," *MLR*, xlviii (1953), 293–300.

Bruce W. Wardropper, "*Apenas llega cuando llega a penas*," *MP*, lvii (1960), 240–244.

* William M. Whitby, "Rosaura's Role in the Structure of *La vida es sueño*," *HR*, xxviii (1960), 16–27.

* E. M. Wilson, "*La vida es sueño*," *Revista de la Universidad de Buenos Aires*, Tercera época, Año ɪv, Nos. 3 & 4 (1946), 61–78.

OTHER PLAYS

Edward Glaser, "Calderón de la Barca's *La sibila del Oriente y gran reina de Saba*," *RF*, lxxii (1960), 381–403.

Everett W. Hesse, "*El arte calderoniano en El mayor monstruo los celos*," *Clavileño*, vii, No. 38 (1956), 18–30.

———, "*Estructura e interpretación de una comedia de Calderón*: Eco y Narciso," *BBMP*, xxxix (1963), 57–72.

———, "The 'Terrible Mother' Image in Calderón's *Eco y Narciso*," *RomN*, ɪ, No. 2 (1960), 1–4.

Edwin Honig, "Flickers of Incest on the Face of Honor: Calderón's *Phantom Lady*," *TDR*, vi, iii (1962), 69–105.

A. A. Parker, "Henry VIII in Shakespeare and Calderón: An Appreciation of *La cisma de Ingalaterra*," *MLR*, xliii (1948), 327–352.

———, "History and Poetry: The Coriolanus Theme in Calderón," in *Hispanic Studies in Honour of I. González Llubera* (Oxford, 1959), pp. 211–224 [on *Las armas de la hermosura*].

E. M. Wilson, "*La discreción de Don Lope de Almeida*," *Clavileño*, ii, No. 9 (1951), 1–10 [on *A secreto agravio secreta venganza*].

Notes on the Contributors

PETER N. DUNN is a Lecturer in Spanish at the University of Aberdeen. Born in London in 1926, he was educated at the Sir George Monoux School and the University of London. His publications include the book *Castillo Solórzano and the Decline of the Spanish Novel* (Oxford, 1952) and articles not only on the Spanish theatre but also on the *Poema de mio Cid* and the lyric poets, Jorge Manrique and Garcilaso de la Vega. In 1965 his critical edition of *El alcalde de Zalamea* will be published by Macmillan in this country and the Pergamon Press in Oxford. In 1964–65, Mr. Dunn is a Visiting Professor at Western Reserve University.

EVERETT W. HESSE is Professor of Spanish at the University of Southern California. Born in Brooklyn in 1908, he obtained the A.B., A.M., and Ph.D. degrees from New York University, where he served for a time as an instructor. From 1941 to 1960 he progressed through the ranks to that of Professor at the University of Wisconsin. Since 1955 he has been a Corresponding Member of the Hispanic Society of America. He is a past President of the American Association of Teachers of Spanish and Portuguese. In addition to writing many articles on the Spanish theatre, Professor Hesse has edited Calderón's *El mayor monstruo los celos* (University of Wisconsin Press, 1955) and *La vida es sueño* (Scribner's, 1961). In collaboration with Harry T. Williams he produced in 1948 an edition of the picaresque novel *Lazarillo de Tormes*, for which Américo Castro wrote an important prologue.

EDWIN HONIG is Professor of English at Brown University. Born in New York in 1919, he studied at the Universities of Michigan and Wisconsin, and at Columbia. He has taught at New York University, Illinois Institute of Technology, Purdue, New Mexico, Wisconsin, Claremont College, and Harvard. He is a

Fellow of the Guggenheim Foundation. His chief interest is writing. He has published two volumes of verse: *The Moral Circus* and *The Gazabos*; he has some plays in the making. His translations include not just the plays of Calderón but the *entremeses* of Cervantes, published as *Interludes* in the Signet Classics series (1964). His book *García Lorca* is one of the first critical studies of this poet; it appeared in London in 1945, and has since been revised (New Directions, 1963). His latest book of criticism is *Dark Conceit: The Making of Allegory* (North-western University Press, 1959). In the first semester of 1964–65 Professor Honig will be on the Davis campus of the University of California.

CYRIL A. JONES is a Fellow of Trinity College, Oxford, and a Lecturer in Spanish at St. John's and Worcester Colleges. Born in 1924, he has studied and taught at Oxford except for one brief spell as a master at Launceston College in Cornwall (1944–45) and another as a Visiting Lecturer at the University of Pennsylvania (1959–60). He served as organizing secretary of the First International Congress of Hispanists, which was held at Oxford in 1962; he is a member of the committee of the International Association of Hispanists which was born at that conference. In addition to his articles on the Golden-Age drama he has written on the nineteenth-century novelist, Galdós, and on the medieval debate between the body and the soul. His edition of *El médico de su honra* was published by the Oxford University Press in 1961.

ALEXANDER A. PARKER is Professor of Hispanic Studies at the University of Edinburgh. Born in Montevideo in 1908, he studied at the Hawkesyard School (now the Blackfriars School, Laxton) and at Gonville and Caius College, Cambridge. After obtaining First Class Honours in both parts of the Modern and Mediaeval Languages Tripos, he was appointed a Fellow of his college, where he remained until 1939. From then until 1953, with two years out for war service, he was a Lecturer, and later Reader, at the University of Aberdeen. In 1953 he became Cervantes Professor of Spanish at the University of London. During the academic year 1960–61 he was seconded to the

University College of the West Indies (in Jamaica) as Professor of Modern Languages. In 1963 he was called to the new chair of Hispanic Studies in the Scottish capital. For the first trimester of 1964–65, he is Visiting Mellon Professor of Spanish at the University of Pittsburgh. Professor Parker is a Commander of the Order of Isabel la Católica, and a Corresponding Member both of the Hispanic Society of America and of the Real Academia Española de la Lengua. He has written on numerous subjects besides Calderón: the *Libro de buen amor*, Garcilaso, Quevedo, Church and State in nineteenth-century Spain. . . . Readers of this book will be particularly interested in his pamphlet *The Approach to the Spanish Drama of the Golden Age* (London: Diamante, 1957; reprinted in *TDR*), a work which has revolutionized our thinking about the *comedia*. A collection of Professor Parker's Calderonian studies will shortly be issued, in Spanish, by Gredos of Madrid.

ARNOLD G. REICHENBERGER is Professor of Spanish at the University of Pennsylvania and an editor of *Hispanic Review*. Born in Karlsruhe in 1903, he has a doctorate in classics from Heidelberg, another in classics from Milan, and still another—in Spanish!—from Ohio State. Before going to Philadelphia, he taught at the University of Milan, the New School of Social Research, Capital University, and Ohio State. He has been a Fulbright Lecturer at the University of Munich. His extensive publications include works on Livy and Confalonieri, articles on the Spanish theatre and the poet Boscán. His editions of Vélez de Guevara's *El embuste acreditado* and Lope's *Carlos V en Francia* are models of scholarship.

ALBERT E. SLOMAN has been Vice-Chancellor of the new University of Essex since 1962. Born in Cornwall in 1921, he read Mediaeval and Modern Languages at Wadham College, Oxford. In the war he served as a night-fighter pilot, and was mentioned in despatches. After a year teaching at the University of California (Berkeley), he went in 1947 to Trinity College, Dublin, where he was Reader in Spanish. In 1953 he was appointed Gilmour Professor of Spanish and editor of the *Bulletin of Hispanic Studies* at the University of Liverpool. In addition to his

two books on Calderón and his many articles, he has edited
La vida es sueño (Manchester University Press, 1961). His
Reith Lectures, delivered in 1963 over the BBC, were published
in the following year under the title A *University in the Making*.

LEO SPITZER was Professor of Romance Languages at the Johns
Hopkins University from 1936 until his death in 1960. One of
the great, almost mythical figures of Romance scholarship, he
appeared to have read everything, to have known all languages,
to have written on every conceivable philological subject. His
articles covered the language and literature of all Romance
countries and provinces, and also of England, America and
Germany; he was a great scholar in medieval and Renaissance
Latin. Born in Vienna in 1887, he studied at the Universities of
Leipzig and Paris, getting his Ph.D. from Vienna in 1911. He
taught at Vienna and Bonn before going to his beloved Mar-
burg as Professor in 1925. From 1930 to 1933 he occupied the
chair of Romance Philology at Cologne. As a result of Hitler's
policies he accepted in 1933 a call to Istanbul. Several collec-
tions of his scholarly articles exist. For English-speaking readers
the best approach to his work is through *Linguistics and Literary History: Essays in Stylistics* (Princeton, 1948).

A. IRVINE WATSON is a Lecturer in Spanish at Birkbeck College,
London. Born at Surbiton in 1926, he was educated in Argen-
tina and at King's College School in Wimbledon. His under-
graduate years were spent at King's College, London. He has
taught at Trinity College, Dublin, and at University College,
Cardiff.

WILLIAM M. WHITBY is Associate Professor of Spanish at the
University of Arizona. Born in Philadelphia in 1920, he studied
at Haverford and at Yale, where in 1954 he finished a disser-
tation on "Structural Symbolism in Two Plays by Pedro Calderón de la Barca." He taught at the University of Southern
California for three years before going to Tucson. He has
written on the drama of Cervantes and Rojas Zorrilla as well as
on Calderón. He is editor of the *Bulletin of the Comediantes*.

EDWARD M. WILSON is Professor of Spanish at Cambridge University and Vice-Master of Emmanuel College. Born in Kendal in 1906, he attended Windermere Grammar School and went up to Trinity College, Cambridge, where he received the Ph.D. in 1934. In 1929–30, he was at the Residencia de Estudiantes in Madrid, and in 1932–33 at Princeton University as a Jane Eliza Proctor Visiting Fellow. He taught at Cambridge from 1933 to 1945, with three years out for war service. In 1945, he was elected Cervantes Professor of Spanish at the University of London. In 1953, he returned to Cambridge. Professor Wilson is a past President of the Association of Hispanists of Great Britain and Ireland; in this capacity he played host to—and presided over—the First International Congress of Hispanists in 1962. He is a Corresponding Member of the Real Academia Española de la Lengua, and a Fellow of the British Academy. His translation *The Solitudes of Don Luis de Góngora* appeared in 1931. His theatre criticism covers Lope as well as Calderón. He has written on English and Spanish folklore (chap books, ballads, motifs, etc.) and on bibliographical matters. He is an enthusiastic bibliophile.

THE GOTHAM LIBRARY

Oscar Cargill, General Editor

Robert J. Clements, Associate Editor for Modern Languages

A paperback series devoted to major figures in world literature and topics of enduring importance

The Art of Paul Verlaine *by Antoine Adam (translated by Carl Morse)* $1.95

Shakespeare's Life and Art *by Peter Alexander* $1.95

Gabriela Mistral: The Poet and Her Work *by Margot Arce de Vázquez (translated by Helene Masslo Anderson)* $1.75

Borges the Labyrinth Maker *by Ana María Barrenechea (translated by Robert Lima)* $1.95

The Landscape of Nightmare: Studies in the Contemporary American Novel *by Jonathan Baumbach* $1.95

The Importance of Scrutiny *edited by Eric Bentley* $2.25

Balzac and the Human Comedy *by Philippe Bertault (English version by Richard Monges)* $2.25

Virginia Woolf *by Dorothy Brewster* $1.75

Passages from the Prose Writings of Matthew Arnold *edited by William F. Buckler* $1.95

Stendhal *by Armand Caraccio (translated by Dolores Bagley)* $2.25

O'Neill and His Plays *edited by Oscar Cargill, N. Bryllion Fagin, and William J. Fisher* $2.95

The Imagination of Charles Dickens *by A. O. Cockshut* $1.95

The Modern Spanish Novel *by Sherman H. Eoff* $1.95

Dante and His Comedy *by Allan Gilbert* $1.95

Kipling and the Critics *edited by Elliot L. Gilbert* $1.95

The Three Jameses *by C. Hartley Grattan* $2.75

A Short History of Literary Criticism *by Vernon Hall, Jr.* $1.95

A Thoreau Handbook *by Walter Harding* $1.95

Explorations *by L. C. Knights* $1.95

Bergson and the Stream of Consciousness Novel *by Shiv K. Kumar* $1.75

The Great Tradition *by F. R. Leavis* $1.95

Robert Penn Warren: A Collection of Critical Essays *edited by John Lewis Longley Jr.* $2.25

Mallarmé *by Guy Michaud (translated by Marie Collins and Bertha Humez)* $1.95

F. Scott Fitzgerald: His Art and His Technique *by James E. Miller* $1.95

A Definition of Tragedy *by Oscar Mandel* $1.95

Horace *by Jacques Perret (translated by Bertha Humez)* $1.95

A History of German Literature *by Ernst Rose* $2.75

The Art of Bertolt Brecht *by Walter Weideli (English version by Daniel Russell)* $1.95

The Theater of Protest and Paradox: Developments in the Avant-Garde Drama *by George E. Wellwarth* $2.25

Art and Order: A Study of E. M. Forster *by Alan Wilde* $1.95

Critical Essays on the Theatre of Calderón *edited by Bruce W. Wardropper* $2.25

If these titles are not available at your bookstore, you may order them by sending a check or money order direct to: New York University Press, 32 Washington Place, New York 3, New York. The Press will pay postage.